7/98

 St. Louis Community College

Forest Park
Florissant Valley
Meramec

Instructional Resources
St. Louis, Missouri

COLETTE (1873–1954) IN HER TEENS
Photograph used by permission of Archive Photos.

Colette

Updated Edition

Twayne's World Authors Series

David O'Connell, Editor
Georgia State University

TWAS 679

Colette

Updated Edition

Joan Hinde Stewart

North Carolina State University

Twayne Publishers
An Imprint of Simon & Schuster Macmillan
New York

Prentice Hall International
London   Mexico City   New Delhi   Singapore   Sydney   Toronto

Twayne's World Authors Series No. 679

Colette, Updated Edition
Joan Hinde Stewart

Twayne Publishers
An Imprint of Simon & Schuster Macmillan
1633 Broadway
New York, New York 10019

Library of Congress Cataloging-in-Publication Data

Stewart, Joan Hinde.
    Colette / Joan Hinde Stewart.—Updated ed.
      p.   cm. —(Twayne's world authors series ; TWAS 679)
    Includes bibliographical references and index.
    ISBN 0-8057-4552-1 (cloth)
    1. Colette, 1873–1954—Criticism and interpretation.   2. Women and
literature—France—History—20th century. I. Title. II. Series.
PQ2605.028Z834   1996
848'.91209—dc20   96-24266
                                                  CIP

10 9 8 7 6 5 4 3 2 1

Printed in the United States of America

For Philip

Contents

Preface

Like the more famous of male writers, Sidonie-Gabrielle Colette is known to the public by her family name alone. One of the most widely read authors of the modern period, she is in some ways as little understood as she is well loved. She led a life that was startling in its multiformity and resonances as well as its symmetries, and exercised the professions not only of writer, but of mime, actress, dancer, and beautician as well. She was married three times in neat progression, at intervals of about 20 years: first to a man 13 years her elder, then to one three years younger than she, and finally to one by 16 years her junior. Each of these marriages lasted between 10 and 20 years, the third one ending only with her death. Between her first two husbands, she made a well-publicized excursion into Lesbos. Nine months after the death of her mother, Colette gave birth to her only child, a daughter whom she also named Colette. When the author died at 81, she was a member of the Legion of Honor and the Royal Academy of Belgium, and the first woman president of the Académie Goncourt. She was also the first woman in French history to be accorded a state funeral, although she was refused a religious burial. Hers was a life, in short, so rich in anecdotal material that biography threatens to submerge the works.

During her last years, Colette was a grande dame and a kind of national icon, whose very presence in some sense eclipsed her writings: over 70 volumes including novels, short stories, plays, animal dialogues, reminiscences, newspaper articles, theater criticism, and letters. Only after her death did her reputation become more solid and serious. On balance, nevertheless, it seems that more words may have been devoted to the biography than to the literary creation. Two of her husbands (the first and the third), like two of her secretaries (Claude Chauvière and Germaine Beaumont), wrote about her, and nearly everyone else acquainted with her, intimately or casually, seems to have done the same. Biographies, memoirs, and interviews have appeared unabated, explaining Colette's personality, her likes and dislikes, encounters, travels, friends.

Those attempting to define Colette's art have often tended to regard it as subjective, judging the writing—fiction and nonfiction alike—in terms of the biography, searching for the woman in her works. In spite of her expressed hostility toward those who expect to find her true to life in her novels, critics and biographers are inclined to put into her own mouth the lines of her heroines. Only with the critical developments of the last few years has it become more common to speak of Colette in a resolutely literary manner, without patronizing or trivializing. It is increasingly apparent that Colette's uniqueness is a matter of proportion and definition, of perspective and emphasis. If she belongs to the classical French tradition, her fictional and autobiographical constructs, essentially feminine, are a distinct break with tradition.

I do not mean to suggest that biographical data can be dogmatically excluded or entirely dissociated from what she wrote; in unusually obvious ways, Colette continually exploited the material of her private existence. But if one can hardly speak of her life without drawing extensively on her characterizations of it in journals and memoirs, it does seem possible, while acknowledging and exploring the debt her fiction owes her biography, to discuss her literary works in literary terms. For the most part, then, after my introductory pages, I have resisted the temptation to explicate her fiction on the basis of biographical information.

The ordering of this study is generally (but not rigorously) chronological—which, because of the lines of development of Colette's writing, favors rather than precludes thematic and structural groupings. The size of the corpus made some selection necessary, and I have preferred to treat the works available in English translation and to deal principally with the most representative and some of the more neglected, rather than devoting a paragraph or two to each book while exploring none at length.

Joan Hinde Stewart
North Carolina State University

Preface to the Updated Edition

The years since this study originally appeared have seen not only the publication of three of the four planned volumes in the monumental Pléiade edition of Colette's works, but also the appearance of an enormous number of books and essays devoted to her, many of them in English. Although much of this new criticism is psychoanalytical or feminist in tone, the variety of approaches and concerns testifies to the richness of Colette's writing and to her power to inspire readers of all stripes, persuasions, and disciplinary backgrounds.

I have not tried here to inventory this new criticism systematically, but have referenced only the works most useful for my purposes. It remains essential to ground one's reading of Colette in the author's own world, her own perspectives, and, above all, the specific qualities of her literary achievement. I see this book as a useful preface, a basic map to territory currently being occupied by more self-consciously theoretical approaches. For this edition, then, the Selected Bibliography has been updated, and additions to the Notes and References section point to recent critical work. I have added chapter 8 on Colette's letters, and have occasionally corrected or clarified a biographical fact or reading.

Acknowledgments

Permission is gratefully acknowledged for reprinting the following pages, originally published elsewhere in slightly different form: the section on *The Vagabond* and *Mitsou,* which first appeared as "Colette: The Mirror Image" in *French Forum* 3, no. 3 (September 1978):195–205, and was reprinted as "Colette and the Epistolary Novel" in *Colette: The Woman, The Writer* (University Park: Pennsylvania State University Press, 1981), pp. 202–13; the section on *Chéri* and *The Last of Chéri,* originally published as "Colette and the Hallowing of Age" in *Romance Notes* 20, no. 2 (Winter 1979–80):172–77; and the pages on *Duo* and *Le Toutounier,* which appeared as "Colette's Gynaeceum: Regression and Renewal" in the *French Review* 53, no. 5 (April 1980):662–69. Parts of chapters 1 and 2 were published as "The School and the Home" in *Women's Studies* 8, no. 3 (1981):259–72. Portions of chapter 6 appeared in modified form as "Willy, Sido: une géographie morale" in *Europe* 59, no. 631–32 (November–December 1981): 61–71.

Quotations from *Evening Star,* © 1974, and *Duo and Le Toutounier,* © 1975, by Colette, used with permission of the publisher, The Bobbs-Merrill Company, Inc.

Grateful acknowledgment is made to Farrar, Straus and Giroux, Inc., for permission to quote from the English translations of the following works by Colette: *The Blue Lantern,* translated by Roger Senhouse, © 1963 by Martin Secker and Warburg, Ltd.; *Break of Day,* translated by Enid McLeod, © 1961 by Martin Secker and Warburg, Ltd.; *Chéri and The Last of Chéri,* translated by Roger Senhouse, copyright 1951, © 1979 by Farrar, Straus and Giroux, Inc.; *The Complete Claudine,* translated by Antonia White, © 1976 by Farrar, Straus and Giroux, Inc.; *Gigi/Julie de Carneilhan/Chance Acquaintances,* translated by Roger Senhouse and Patrick Leigh Fermor, copyright 1952, © 1980 by Farrar, Straus and Giroux, Inc.; *The Innocent Libertine,* translated by Antonia White, © 1968 by Martin Secker & Warburg, Limited; *Letters from Colette,* translated by Robert Phelps, © 1980 by Farrar, Straus and Giroux, Inc.; *Mitsou* and *Music-Hall Sidelights,* translated by Raymond Postgate and Anne-Marie Callimachi, © 1957 by Farrar, Straus and Cudahy, Inc. (now Farrar, Straus and Giroux, Inc.); *My Apprenticeships,* translated by Helen Beauclerk, © 1957 by Martin Secker & Warburg, Ltd.; *My*

Mother's House and *Sido,* translated by Una Vincenzo Troubridge and Enid McLeod, copyright 1953, © 1981 by Farrar, Straus and Giroux, Inc.; *The Other One,* translated by Elizabeth Tait and Roger Senhouse, © 1960 by Martin Secker and Warburg, Ltd.; *The Pure and the Impure,* translated by Herma Briffault, © 1966, 1967 by Farrar, Straus & Giroux, Inc.; *The Ripening Seed,* translated by Roger Senhouse, © 1955 by Farrar, Straus & Cudahy (now Farrar, Straus and Giroux, Inc.); *Seven by Colette,* translated by Antonia White, © 1955 by Farrar, Straus & Cudahy (now Farrar, Straus and Giroux, Inc.); *The Shackle,* translated by Antonia White, © 1964 by Martin Secker & Warburg, Ltd.; *The Tender Shoot,* translated by Antonia White, © 1958 by Martin Secker & Warburg, Ltd.; *The Vagabond,* translated by Enid McLeod, © 1955 by Farrar, Straus and Young (now Farrar, Straus and Giroux, Inc.); and *Creatures Great and Small,* translated by Enid McLeod, copyright 1951, © 1979 by Martin Secker & Warburg, Ltd.

A leave from North Carolina State University in 1978–79 and a fellowship at the Fondation Camargo, Cassis, allowed me to begin research on this study. A 1980 Summer Seminar Fellowship from the National Endowment for the Humanities, which I spent at Princeton University working with Albert Sonnenfeld, gave me the freedom and the context to complete several chapters.

I am grateful to the late Colette de Jouvenel (1913–81) for graciously receiving me in her mother's last apartment.

A number of generous friends have read portions of the manuscript. I am much indebted to the late Reinhard Kuhn, to Steven Winspur, to Erica Eisinger, and to Janet Whatley; and more than grateful to Linda Stillman for her sustaining interest in my work and for her invaluable comments on every chapter. Without the encouragement and patient readings of Sandy Petrey, who has long been a source of counsel and support, this would be a different book. My children, Anna Faye and Justin, have been an inspiration and a distraction at every stage. Finally, to Philip Stewart, for his example and help, my debt is too great to name.

For the updated edition, I want to thank Philip Stewart and Sandy Petrey once more for the encouragement that led me to undertake it; Alex DeGrand, Michel Mercier, Linda Stillman, Jean Vaché, and Janet Whatley for helpful comments; and Susan Marston for crucial research and editorial assistance.

Note on Translations

Several factors greatly complicate cross-language identification of Colette's works. In the first place, while some have never been published in English translation, a large number have appeared in more than one English or American version. And while several of Colette's books are themselves collections of earlier separate publications, translators and editors have frequently cut, excerpted, recombined, and retitled the French volumes.

For works of Colette that have not been translated, I have supplied English titles in my text, placing them in quotation marks to indicate that the translated title is mine. For the most part, however, references are based on translations readily available (many of which are, in fact, recent reprints of volumes originally published decades ago). At my first mention of each work, as well as at the beginning of a major discussion of a work, I have given the original French title in parentheses. My bibliography of Colette's works parenthetically indicates translations used in this study. Page references in the text are to these editions.

For a history of Colette in English to 1977, see Eleanor Reid Gibbard, "A Chronology of Colette in English Translation," *West Virginia University Philological Papers* 23, no. 7–1 (January 1977): 75–93.

Chronology

English titles are given for published translations only.

1873   28 January: Sidonie-Gabrielle Colette born in Saint Sauveur-en-Puisaye (Burgundy), daughter of Jules-Joseph Colette (born 1829) and Adèle-Eugénie-Sidonie Landoy, "Sido" (born 1835), widow of Jules Robineau-Duclos. She has an older brother, Léopold, "Léo" (born 1866); a half brother, Achille (born 1863); and a half sister, Juliette (born 1860).

1891   Family moves to Châtillon-Coligny, to the home of Achille.

1893   15 May: marries Henry Gauthier-Villars, "Willy" (born 1859). Moves to Paris.

1894   Suffers a long illness.

1895   Meets Marguerite Moreno. July: travels with Willy to Saint-Sauveur. Begins writing *Claudine à l'école (Claudine at School)*.

1900   *Claudine à l'école*, signed by Willy.

1901   *Claudine à Paris (Claudine in Paris)*, signed by Willy.

1902   *Claudine en ménage (Claudine Married)*, signed by Willy.

1903   *Claudine s'en va (Claudine and Annie)*, signed by Willy.

1904   *Minne,* signed by Willy. *Dialogues de bêtes (Creature Conversations)*, signed Colette Willy, a signature she continues to use until 1923.

1905   *Les Egarements de Minne,* signed by Willy. *Sept Dialogues de bêtes*. 17 September: death of Jules-Joseph Colette. Begins studying mime with Georges Wague.

1906   Begins acting professionally in mimodramas, which she continues doing until 1913. Separates from Willy and begins living with Missy, Marquise de Belbeuf.

1907   *La Retraite sentimentale (Retreat from Love)*. Moulin Rouge scandal, Colette playing opposite the Marquise de

Belbeuf in *Rêve d'Egypte*. Willy sells the rights to the Claudine novels.

1908   *Les Vrilles de la vigne*.

1909   *L'Ingénue libertine (The Innocent Libertine:* a reworking of *Minne* and *Les Egarements de Minne)*. Performs in *En camarades*.

1910   *La Vagabonde (The Vagabond)*. 21 June: divorce from Willy. Begins publishing in *Le Matin* and meets Henry de Jouvenel, editor-in-chief (born 1876). Travels with Auguste Hériot to Nice and Italy.

1912   25 September: death of Sido. 19 December: marries Jouvenel.

1913   *L'Entrave (The Shackle)*. *L'Envers du music-hall (Music-Hall Sidelights)*. *Prrou, Poucette et quelques autres*. 3 July: birth of Colette de Jouvenel, "Bel Gazou." 31 December: death of Achille Robineau-Duclos.

1916   *La Paix chez les bêtes (Creature Comfort)*.

1917   *Les Heures longues*. *Les Enfants dans les ruines*.

1918   *Dans la foule*.

1919   *Mitsou ou comment l'esprit vient aux filles,* followed by *En camarades*. Appointed literary editor of *Le Matin*.

1920   *Chéri*. Named chevalier of the Légion d'honneur. Begins liaison with stepson Bertrand de Jouvenel in Rozven.

1921   *La Chambre éclairée*. Premiere of stage version of *Chéri*.

1922   *La Maison de Claudine (My Mother's House)*. *Le Voyage égoïste*. Plays Léa in the hundredth performance of *Chéri*. April: travels to Algeria.

1923   *Le Blé en herbe (The Ripening Seed)*, signed Colette. *Rêverie de nouvel an*. Premiere of stage version of *La Vagabonde*. December: separates from Henry de Jouvenel.

1924   *La Femme cachée (The Other Woman)*. *Aventures quotidiennes*.

1925   Meets Maurice Goudeket (born 1889). 21 March: premiere in Monte-Carlo of *L'Enfant et les sortilèges (The Boy and the Magic)*, with libretto by Colette and music by Maurice Ravel. April: divorce from Jouvenel.

1926   *La Fin de Chéri (The Last of Chéri)*. Purchase of La Treille Muscate in Saint-Tropez.

1927   Moves to *entresol* apartment at 9, rue de Beaujolais, where she lives until February 1930.

1928   *La Naissance du jour (Break of Day)*. *Renée Vivien*. Named officer of the Légion d'honneur.

1929   *La Seconde (The Other One)*. *Sido ou les points cardinaux*.

1930   *Histoires pour Bel-Gazou*. *Sido* (edition expanded to include third part: "Les Sauvages" ["The Savages"]), *Douze Dialogues de bêtes*.

1931   12 January: Willy dies. February–April: lectures in Austria, Romania, and North Africa. September: fractures her leg.

1932   *Paradis terrestres. La Treille Muscate. Prisons et paradis. Ces Plaisirs* (reedited in 1941 as *Le Pur et l'impur* [*The Pure and the Impure*]). June: opens a beauty institute.

1933   *La Chatte (The Cat)*.

1934   *Duo*.

1934–38 Drama criticism published as *La Jumelle noire*.

1935   Elected to the Académie royale de langue et de littérature françaises de Belgique. 3 April: marries Maurice Goudeket. May–June: sails to New York. 10 August: marriage of Colette de Jouvenel. 5 October: death of Henry de Jouvenel.

1936   *Mes Apprentissages (My Apprenticeships)*. 4 April: acceptance speech at the Académie royale de Belgique. Becomes commander of the Légion d'honneur.

1937   *Bella-Vista*.

1938   Moves to second floor at 9, rue de Beaujolais, where she remains until her death. Sells La Treille Muscate. Travels to Fez.

1939   *Le Toutounier*.

1940   *Chambre d'hôtel (Chance Acquaintances)*. 7 March: death of Léopold Colette. 12 June: during wartime exodus, goes to her daughter's estate at Curemonte (Corrèze district). 11 September: returns to Paris.

1941   *Journal à rebours (Looking Backwards). Julie de Carneilhan. Mes Cahiers.* 12 December: Goudeket arrested by the Germans.

1942   *De ma fenêtre (From My Window).* 6 February: Goudeket released.

1943   *Le Képi (The Kepi). De la patte à l'aile. Flore et Pomone. Nudité.*

1944   *Gigi et autres nouvelles. Trois... six... neuf.... Broderie ancienne.*

1945   *Belles Saisons.* Elected to the Académie Goncourt.

1946   *L'Etoile Vesper (The Evening Star).* Travels to Geneva for treatment of arthritis, where she returns in 1947.

1948   *Pour un herbier (For a Flower Album).* 14 July: death of Marguerite Moreno.

1948–50 *Oeuvres complètes,* under the direction of Maurice Goudeket.

1949   *Le Fanal bleu (The Blue Lantern).* Collects her newspaper articles into *Trait pour trait, Journal intermittent, La Fleur de l'âge, En pays connu.* October: elected president of the Académie Goncourt.

1950   Travels to Monte Carlo, where she returns yearly.

1953   Named grand officer of the Légion d'honneur.

1954   3 August: dies; 7 August: secular state funeral in the Palais Royal, followed by burial in Père Lachaise cemetery.

Chapter One
Redemption

"The Priest on the Wall"

In a passage of *My Mother's House (La Maison de Claudine)*, Colette is reminded by the silent impenetrability of her small daughter, whom she called Bel Gazou, of the generative but ephemeral magic of her own intimate childhood universe. The episode illustrates the primordial role of language in organizing and possessing the world and suggests a privileged relation with words.

At the age of about eight, the child Colette hears the mysterious word "presbytery" for the first time and it enchants her. She initially supposes that it must be some kind of malediction: "Begone! You are all presbyteries!" (31), she bellows from the top of a narrow wall-like terrace behind her house where she likes to play. A little later, she decides that the word is likely the scientific name for a certain yellow and black striped snail. When her mother disabuses her, she is sorely disappointed, but eventually yields to the adult verdict: a presbytery is only a priest's house. She embraces the lovely word, climbs to her terrace, christens it the Presbytery, and inducts herself as "priest on the wall."

The account is exemplary, containing in miniature a life's drama: the necessity of compromise and renunciation, the inevitable coming to terms with reality. It enciphers a temporary refusal of a whole sociolinguistic heritage and the attempt to recreate a world with free-floating signifiers. It also suggests the opposition between the autonomy, magic and mystery of the child's universe—where anything can mean anything, and words are material, tactile, voluptuous, and mutable—and the arbitrary rules and boundaries imposed by the code of adults. This passage evidences an embryonic literary fantasy in the word play of the eight-year-old, for writer and child use signs similarly, in an aesthetic and nonutilitarian manner,[1] not merely to designate but to suggest and create. While Colette was not a believer, a religious vocabulary imbues "The Priest on the Wall," and her forced awakening to the function of language as naming is semi-religious, just as writing would become the vocation she initially refused to acknowledge, and a sort of redemption, too.

Saint-Sauveur[2]

"An inexpressible state of grace" (*Sido,* 156): this is the metaphor she would use to describe her childhood. The fall from grace reverberates throughout her writings.

She grew up in the Burgundian village of her birth, Saint-Sauveur-en-Puisaye, a town whose very name has religious connotations that reinforce the literary use Colette was to make of it. Her native village became for her a lost paradise, a world of which she somehow "ceased to be worthy," and her recollections of it and of the mother she called "Sido" inform her work from middle age until death. Colette was the last child and cherished daughter of an uncommon couple. Captain Jules Colette, one-legged veteran of the Italian expeditions of the Second Empire and member of the Legion of Honor, was a tax collector in Saint-Sauveur, a passionate man who fell in love once and for all with Sidonie Landoy. Sido had been born in Paris and lost her mother when she was still young. She was raised first by farmers near Saint-Sauveur, then by her father, a chocolate-maker called "the Gorilla," and then by her journalist brothers in Brussels. On a visit to the farm of her old nurse, she met and then married a man nicknamed "the Savage": Jules Robineau-Duclos. Twenty-one years older than she, he was an alcoholic who left her a widow at 29 with two children, Juliette and Achille, and a handsome fortune in property in Saint-Sauveur. She promptly remarried and bore two more children to Captain Colette: Léopold and Sidonie-Gabrielle, our Colette, whom they called "Gabri" or "Minet-Chéri."

Colette compellingly celebrates her childhood and adolescence, especially in *My Mother's House* and *Sido.* Their nostalgic prose evokes the child's love of nature and books, and her development in an atmosphere of warmth and affection, created principally by Sido. Colette the writer makes of her remarkable mother a character of legendary proportions.[3] It is Sido's characteristic chant, "Where are the children?" with its connotations of mystery and solicitude, that Colette adopts as the title of chapter one of *My Mother's House*—and the question rings throughout her work. If Sido, incurably irreligious, pleasantly harassed the village priest during his sermons, she was also ready to brave public opinion to comfort and shelter unwed mothers and lost animals. From an ever-alert and valiant Sido, Colette inherited an enduringly positive outlook on life: "I believe," she would note in a radio talk in 1937, "that there are occupations more urgent, and more honorable, than that unequaled waste of time we call suffering."[4]

In Sido's orbit moved a colorful array of family members and adjuncts. There were the servants, generations of pets of various species, and Juliette with the "mongol eyes," whom Colette dubs "my long-haired sister." (Anyone who has seen the picture of a teenaged Colette, seated in a hammock, with her braid almost sweeping the ground, can only marvel at what must have been the length of the tresses that gave such an epithet to Juliette.) A silent adolescent immersed in fiction and romance, whose marriage in 1885 would estrange her even more radically from the family, Juliette was later to commit suicide. There were also two brothers, considerably older than Sidonie-Gabrielle, whose hilariously macabre games she shared. Léo at age 13 was laying out mock cemeteries in attic and garden, and composing the epitaphs that embellished the tombstones of his imaginary dead.

And, of course, there was the Captain. Colette was to regret not having known her father better, this complicated man, jovial but disillusioned. He had trained at Saint-Cyr, the nation's foremost military academy, and fought in the Crimea and Italy, only to be confined by the loss of a leg to an uneventful life in the provinces. A keen reader and sometime poet, he devoured the periodicals of the day and had aspirations both political and literary: but on both these scores he was sadly unproductive. One of the highest shelves in his library sported a handsome array of notebooks, skillfully bound in black fabric by the Captain himself, and each bearing a title in Gothic lettering: "My Military Campaigns," "The Lessons of '70," "Marshal McMahon Seen by a Fellow Soldier," "From Village to Parliament," and more. In *My Mother's House*, Colette tells how the library was converted into a bedroom after his death and the family took the volumes down from their shelf, only to discover several hundred blank pages in each one. A single tome contained writing—the dedication page: "To my dearest soul, her faithful husband: Jules-Joseph Colette." The Captain's opus was a mirage; only his daughter remained to redeem his literary failures.

Willy

In her eighteenth year, the paradise disintegrated and Sidonie-Gabrielle was forced to "take leave alike of happiness and my earliest youth" (*Sido*, 174). The Captain's mismanagement of the Robineau-Duclos estate had already netted them one disaster: a lawsuit on the part of Juliette's husband that had made the family fair game for the village scandalmongers.

Now their debts obliged them to leave the Saint-Sauveur house and garden and move in with Achille, who was practicing medicine in the neighboring town of Châtillon-Coligny. Here Colette learned some vivid lessons about misery and poverty, for she would climb into her brother's victoria and make the rounds with him. In a fine short piece called "The Patriarch" ("Le Sieur Binard"), she speaks of her brother's hard life as a country doctor, of his splendid good looks, and of his silent affair with an 18-year-old peasant girl and the beautiful child it produced.

It was in Châtillon-Coligny that Colette fell in love. The son of an acquaintance of the Captain had put his own illegitimate son to nurse in the area and came from Paris to visit. In 1893, after a two-year engagement during which she hardly saw him, but wrote and received frequent letters, he became her first husband. He was Henry Gauthier-Villars, already well known as "Willy." An extraordinary figure of a remarkable age, Willy—with his beard, his balding head, his incipient paunch, and his flat-brimmed hat—was not handsome at 33, when Colette married him. But he was erudite, fashionable, and immensely active, with the originality to transplant into the company of the foremost writers, musicians, artists, and critics of the day, an unknown young provincial with an absurdly long braid down her back. (Willy loved to surprise.) His coterie included the poet Catulle Mendès, and Paul Masson and Marcel Schwob, scholars and writers who befriended the exile from Saint-Sauveur. She met Marguerite Moreno as well, her elder by two years, for a time the mistress of Catulle Mendès and later the wife of Schwob. Moreno became one of the period's distinguished actresses and a precious lifelong friend to Colette. But the young woman's awakening in Willy's bachelor apartment was nonetheless rude:

> I have never been able to forget that attic and its murky, rattling double windows. Painted in bottle green and chocolate brown, filled with unspeakably sordid cardboard files, soaked in a sort of horrible office gloom, it looked uninhabited, utterly forsaken. The draughts crept over the creaking boards. . . . Heaps of yellowing newspapers occupied the chairs; German postcards were strewn more or less everywhere, celebrating the attractions of underclothes, socks, ribboned drawers and buttocks. (*My Apprenticeships* [*Mes Apprentissages*], 21)

If Willy seemed to love her as she did him, he was all the same an irrepressible womanizer, an egomaniac, a publicist and worshiper of publicity, and he operated in an atmosphere of bohemianism, artifice, and perversion. Before him, "except for my parents' ruin, the money gone, the furniture sold by public auction—it had been roses" (*My Appren-*

ticeships, 17). Colette fell ill, to be slowly nursed back to health by Sido, while Paul Masson visited and Marcel Schwob read his translations of Twain, Defoe, and Dickens aloud at her side.

Willy was a critic of music and drama, an influential supporter of Wagner and the musical avant-garde, and, if not much of a writer, at least a known author of books. He maintained a stable of ghostwriters—the "secretaries" whose efforts he orchestrated laboriously, compensated, and published under his own numerous pseudonyms. Eternally broke but prodigiously resourceful, Willy urged his wife to write. As she tells the story in *My Apprenticeships,* they had been married for a year or two and she was lazily emerging from her illness. Willy was characteristically complaining about the state of their finances: "You ought to put down what you remember of your board-school days. Don't be shy of the spicy bits. I might make something of it. Money's short." She docilely went out and bought some notebooks, exactly like those she had used as a schoolgirl:

> The heavy grey-ruled pages, the vertical red line of the margins, the black cover and its inset medallion and ornamental title, *Le Calligraphe,* reawakened the urge, a sort of itch in my fingers, to do an "imposition," to fulfil a prescribed task. A well-remembered water-mark in the thick, laid paper, took me back six years. Diligently, with complete indifference, perched at the corner of the desk, the window behind me, one shoulder hunched and my knees crossed, I wrote. (19)

When she finished the manuscript, she gave it to Willy, who pronounced it of no use whatever, and Colette returned to the sofa and the cat. Then one September, on returning from vacation, Willy decided to straighten up his desk. He found the school notebooks that he thought he had thrown away, reread them, declared himself a bloody fool, grabbed his flat-brimmed hat, and rushed off to see a publisher. "And that is how I became a writer" (58).

The pace of life changed dramatically. Under Willy's supervision, she worked the story over, adding a bit of slang and some lesbian episodes. The book was signed "Willy" and published in 1900 as *Claudine at School (Claudine à l'école),* with an alluring cover design by Emilio della Sudda: a long-haired adolescent girl in a red riding cape, striped stockings, and yellow sabots sits cross-legged on the edge of a desk and writes in a notebook on her lap. The novel's formula was inspired: an irreverent narrator, a host of nubile and excited girls, and the school setting. It had a stupefying success. In its impact, it might be compared to *Werther.* Like

Goethe's hero a century and a quarter earlier, Colette's heroine was to capture the imagination of an enormous readership, and to enjoy a durable and tumultuous vogue. If the European public of the mid-1770s reveled in Werther's misfortunes, sporting Werther outfits and buying china and shaving mugs with his name and supposed likeness, that of 1900 was equally bedazzled by Colette's unorthodox schoolgirl. Claudine outfits and short hair became the rage, and a dizzying proliferation of products bore the name of Claudine; there were Claudine collars, perfumes, lotions, soaps, cigarettes, and ice cream. Willy, extraordinarily adept at manipulation and self-promotion, did everything in his power to foster the heroine's notoriety. This included the somewhat scandalous gesture of dressing in twin outfits his wife and Polaire, the young actress who created the stage role of Claudine, and parading them around the capital on his arms, as if both to certify suggestions of lesbianism and to authenticate his paternity of the character.

Since the manuscript has disappeared, Willy's role in the composition of *Claudine at School* cannot be easily assessed. While Colette considered Claudine as her own creation as well as a kind of literary alter ego, an article by Richard Anacréon in *Le Figaro Littéraire* of 20 January 1973 ("The Mystery of the Claudines Finally Solved") cites evidence that does not entirely mesh with the account in *My Apprenticeships,* but suggests that Willy's part was actually quite a considerable one. The *Figaro* produces a 1900 letter addressed by Willy to Rachilde, codirector of the *Mercure de France,* in which he explains that after a visit to Colette's village school, where he cavorted in a dormitory full of adolescents, he resolved to write about it and finally realized that the best thing would be to boil down his wife's own notes and conversations. According to Willy, he and Colette invented Claudine together.[5]

Whatever the degree of his contribution to the writing of the book, the essential thing is that Willy intuited in Colette a talent and nurtured it, even if his methods were not the tenderest. With the sale of *Claudine at School* having brought huge profits, he took to locking his wife in her room (by her account) for a few hours each day so that she would continue to produce best-sellers—which he continued to publish under his name. Three more "Claudines" followed, taking the heroine from her country school to Paris and marriage. The notebooks in which two of them were composed, with Willy's emendations in the margins, can be consulted at the Bibliothèque Nationale. Colette was launched as a writer—if not as an author—and in the wake of the Claudine series appeared *Minne* and *"Minne's Escapades" (Les Egarements de Minne),* written in a similar vein. In 1904 she also published a whimsical book about animals, *Creature Conversations* (*Dialogues de bêtes*), a flattering preface by poet Francis Jammes enhancing the second edition. It appeared under the name "Colette Willy," which she would continue to use for a number of years, even after divorce and remarriage.

Life with Willy was never dull: there were his duels, his lawsuits, and his infidelities; concerts, plays, receptions, and late-night stints in cafés; the musical criticism on which she collaborated, and the proofreading sessions. Colette wrote a good deal about this period, depicting the complexity of her reactions to life away from Sido, to the excitement of Paris around the turn of the century, and to marriage with this mature "Monsieur Willy," who supervised her dress, her writing and her activities, while fashioning her into a kind of libertine plaything. "What is known as the Bohemian life," she declared, "has always suited me about as badly as a hat trimmed with ostrich feathers" (*My Apprenticeships,* 44).

From 1902 to 1904, she spent a good deal of time writing in a country house Willy had bought at Les Monts Boucons in the Jura. Photographs of Colette and Willy about this time do not show her smiling; the small triangular face appears generally wistful and distant. In a provocative review-article entitled "Three Photos of Colette," William Gass comments on a photograph of the couple at table:

> Her stare is nowhere, and her unnaturally pale face seems fastened to her head like a mask. . . . Who but Willy would have posed for such a domestic picture, or permitted Colette's unhappiness or his own indifference—their total estrangement—to be so nakedly stated?[6]

However far apart they eventually grew, and however harshly Colette was in later years to portray her marriage to Willy, there is also evidence that she was for a long time in love with him. She endured the union for 13 years; and it was at Willy's rather than her own initiative that it came to an end in 1906. The breakup was a blow to her ego, but it was still freedom. On the verge of separation, Colette effectively exorcised Willy—appropriately enough in the last of the series of books she had begun to write under his direction. In *Retreat from Love* (*La Retraite sentimentale*), Claudine makes her final appearance as fictional protagonist. The fact that her name does not occur in the book's title is the first novelty, setting this work apart from the preceding ones; the signature under which it was published, "Colette Willy" (the first of her novels to be so signed), is another. And finally, the plot neatly disposes of

Claudine's "daddy-husband" Renaud, a character incarnating certain aspects of Willy. In one of her last books, *The Evening Star* (*L'Etoile Vesper*), Colette comments that Renaud's death gave her the sense of having attained "literary puberty."

Emancipation

Willy of course was still alive, although his best years were behind him; the divorce would be pronounced in 1910 and he would go on to remarry a woman of English origin whom he set to writing about the adventures of a schoolgirl called Peggy. Colette herself had taken a ground floor apartment on the Rue de Villejust, which she would later describe nostalgically in *"Three... Six... Nine..."* (*Trois... six... neuf...*). At the age of 33, she was faced for the first time with the necessity of earning her livelihood. She turned dancer and mime, working with the talented Georges Wague, and going so far as occasionally to appear on stage all but nude. But she zealously guarded her right to privacy and refused, as she would all through her life, to make any intimate revelations not willfully calculated.

Her heady freedom notwithstanding, the imperative to write had by this time been internalized, and she indefatigably continued publishing. Her literary activities in fact fed on her stage career, and in the short pieces that make up *Music Hall Sidelights (L'Envers du music-hall)* she evokes some of her experiences as a performer and depicts her colleagues in their combination of impecuniousness, nonchalance, professionalism, and discretion. Two novels—*The Vagabond (La Vagabonde)* and its companion piece *The Shackle (L'Entrave)*—also belong to this period; their heroine, Renée Néré, contains much of Colette herself, and the dilemma of the fictional character is not unlike the one the author faced after her divorce.

During her years of marriage to Willy, Colette had frequented some of the most important women writers in Paris: Lucie Delarue-Mardrus, Renée Vivien, Natalie Clifford-Barney, Anna de Noailles (to whose seat in the Royal Academy of Belgium she would in later life succeed). Rachilde, the influential literary critic of the *Mercure de France,* was a family friend to the Gauthier-Villars. Just after the separation, Colette's companion, financial and emotional mainstay, and her occasional housemate, was the Marquise de Belbeuf, also called the Marquise de Morny and nicknamed Missy—one of the principal figures of the Parisian lesbian milieu. Their liaison continued for half a dozen years. Two important texts speak of Missy: in *"The Tendrils of the Vine" (Les Vrilles de la vigne)*, there are evocations of Colette's physical attachment to the Marquise; and in a later work, *The Pure and the Impure (Le Pur et l'impur)*, Colette recounts portions of Missy's story, calling her "La Chevalière." Missy bought and furnished for Colette a house in Brittany called Rozven, where they often vacationed. She was also coached by Wague to play a man's role opposite Colette in a mimodrama called *Rêve d'Egypte*. The 1907 premiere at the Moulin Rouge, in which the women, who were known to be lovers in real life, exchanged a long kiss, was a scandal; it was attended by Willy as well as the ex-husband of Missy—the one applauding, the other hissing, and both obliged to make rapid exits from the theater. Colette's marginality, both social and sexual—her divorce, her dancing, her involvement with women as well as men, her apparently unselfconscious rejection of conventional codes—finds continuing echoes in her work.

Much of the documentation regarding these years is contained in her correspondence; her letters to her principal confidant, Léon Hamel, which have been published along with those to Georges Wague under the title *Letters of the Vagabond (Lettres de la Vagabonde)*, are especially precious. (Hamel and Wague both inspired characters in *The Vagabond:* Hamond and Brague.) Until her mother's death in 1912, Colette also wrote regularly to her (although these letters were later destroyed), and later identified part of her grief at the loss of Sido with the torment she experienced at the idea that she would no longer be able to write to her.

By then, she had a new emotional involvement with the editor-in-chief of an important Parisian newspaper, *Le Matin:* Baron Henry de Jouvenel des Ursins, who was to be a distinguished diplomat and eventually French ambassador to Rome. In a letter to Léon Hamel in the summer of 1911, Colette recounts the cataclysmic events she was living through: she and Jouvenel—"Sidi," as she called him—were falling in love, while his ex-mistress was going through a jealous and murderous rage, and Missy, who disliked Jouvenel, was pressing the suit of another of Colette's admirers, Auguste Hériot. It was a period of elation and upheaval, and Colette was at the same time writing for *Le Matin*. She became literary editor in 1919 and continued to publish weekly until 1924, when her work started appearing regularly in other Parisian periodicals. A few months after Sido's death, Colette and Jouvenel were married. Her only child, Colette de Jouvenel, was born in July 1913, and Colette gave up dancing to lead a more bourgeois existence, although she continued to write. The marriage was rocky. She had by now grown used to independence, and the demands of Jouvenel's career were not always compatible with those of her own. In the summer of 1920, moreover, she began an affair with Bertrand de Jouvenel, who was almost 17 and her husband's son by a first marriage. Henry de Jouvenel, meanwhile, had affairs of his own. In 1923, after discovering his wife's ongoing liaison with his son, he left her. The following year saw the appearance of a collection of very short stories entitled *The Other Woman* (*La Femme cachée;* literally, "The Hidden Woman"), dealing partly with what she calls the mold of married life—the unpleasant surprises, gnawing jealousy, monstrous compromises, and woman's secret aspirations toward a more private existence.

During the 1920s Colette published some of her most important works, including *My Mother's House* and *Sido,* and her best-known novels. In 1925 a project initiated years earlier culminated with the premiere, in Monte-Carlo, of a fairy-tale ballet-opera called *The Boy and the Magic* (*L'Enfant et les sortilèges),* with libretto by Colette and music by Maurice Ravel. This delightful story of a little boy's temper tantrum is one of Colette's best works for theater.

As though her writing were not enough, Colette did some acting, appearing a number of times, for example, in the stage version of *Chéri* (in 1925 she played Léa to Marguerite Moreno's Charlotte Peloux) and as Renée Néré in a production of *The Vagabond.* She occasionally did translations as well, or wrote the French subtitles for foreign films, while she continued to work as drama critic for several newspapers. In the mid-1920s, she met a man considerably younger than she, a pearl broker named Maurice Goudeket. Never bound by convention, she embarked in 1932 with Goudeket's support on another unlikely adventure, the sale of beauty products. She hung out a shingle in the Rue de Miromesnil in Paris, announcing, "My name is Colette and I sell perfume," and the following year opened a branch in Saint-Tropez. But the excursion into beauty sales was less lucrative than they had hoped. In a highly competitive business world, customers proved more interested in her autograph than her cosmetics; the enterprise was short-lived.

Palais-Royal

In 1935 she married Goudeket, who was to remain at her side for her last 19 years. Colette, whose attachment to her "mother's house" in Saint-Sauveur was so deep, had by now inhabited a vast number of homes—a variety of Paris apartments and hotels, country residences, and seaside villas from Brittany to Saint-Tropez, the images of which reappear throughout her work. From 1938 on, she was to live in her last apartment, the one most closely associated with her in the public mind: the second floor at 9, rue de Beaujolais in the Palais-Royal. Here she did some of her most representative writing and, surrounded by her photographs and collections of butterflies and paperweights, received a growing number of admirers. She had become friends with her neighbor Jean Cocteau and enjoyed visits from the actor Jean Marais.

With Goudeket, she traveled and lectured, sailing to New York in 1935 on the maiden crossing of the *Normandie*. In *Close to Colette,* Goudeket describes her fascination with Woolworth's and her delight at coming across a cat in the streets of Manhattan: "At last someone who speaks French," she exclaimed.[7] In 1938 they flew to North Africa, which Colette had previously visited and evoked in parts of *"Prisons and Paradise" (Prisons et paradis)*. This time they went as reporters for *Paris Soir,* covering the sensational murder trial in Fez of a Moroccan prostitute; Colette's account of the affair appears in *Looking Backwards (Journal à rebours)*. With Henry de Jouvenel she had lived through World War I, in which he fought and was slightly wounded, and had woven some of her war memories into *Mitsou* and *The Last of Chéri;* with Goudeket she experienced the horrors of World War II. *Looking Backwards* contains recollections of their flight during the German invasion of Paris and their temporary retreat at Curemonte, her daughter's estate in the Corrèze district of France. After their return to Paris, Goudeket, who was Jewish, was arrested and detained for two months at Compiègne. Colette gave radio broadcasts, and in a series of articles eventually to be published as *"From My Window" (De ma fenêtre,* included in *Looking Backwards),* she chronicles the reactions, sacrifices, and wartime expediencies of the Parisians.

Her last work of fiction, the novelette *Gigi,* appeared in 1944. At nearly 50 years distance, this heroine recalls Colette's first; and like Claudine, the adolescent protagonist of *Gigi* had an immense success. Colette herself noticed an unknown young actress in Monte Carlo and recommended her for the role of Gigi in the Broadway musical comedy version: it was Audrey Hepburn. A good number of Colette's novels were successfully turned into plays or films. During her lifetime, movies were made not only of *Gigi,* but also of *The Innocent Libertine (L'Ingénue libertine), The Vagabond, Claudine at School, Julie de Carneilhan,* and *Chéri. The Ripening Seed (Le Blé en herbe)* was released in 1954, and *Mitsou* in 1956. In 1958, there was an American version of *Gigi,* in which the male lead was played by Maurice Chevalier, whose path Colette had crossed decades earlier during their music-hall days.[8]

She had broken her leg in 1931, and arthritis gradually immobilized her in the bed she liked to call her "raft." She grew old writing. In the tinted light of the "blue lantern" (a lamp she had fitted with two sheets of blue writing paper), she collected and composed chronicles, journals, reminiscences—half a dozen books appearing in 1949 alone. She who, in her youth, had "never wanted to write," could not stop once she had begun; "for writing," she notes in her last major work, *The Blue Lantern (Le Fanal bleu),* "leads only to writing" (161).

Her literary production, embracing a multitude of forms of expression, is as unique and varied, as surprising as her life. She wrote during the entire first half of the twentieth century, a period characterized by a plethora of literary and artistic movements, yet she never associated with any. She was a popular writer and her books were her source of income—the sheer quantity of her publications corresponding to her constant need for money—but her art was all the same of capital importance to her. She composed slowly, perfecting her style and occasionally complaining about the difficulty she had in writing. From childhood, her favorite author was Balzac, but she characteristically refused to talk about literature in general or her own books in particular. Acutely intelligent, she was not an intellectual, and wrote about neither philosophy, politics, religion, morality, nor public causes.

She readily found her inspiration in the events of daily life and in her past. Throughout her career, her heritage and youth were vividly present to her, and until 1940 they had a living symbol in her brother Léo—the "old sylph," as she called him—who led a nostalgic life mentally and emotionally centered on Saint-Sauveur. In his last years Léo would slip into his sister's Palais-Royal apartment, play a few tunes on the piano, drink a hot toddy, and with his sure memory plunge her into the landscape and events of her childhood. In *The Evening Star* she laments his death as the eternal sealing of certain treasures of their youth which he alone held: "our ritual songs, the topography of our natal village, the names of the departed commended in the sermon every Sunday" (65).

Léo was only one of the ways in which Colette's past reclaimed her present. In *Break of Day (La Naissance du jour)* she recounts how in middle age she grows marvelously more like her mother every day—the mother whom she had mythologized and, as it were, sanctified. But Colette was the Captain's child as well, and in *Sido* she reports the observation of a medium: "You are exactly what he longed to be. But he himself was never able" (194). It is curious to note (and Colette herself does not seem to have done so) that by the mid-1920s her identity with the Captain too was in some sense complete: she was then signing her works as well as her correspondence with a single name, his name—the one by which Sido used to call him: "Colette."[9]

Willy had died in 1931, Henry de Jouvenel in 1935, and her dear friend Marguerite Moreno in 1948. Colette herself slipped quietly away in the famous apartment, an object of national adulation, on 3 August 1954. She was attended by her "best friend" Maurice Goudeket, her daughter Colette de Jouvenel, and her faithful servant Pauline Tissandier. If her exceptionally productive and successful career can in some sense be equated with redemption—both of the unworthiness she imputed to herself and of her father's delusions of authorship—there was to be a curious afternote: her burial in Père Lachaise cemetery took place without benefit of public prayers. The Church refused her a religious burial on the grounds that she had been twice divorced and had not received the last sacraments. Its stance triggered protests from all over the world, while Colette's state funeral in the Palais Royal gardens was a national event. The square by the Comédie Française, in front of the Palais-Royal, was later renamed "Place Colette."

Chapter Two

Apprenticeship

Vocation

In a day when critics and theoreticians explore the special nature of the female experience of writing and emphasize the fire, drive, and consciousness required of the *woman* who accedes to the pen, Sidonie-Gabrielle Colette's itinerary into literature appears all the more exceptional, and her analysis of it even somewhat disconcerting. For she insists on the original *absence,* in her case, of a literary vocation:

> Vocation, holy signs, childhood poetry, predestination? . . . I can find nothing of the sort in my recollections. . . . In my youth I never, *never* wanted to write. No, I did not get up at night in secret to write verses in pencil on the lid of a shoe-box! No, I did not get nineteen or twenty [high grades] for style in an exercise between the ages of twelve and fifteen! For I felt, more so every day, I felt that I was made precisely *not* to write. (*Looking Backwards* [*Journal à rebours*], 15–16)

She eventually began to write neither in anguish, nor in response to a powerful inner impulse, nor with any sense of defiance of a bastion of male ascendancy, but constrained to do so by one particular male, the amazing Willy. "The day when necessity put a pen in my hand and I was given a little money in return for the pages I had written, I understood that I should have to write slowly, submissively, each day, patiently reconcile sound and number, rise early by preference, retire late from duty" (*Looking Backwards,* 17). Monitored by Willy, she gradually acquired both the discipline and the taste for writing.

The School

A child of Willy's insistent direction and his wife's inspired compliance, Claudine was born with our century. Bearing with deceptive simplicity the signature of Willy alone, *Claudine at School (Claudine à l'école)* was brought out by Ollendorff in 1900 and took the public by storm. This first work of fiction, published before Colette was 30 years old, is a literary transposition of some of her recollections of primary school. Saint-Sauveur-en-Puisaye has become Montigny-en-Fresnois; Captain Jules Colette, dreamer and author of unwritten books, has merged with her scientific elder brother Achille to become a distracted father, preoccupied with his experiments in malacology and composing a treatise on slugs; Gabrielle's own teacher, Mademoiselle Olympe Terrain, has become Mademoiselle Sergent. And Sidonie-Gabrielle has become Claudine. For her first fictional incarnation, Colette chose a name alliterating with her own and ending in a suffix which is semantically similar—the feminine "-ine," comparable both to the "-ette" of Colette and to the "-elle" of Gabrielle. And, as if anticipating the Colette of later years, Claudine goes by a single name.

The book recounts the events of the 15-year-old heroine's last year of studies in a village school. The theater of her adventures is a schoolhouse consisting partly of the shaky remains of a dilapidated and half-demolished building, partly of the beginnings of a new edifice. This symbolic structure is not obtrusively allegorical, but it discreetly informs the work: the contrast between the fall of one building and the rise of the other finds echoes in descriptions and episodes throughout the novel, while the transitional nature of the premises parallels the transitional role played by the school in Claudine's life. And finally, the disruptions associated with the construction project account in part for the chaos and promiscuity characterizing the environment.

Insolent and irreverent, Claudine is surrounded by an hilarious array of cohorts. They are Mademoiselle Sergent, the stern red-headed schoolmistress, and Aimée Lanthenay, her golden-eyed paramour and assistant. The debonair Dutertre, whose dual function of medical doctor and cantonal representative creates a pretext for his fondling of the nubile schoolgirls, makes frequent appearances. About half a dozen girls finishing their primary studies complete the cast: the insipid Jaubert twins; the languid and rattlebrained Marie Belhomme; Aimée's younger sister, masochistic Luce Lanthenay, who is irrepressibly in love with Claudine; and tall Anaïs, ungainly, comical, vicious, eternally munching on chalk, paper, and erasers and tormenting the younger and weaker girls.

Self-styled prettiest and cleverest, Claudine associates with teachers and comrades, but remains intellectually, and for the most part emotionally, aloof. She lacks authentic bonds: motherless, functionally fatherless, she has no siblings or other family attachments. Being from the upper middle class, she is out of place among these daughters of grocers, farmers, and laborers. "If I had a Mamma," she notes, "I know very well that she would not have let me stay here twenty-four hours" (*Claudine at School*, 4).

Claudine's loosely constructed diary constitutes the novel. Its use as a narrative device means that events are filtered through the consciousness of this protagonist-spectator, and that the essentially linear and thereby potentially tedious plot developments are reported with apparent spontaneity, fervor, and artlessness. The technique, however, is imperfect, for journal entries are neither dated nor otherwise delineated, and the text is not always internally coherent in terms of chronology. The sequence of events is clear, but there is some oscillation in their relation to the present, in the writer's temporal distance from them. For example, Claudine occasionally begins a passage with "yesterday," "today," or even "this morning," only immediately to move farther away from it, assessing the episode from the standpoint of several days or weeks in the future.

The composition of her journal is a crucial part of Claudine's present. So much so that her activities and her writing sometimes impinge upon each other: "The town and the School are upside down," she comments. "If it goes on like this, I shall no longer have time to describe anything in my diary" (167–68). The events reported are in the process of taking form. Their full value cannot be immediately assigned, owing to their problematic and undulating nature, but the journal confers unity on them. Only with the novel's last line, only therefore as she closes her journal, does the school year become something recognized as integral. Only then, moreover, is there an opening out from the school and onto the world and Claudine's future.

The novel begins with a vertiginous plunge, its first sentence evoking the ineluctable downward course of life and initiating a continuing descending movement. "My name is Claudine, I live in Montigny; I was born there in 1884 . . . ," she begins, using a standard autobiographical formula. But the sentence's curt final clause—"I shall probably not die there"—puts a sudden distance between her narrational stance and the traditional autobiographical posture, even insinuating a parody of the latter. The passage continues:

> My *Manual of Departmental Geography* expresses itself thus: "Montigny-en-Fresnois, a pretty little town of 1,950 inhabitants, built in tiers above the Thaize; its well-preserved Saracen tower is worthy of note." . . . Montigny "built in tiers"? No, that's not how I see it; to my mind, the houses just tumble haphazard from the top of the hill to the bottom of the valley.

> They rise one above the other, like a staircase, leading up to a big chateau that was rebuilt under Louis XV and is already more dilapidated than the squat, ivy-sheathed Saracen tower that crumbles away from the top a trifle more every day. Montigny is a village, not a town; its streets, thank heaven, are not paved; the showers roll down them in little torrents that dry up in a couple of hours. (*Claudine at School*, 1)

Expressions like "tumble haphazard," "top . . . to bottom," "crumbles away from the top," and "roll down" accentuate the bathetic thrust. This simultaneously suggests the descent of the female *I* into herself and her past, and translates Claudine's characteristic posture: mockery and undercutting. At the very outset, she challenges the practice of traditional autobiography, standard geography, conventional sight and discernment, schoolbooks, and, by extension, education. In *Claudine at School* there is an immense emphasis on the visual, both figuratively and literally: on the level of characterization, eyes have an extreme importance, and ultimately, the book's interest resides in its proposing an original and satirical view of the familiar.

Its criticism is directed chiefly against a system of formal education on which Claudine has a privileged perspective. The schools are administered by the elderly, the insensitive, and the lecherous, and classes taught by underpaid instructors who, "in order not to work in the fields or at the loom . . . preferred to make their skins yellow and their chests hollow and deform their right shoulders" (124). *Claudine at School* is a novel about growing up and acquiring knowledge, and simultaneously a kind of parody of the *Bildungsroman*. Claudine is commendably avid for learning, but her eagerness to absorb experience is so great that it finds some unsavory outlets: she continually creeps up staircases, listens at doors, hides in bushes, and thereby overhears conversations or witnesses scenes not intended for her. Without exception, these are of a sexual, or at least a sensual, nature. For Claudine seeks a sexual identity, and in her day she was one of the rare female protagonists in fiction to embark on such a search.

As the book opens, Claudine is prepared to bestow her affections on a new arrival, the alluring assistant teacher. But so, alas, is the headmistress, and in the struggle for Aimée, Mademoiselle Sergent—who can offer desirable teaching hours, comfortable lodging, and various privileges—shortly comes out the winner. The prize of the match between two strong minds (Claudine's and Mademoiselle Sergent's) is consistently evoked in the minor key. Aimée's traits are diminutive; she is not beautiful, but supple, caressing, wheedling, fickle.

Claudine at School is an entertaining book. Not only are the percep-
tions of the adolescent narrator amusing, her analyses of people and
institutions are dependably comical. Much of the humor comes from her
epithetic characterizations: "Anaïs," for example, never goes unqualified
by "tall," and the names of Aimée and Luce Lanthenay reliably elicit
suggestions of their common feline nature: they are clawing, meowing,
cute, dissimulating, lazy. Claudine's malacologist father, although essentially benevolent (unlike Aimée and Anaïs), is nonetheless an instant
humorous motif. All allusions to him are ironic, and they generally entail
reference to his droll scientific pursuits; during an illness, he nurses
Claudine tenderly, "like a rare slug." Most of all, there is a humorous
putdown of school procedures—for example, the silly problems:

> And the number of needles a seamstress uses in 25 years when she uses
> needles at 50 centimes a packet for 11 years, and needles at 75 centimes
> for the rest of the time but if the ones at 75 centimes are... etc., etc....
> And the locomotives that diabolically complicate their speeds, their times
> of departure and the state of health of their drivers! (25)

And the idiotic essay questions: " 'Imagine the thoughts and actions of a
young blind girl.' (Why not deaf and dumb as well?)" (16), the so-called
medical visits, the pawing of the older girls by the cantonal representative, the absurd punishments.

On the rhythm of a school year punctuated by such exercises, the
book builds from the decrescendo of the first paragraph to two succes-
sive climactic moments. First, the logical climax, the final examinations
of Claudine and her schoolmates in the county seat, terminating in the
predictable (and predictably unorthodox) success of Claudine, the failure
of Marie Belhomme, and the fair showing of the rest. Second, the anti-
climax: a stunning sex scandal involving the school administration,
grafted in Flaubertian style onto the account of an agricultural fair and
of the simultaneous dedication of the new school building. Claudine
views the explosion as an appropriate conclusion to her zany education
and declares herself "completely happy at having crowned [her] school-
days with such a memorable night" (206).

The school is the principal of the book's three foci, the two lesser ones
being nature (especially the woods of Montigny, on which Claudine lav-
ishes considerable lyricism) and her cat Fanchette. The Church, that oft-
parodied institution in France, is conspicuously absent. And her home,
which might normally be expected to function as a pendant to the

school, is a nonplace. If it has no negative associations, it is at best neutral, ultimately boring; nothing ever goes on at home, except for fond encounters with the cat. The woods supply a place for solitary meditation and the cat provides an outlet for affections, but only in the context of the school does anything genuine *happen.*

Education is an area on which novelists have expended a great many words and a great deal of criticism. While Colette is thus working in a traditional framework—the novel of education—her attitude is starkly nontraditional. The stress does not fall on the wretchedness and trauma that a lamentably inadequate school causes in its victims, for Claudine refuses the status of victim. On the contrary, her exuberance feeds on the very abuses of the educational system, and she contemplates with joy (and even profit) the mischief surrounding her. Here the school is not the hell that Colette's predecessors normally make of it, but a paradise—though of a particular sort. It is not a place of beauty, certainly not of virtue, nor of stability (Claudine repeatedly ironizes on the officially "provisional" nature of unsuitable arrangements, quarters, activities): the school is a place of good times. The notion of good times—"amusement" in French—is a dominant leitmotif. For example, the older girls, as we have seen, do not divulge the irregularities of their education because they are "having a good time." Claudine equates the school with amusement: "Tomorrow would be Sunday. No school. What a bore! It's the only place I find amusing" (21). Mishaps, successes, scandals, disasters—all are assessed in terms of the amusement they provide. When, at the end, Claudine is obliged to forsake class, companions, and teachers and wonders what society will offer in compensation, she prejudges it negatively: "I shall be very much astonished if I enjoy myself there as much as I have at school" (206).

The last sentence of the French text, like the first, begins with the word *je,* and the identification of this "I" has troubled not just students of Claudine, but the author herself. In a section of *"The Tendrils of the Vine"* entitled "The Mirror" ("Le Miroir"), Colette declares that she frequently chances to meet Claudine. She describes with bemused resignation one encounter with the alter ego who regularly emerges from the mirror to converse on an equal-to-equal basis. Colette and Claudine lament the confusion in the mind of the public and the impossibility, even for themselves, of separating the strands of the two lives, so much alike, but one real and the other fictional. For if Claudine is an imitation of her author, the reverse is also true: the character reminds the creator that she, Claudine, was the first of the two to have her long tresses cut.

With Claudine, Colette had created not merely a literary type, but a myth, and one that would haunt her.

The Later *Claudines*

Claudine at School was rapidly followed by three other Claudine books: *Claudine in Paris (Claudine à Paris,* 1901), *Claudine Married (Claudine en ménage,* 1902; originally entitled *Claudine amoureuse*), and *Claudine and Annie (Claudine s'en va,* 1903). The first two continue Claudine's journal, but the main protagonist and narrator of the third is not Claudine herself, but her friend Annie, and the novel is *her* journal. The appearance of Claudine's name in the title—the original French means "Claudine leaves"—attests to the viability and salability of the myth. Claudine herself returns as principal character and narrator of a somewhat later work as well, *Retreat from Love (La Retraite sentimentale,* 1907).

With pervasive autobiographical echoes, these books take the heroine from the isolation and precocious independence of a spoiled child to authentic solitude and liberty. After finishing school, Claudine successively experiences loneliness, love, marriage, jealousy, reconciliation, and widowhood. *Claudine in Paris* forms the appropriate continuation to *Claudine at School:* the child of nature makes her entrance into Parisian society, which is represented by characters as bizarre as those who peopled the school (and a number of whom are ruthless caricatures of Willy's acquaintances and enemies). Tante Coeur, the sister of Claudine's father, is a pretentious Parisian hostess with a homosexual grandson named Marcel. A Proustian figure of the same age as Claudine, Marcel is impeccably groomed and gloved, his principal talent the graceful pouring of tea. As phlegmatic in Paris as she was galvanized in Montigny, Claudine turns initially to Marcel for companionship, then her knight appears in the form of his 40-year-old father, Renaud—disabused and philandering, but handsome, tender, and easygoing. Groping for a term of address for the father of a first cousin once removed, Claudine christens him her "cousin Uncle." A brief and poetical courtship culminates in their engagement. The ambiguous romantic/avuncular relation of Renaud to Claudine carries most of the novel's humor. A distressing note is sounded in the appearance of Luce, one of Claudine's schoolmates, who has run away from Montigny and into the bed of an elderly Parisian uncle of her own: they inevitably suggest a caricature of Claudine and Renaud.

Claudine in Paris focuses more closely than the previous novel on female awakening to sexuality. It inventories sources of physical pleasure: her nurse Mélie's taste for the role of go-between, her cat Fanchette's blissful maternity, Marcel's homosexuality, Luce's lesbianism and prostitution, Luce's uncle's lechery and bizarre sexual sports. Each repels and titillates the 17-year-old heroine. Her coupling with Renaud by no means appears the healthiest formula, for Claudine's attraction to him is the consequence of her determination to swear, not fidelity, but obedience, to a male: "My liberty oppressed me, my independence exhausted me; what I had been searching for for months—for far longer—I knew, with absolute clarity, was a master. Free women are not women at all" (*Claudine in Paris,* 352–53). This book attempts a definition of woman's sexual fulfillment as domination by the male: Claudine exults in having found a comfortable place for her head on Renaud's shoulder and falls into his arms at the end, hoping that never again will she have to make an autonomous decision.

The sequel, *Claudine Married,* is, along with *Claudine at School,* the best of the series. One contemporary reviewer, Jean Lorrain, dubbed it "the *Liaisons dangereuses* of the twentieth century."[1] Continuing her journal, Claudine evokes the disappointments of marriage to the overly accommodating "cousin Uncle" who became her "daddy Husband." Renaud's dubious proclivities are revealed during the couple's overnight stay in Claudine's old school at Montigny. Clad in nightclothes, they pay a sunrise visit to the girls' dormitory, where they dispense sweets in return for embarrassed kisses from the sleepy adolescents. Back in Paris, Renaud instinctively recognizes a possibility for providing a distraction for his wife, and a spectacle for his own voyeurism, when Claudine meets a ravishing young woman named Rézi. Exquisitely dressed and made up, delicate, quintessentially feminine, Rézi displays blond and serpentine charms that are an obvious foil for the boyish grace of the olive-skinned, short-haired Claudine. Renaud takes a vicarious pleasure in supplying the two women with a bachelor apartment, to which he ceremoniously conducts them several times a week. In love with Rézi, Claudine is nonetheless vaguely ill at ease with her husband's libertine complaisance. As the scenes shift to the small apartment where the liaison takes place, the atmosphere becomes increasingly claustrophobic. The climax occurs when Claudine, who is supposed to be sick in bed, goes out for a breath of air and strolls to the trysting place, only to discover her husband in the arms of her mistress. Contrite and nauseated, she flees to Montigny and later invites Renaud to come live with her in her beloved countryside.

Less well constructed than the three previous novels, *Claudine and Annie* attempts to widen the focus of the Claudine story by weaving it with another story, Annie's. She is a kind of double of Claudine, incarnating both the latter's temptation toward submission and her growing taste for independence. Some time has passed since Claudine's retreat to Montigny; she and Renaud are together again and making the circuit of the chic watering places and opera houses of Europe. (Parts of the novel are set in Bayreuth, where Colette and Willy had attended the Wagner festival in 1895.) In their social circle is Annie, a timid young woman, her husband's creature. When he leaves her for several months of business in South America, she painfully assumes her own liberty and the responsibility for her life, going off alone at the end.

Annie returns in *Retreat from Love* (1907) to Casamène, the country estate she owns and where Claudine has been staying while an ailing Renaud languishes in a mountain sanatorium. This is the most diffuse and the least satisfactory novel of the group: there is no real plot, but rather a series of conversations in which Annie details her adventures and promiscuity. Claudine tries to amuse herself by playing go-between for her nymphomaniac friend Annie and her homosexual stepson Marcel. When Renaud finally returns to her side, he is a sick old man in whom Claudine sees only a maimed image of her love: the husband she delighted in calling her daddy now looks like her grandfather. Renaud's humiliation and Claudine's disgust are mercifully short-lived. His death restores her to nature and herself. The series ends where it began—in the country. She has exchanged physical and emotional submission for liberty and nature.

Claudine's Heroinism

The Claudine books are more than the point of departure for Colette's ascent toward literary glory, more than an incondite commentary on her youth, more too than a testimony to the taste for scandal that characterized the Belle Epoque. They are a unique response to an extraordinary demand. In the lines from *Looking Backwards* quoted at the beginning of this chapter, Colette speaks of necessity putting a pen in her hand, of submissiveness, patience, and duty, and of getting a little money for the pages she produced. In French society as it was organized in 1900, Willy as husband—and a husband she loved—was undisputed master, exercising sexual, emotional, and financial control. Colette was left to exercise only the female virtues she names. What is extraordinary is not that she should have so easily acceded to his requiring her to write, but that she should have created an enduring comic heroine and at the same time turned out so original and so sustained a portrait of female strength, sexuality, and lust. Claudine's saga sets unexpected physical priorities for woman and embodies the refusal not only of conventional values and ordinary notions of fidelity, morality, and vice, but even of conventional perspectives on adultery. Her adulterous act, equivalent to Renaud's (Rézi is mistress of both), demands recognition of herself as Renaud's physical equal, and her flight to the country establishes her as his moral superior. In a review of *Claudine Married* in the *Mercure de France,* Rachilde suggests the sense behind the surface perversions: she notes that Claudine "is the great and eternal enemy of man,"[2] and she does not seem far from right. The series implicitly concludes that man can provide neither the control nor the guidance that woman has been taught to seek from him. At best, he can give some pleasure, but not in any ultimate sense. Renaud's death is an appropriate abdication. Family, school, marriage, adultery: Colette addresses society's (and the novel's) most important institutions. But rather than allow her heroine to be determined by their influence, she has Claudine subversively rewrite them, so that each experience is a vehicle for female pleasure and discovery.

The Pendant Redemption

Between her first book, *Claudine at School,* and her best known, *My Mother's House* (a collection of vignettes published in book form in 1922), there exist affinities that have gone unrecognized, for they are both evident and elusive. The French title of *My Mother's House* is *La Maison de Claudine*—*Claudine*'s house: Sido in fact appears importantly within it, but the cover and the title page belong to Claudine. Thus it explicitly attaches itself to Colette's first novels; this fact, and the central role it plays in her opus, justify treating it in conjunction with the Claudine works.

If the striking similarity of the two bipartite titles (*Claudine à l'école* and *La Maison de Claudine*) is revealing, it is also a subterfuge, for in the second work the name of Claudine appears nowhere after the title. And the title was itself urged on Colette by an editor eager to exploit the publicity already enjoyed by the name. But the obvious bears emphasizing: Colette did accept the proposition and the published text does bear

Claudine's name. This circumstance suggests a link that deserves exploring: the autofiction of *Claudine à l'école* may be considered both origin and prophecy of the autobiographical content of *La Maison de Claudine*.[3] The earlier book is, in the photographic sense, a kind of negative for the other.

In the interval between the two works, Colette sometimes turned autobiography into fiction—as, for example, in *The Vagabond* and *The Shackle; La Maison de Claudine* in a certain way does the opposite. It inaugurates a new era in her writing, ostensibly autobiographical and portraying not the present, as do most of the preceding works, but a relatively distant past. The past she treats here, however, is, first of all, a literary past: the book's very title (whatever the historical explanation for its adoption) places it under the sign of her entrance into literature. And the text answers to its title, for the autobiography expands on the earlier fiction, both in its themes of purity, communication, and discovery, and in the problem of the distance between the subject and the content of the discourse: Claudine's proximity to the events of her journal; Colette's relation to the material of her past.

The message of the first page of *Claudine à l'école,* where the diarist takes issue with expressions in her *Manual of Departmental Geography,* may be compared to that of the passage from *La Maison de Claudine* that I discussed in my first chapter: "The Priest on the Wall." In both cases the protagonist finds language as adults use it unfit for her experience. The reaction in the novel is a downward thrust and the insistence on a dilapidated world, while in *La Maison de Claudine,* it is to climb to a multi-hued terrace adorned with lilac trees, polished pebbles, and colored glass. But the downward movement has its figurative counterpart elsewhere: the narrator of *La Maison de Claudine* descends into a past from which many years separate her.

Moreover, while the journal form of *Claudine à l'école* attempts to fix events in an historical present tense, to guarantee the integrity of a school year coextensive with the composition of the journal, the sketches that make up *La Maison de Claudine* embalm the past *as past,* in its oscillations, ambiguities, and repetitions. For the past at issue here is not the simple one of Colette's first novel; now the narrator's youth meshes with that of her mother and daughter, and the protagonist is thus a multiple character, a composite of Gabri/"la petite"/Minet-Chéri, Sido and Bel Gazou. These three rejoin and repeat each other, just as do the sundry household pets of the novel's concluding chapters—the progeny of Claudine's Fanchette. The past is thus cyclical, forever alive and evasive.

To the question resounding in the silence opening *La Maison de Claudine*—"where are the children?"—the answer is: everywhere and nowhere.

Yet even a superficial reading confirms that these are dramatically different texts, distinguished by form of composition, by surface texture, by the degree of something we might call sincerity. If we choose to classify differently these two works of autobiographical inspiration, calling the one a kind of fiction and the other a kind of autobiography, it is because the latter manifests a more complete identification of author and narrator/protagonist.[4] *La Maison de Claudine* is framed, moreover, in a more rigorous critical perspective, and the atmosphere is different. While Claudine moves in a moral vacuum among people of no distinction, no achievement, and no consequence, creating herself out of nothing, the narrator of *La Maison de Claudine* develops her ties to a family and a setting, and emphasizes the transmission of a certain womanly wisdom from one generation to the next. And even the differences are suggested in the titles. If the two works are indissolubly linked by the name of Claudine on the title page, the prepositions differ. Is Claudine posted *at* school, but in possession *of* the house? Does the first case suggest a momentary association, the second a true bond?

The original novel so effectively exorcised the school that the later work (which deals broadly with the question of "education," in the French sense of "upbringing") accords no importance to this institution: the very word appears only a very few times in passing—for example when village schoolrooms, vacated of children, become the site of the Captain's political addresses. In counterpoint, the village church and its curé appear and acquire significance, the word "presbytery" becoming, as we have seen, the vehicle to communicate some of the magic of childhood inventiveness. In *Claudine à l'école*, sex itself is nonproductive and nonfamilial: sex for recreation. *La Maison de Claudine,* on the other hand, concerns itself with the female implications of sex: sex for procreation, whether among animals or humans. Thus the burlesque sexuality permeating the school is consigned in *La Maison de Claudine* to the status of a fantasm that elicits from Minet-Chéri less curiosity than alarm. Unlike Claudine, who is titillated by voluptuousness and lechery, "la petite" in *La Maison de Claudine* faints during a reading of a childbirth scene in Zola and flees in fright from a nuptial chamber. When she chances to discover the family's female dog, the amiable Toutouque, wildly pursuing another neighborhood bitch in a dispute over a mate, she can find no adequate terms to express her dismay "at seeing an evil power, whose very name was unknown to my ten years, so transform the gentlest of creatures into a savage brute" (95).

Most important, in *La Maison de Claudine* the home emerges and the missing mother enters creation. Just as the action of *Claudine à l'école* was predicated on the mother's absence ("If I had a Mamma, I know very well that she would not have let me stay here twenty-four hours"), now the omnipresent Sido is the matrix of the text, the image that encompasses and renders intelligible the others. Her presence and sovereignty constitute the work's axis. Sido reigns over a house spatially and temporally set apart—a paradise. Claudine's house? Sido's house really, morally and legally. And if the mother's absence in the novel allowed freedom for sexual investigation, is not the child's secure place in the maternal home based partially on a denial of sexuality? Does not her sexual reticence, although essentially healthy, harbor a grain of repression?

The paradise, then, while superficially enchanting, is flawed, like the earlier version. The characters who gravitate around Sido—the Captain, Léo, Juliette—are in their own subtle ways as strange and perverse as those of *Claudine à l'école*. They uneasily inhabit a den of eerie silence. The irony of *Claudine à l'école* is directed against the provisional character of the school-paradise, its licentiousness, and the dubious nature of what passes for education. These are paralleled in *La Maison de Claudine* by the subtle incompatibility of some family members, by the alienation of the older sister and by the instability of the home-paradise; but the tone differs dramatically as eulogy displaces parody. The structure and project of the two works mimic one another. They are typified by the predominance of the I (now single, now composite), by its nostalgic plunge (now literal, now figurative) into time or space, and by the arrangement of experience around a privileged and symbolic geographical location (now the school, now the home). Both works trace the attempt to possess a fragmented past and to make it coherent.

We may read *La Maison de Claudine* as the pendant redemption of *Claudine à l'école*. Or, to return to the photographic metaphor, we may view it as the positive image. Mother supersedes father; a presence, an absence; the home, the school. School and house are mutually exclusive, functioning as the coordinates of the space designated as childhood. The first organizes a problematic tutelage, a young woman's receptiveness and the reality of compromise; the second reasserts her integrity and roots. Together they encompass the totality of a female experience.

Out of Colette's compliance with Willy, a genuine vocation had been born, and the autofiction would remain unfinished until the appearance of *La Maison de Claudine*. In Colette's opus it has the special function of exonerating not just an existence, but a troublesome work of fiction, first product and enduring emblem of her life. *La Maison de Claudine* parallels and redeems the maiden writ: it is at once its repudiation and its completion.

Minne

Colette explains in a late preface how *The Innocent Libertine* (*L'Ingénue libertine*) was written in two stages. The first part, *Minne,* inspired by a 1903 news item, was conceived as a short story, in the futile hope that the author might be permitted to sign her own name to it; her spouse's literary cupidity did not normally focus on anything of less than the dimensions of a novel. But the tale's success was its perdition. Willy not only signed the publication in 1904, but also insisted that the heroine's adventures be spun out, and the following year saw the appearance of *"Minne's Escapades"* (*Les Egarements de Minne*), also bearing his name. Only in 1909 were the two volumes welded together, retitled, and published under the new signature "Colette Willy."

Colette herself denigrated *The Innocent Libertine,* displaying as little affection for it as for the Claudine series that immediately preceded it. The novel's weaknesses are undeniable. Both characterization and technique remain imperfect; the first lacks subtlety, the second is at times artificial—as, for example, when Minne monologues in a taxi. The plot is vaguely reminiscent of a comic book. Critics have sometimes invoked its shortcomings as an excuse to shun the explicit treatment of fascination with rape and desire for orgasm, and to disqualify it as a serious novel. But Colette's work as a whole and this novel in particular suggest a reinterpretation of notions of innocence and purity, which are construed in *The Innocent Libertine* in such a way as to admit of calculation, cunning, and even promiscuity. In spite of her relish of inchoate sexual play and the spectacle of deviation, the Claudine of the first book— thanks to her own exigencies—remains paradoxically pure. In the case of Minne, the apparent contradiction between her activities and her fundamentally pure nature is even more remarkable; she is a stunning example of artlessness and dissoluteness.

Like the first volume of the Claudine series, part one of *The Innocent Libertine* is set in the world of adolescent perverseness and innocence, of the intransigence of "fresh, cruel youth" (74), of impatience with the old, the ugly and the infirm. Nearly 15 years old, Minne displays a fragility of appearance that belies her passionate nature. The transparence of her silky hair (alternately described as "silver" and "gold"), the thinness of her body and the profundity of her unfathomable dark eyes—all these conceal the exemplary naughtiness of an adolescent who courts the romantic and the sinister. Stirred by newspaper accounts of the gang wars between two bands of Paris ruffians, Minne is obsessed with ideas of assassination and high drama. She dreams of joining the gang that inhabits the outskirts of the city, of becoming queen of the hooligans, fiancée of their leader, Le Frisé. But summer intervenes and she is whisked off to the country, where she spends the vacation with her mother, her pimply-faced cousin Antoine, and his hypochondriac physician father. The dream lies dormant until after the return to Paris, when it suddenly erupts into reality.

A night prowler outside her window is metamorphosed into the beloved Le Frisé, come to take her away. Feverish, Minne dons the baroque getup which in her mind corresponds to the role she expects to play: a red neck ribbon, a smock, red bedroom slippers, a chignon. She races out, but the prowler has moved along. A nightmarish adventure ensues as Minne chases a shadow down streets and alleyways, far from the safety of her own neighborhood, and grows cold, frightened, footsore, and lost. Instead of Le Frisé, she encounters a belligerent prostitute, a drunken lecher, and several additional characters, as unsavory as they are unromantic. By dawn, she has fortuitously found her way home and collapsed on the doorstep. Mamma and Uncle Paul cannot fathom what has happened to this golden child. With Antoine's reaction to the dirty and disheveled figure of his cousin, part one concludes: "He wept for Minne and he also wept for himself because she was lost, debased, branded forever with a hall-mark of filth" (93).

Several years have passed when we meet Minne in part two. She is married to Antoine, her mother having decreed on her deathbed that a girl who stayed out all night could hardly marry anyone else. Minne is disgusted with this devoted but clumsy husband, who acted on their wedding night like "Pan labouring to seduce a nymph" (105). Two years of marriage have failed to give her the one experience which she has decided is worth having, the experience which will make of her "a woman like other women" (122). Whereas her obsession in part one was fairly abstract, her desire for orgasm in part two is highly specific. Methodically she pursues her goal, first in the bed of a rich young baron, then with the paunchy journalist Maugis (whom the Colette reader has previously met as a friend of Renaud in the Claudine series, and who is based on the more easily caricatured aspects of Willy). Minne's beauty drives men to distraction, and the baron attempts suicide when she leaves him. In an exhilarating ending, she finally discovers sexual fulfillment with her husband Antoine, once each has assimilated lessons of altruism and gentleness.

The book's two parts construct a metaphor where sex represents the unknown. It illustrates Roland Barthes's contention that desire is encoded in and passion born of the written word.[5] At the origin of Minne's search are words: "the passion of which she knew nothing . . . was only a word to her, a hissing word that she whispered under her breath as if testing the new lash of a whip" (26). The novel opens with a schoolgirl ostensibly composing an essay, but surreptitiously *reading* a newspaper article whose purple prose transforms seedy events into high romance. In her suggestibility, Minne is the ideal consumer of such prose, which will literally become for her an event. Her comprehension of the heroic exploits of the gang is furthered by another image, this one also verbal: Antoine's description of the actress Polaire playing the role of a streetwalker. It is her costume, as Antoine reports it, that Minne attempts to duplicate for her nocturnal adventure. And during a languid summer afternoon with Antoine, she casually drops the expression "to rape," in an effort to tease out of the word its real meaning, just as years later she admits that she is determined to find out the meaning of what books call "infamous practices" (104). Polaire turns up again in the second part, an exquisite skater in the Ice Palace, and again Minne tries to imitate her by taking up skating. The Ice Palace may be seen as a mirror which Minne interrogates, while it also symbolizes her sexual frigidity and purity. In *The Pure and the Impure,* Colette would make a sustained inquiry into the elusive meanings of those terms; her sense is already adumbrated here.

Animal Dialogues

In 1904 there also appeared a different kind of book, the first to bear the author's name: *Dialogues de bêtes,* signed Colette Willy. All her life Colette loved animals, and she suggests more than once that she preferred their company to that of her human friends. Her contemporaries testify to her uncanny powers of communication and domination in the presence of animals. In *Break of Day,* she reports that Jouvenel would say to her, "When I enter a room where you're alone with your animals . . . I feel I'm being indiscreet" (44). The four sketches in *Dialogues de bêtes* represent her first attempt to write at length about animals. The book stars a pair whose exploits are less dramatic than Claudine's and Minne's, but who were to be no less enduring and emblematic. Toby-Dog (Toby-Chien) and Kiki-the-Demure (Kiki-la-Doucette) are a brindled bulldog and an angora cat, both males, whose names the public associates with Colette's and whose articulate barks and meows resound through her opus. They demonstrated the versatility of the young author and capitalized on the period's interest in animals. The volume had a fair success, and was expanded and reedited the following year as *Sept Dialogues de bêtes,* with a preface by poet Francis Jammes; in 1930 it became *Douze Dialogues de bêtes.* Of the dozen sketches in the final version, which has been translated as *Creature Conversations,* 11 are in dialogue form (only "The Bitch" ["La Chienne"] is a narrative) and the first nine give the floor to Toby-Dog and Kiki-the-Demure, with several anonymous counterparts occupying the last few pages.

The expression of Francis Jammes (whose own poetry shows a predilection for animals) may be old-fashioned, but his comment is apt: Colette "celebrates with the voice of a pure French stream the sad tenderness which makes the hearts of animals beat so fast."[6] Her characterizations of the household pets are persuasive, their conversations figurative and spirited. She has attributed to the animals subtle—and essentially human—reactions to events like meals, baths, storms, and train travel, and translated them into words.

The dog is entirely his mistress's creature, while the cat reveres the male. The text maliciously dubs the masters "lords of lesser importance" (than the animals), these conflicted humans who wield the power of life and death over their pets. Colette gently mocks herself when the mistress cries out in frustration, "I've had enough of it! I want... I want... I want to do as I please!" and Toby wonders, "And who is preventing You, O You who reign over my life, You who can do almost everything, You who, with a mere frown, can make the sky cloud over?" (107). The masters are designated only as "He" and "She," but their professions, pastimes, and quarrels, even the mistress's illness, echo those of the Gauthier-Villars, and the animals are astute commentators on their moods, foibles, and folly.

These dialogues, then, like the Claudine novels, mythologize Colette's autobiography—one in which the making of literature already plays a major role. The legend of Claudine permeates her literary apprenticeship. Not only are Minne's encounters with Maugis (Renaud's Parisian chum in the later Claudine books) and Polaire (the actress who created the role of Claudine) crucial to her story; Kiki-the-Demure and Toby-Dog also lean gingerly on Claudine for a kind of authentification. In a sketch entitled "Toby-Dog Speaks" ("Toby-Chien parle"), the bulldog describes for his companion their mistress's rantings at her husband's infidelities; she imagines him pursued by "the whole gang of horrid little fans with Peter-pan collars and bobbed hair who edge up to Him, lowering their lashes and wriggling their hips, with: 'O Monsieur, it's I who am the real Claudine'" (108).[7] Toby-Dog is here quoting his mistress, who is herself paraphrasing her husband's would-be protégées with this allusion to the "real Claudine." The mention of Colette's fictional double situates the volume in a temporal framework (the period after the initial success of the novels Willy signed) and a fictional universe (over which Claudine reigns). It also suggests the complexity of relations between fiction and autobiography, life and literature. The fictional Claudine has weight enough to be one of the determining factors of the quality of life for the real Colette, while the aspiring actresses and parvenues of Toby-Dog's world regard the heroine's potential reality as a vehicle for acquiring an identity of their own.

Colette's literary apprenticeship was coming to an end: her divorce from Willy was decreed in 1910. In the books written after this period, Claudine's name and the names of her entourage play a less important role. But on the other hand, many of the later works would be organized around another name: her own. "Colette" was to become a first-person narrator of a great many stories, thus onomastically supplanting Claudine and seeming to guarantee her tales' unity and authenticity not only within the world of fiction, but also in the real world.

Chapter Three
Mirrors and Letters

The Music Hall

The second decade of the twentieth century saw the appearance of four major works by Colette, which can profitably be read with and against each other. A series of vignettes published in 1913, *Music-Hall Sidelights* (*L'Envers du music-hall*), evokes the theatrical milieu that furnishes the background for three frankly feminocentric novels. The French title, which could be rendered literally as "the wrong side" or "the reverse side" of the music hall, indicates the effort to portray the undersurface of theater life; Colette is concerned less with what the public sees from the pit than with what the actors experience backstage. The sketches demonstrate her lifelong capacity for finding interest in routine occurrences and ordinary people.

In these portraits composed in the first person, Colette insists on the destitution, fatalism, and pride of her theatrical colleagues. In their capacity for hard work and their uncomplaining endurance of misery, they heroically rise above their sordid surroundings. Most of all, Colette stresses their dignified silence; they are neither a confiding nor an effusive lot, these children of poverty, and they practice their arts with very little talk. The narrator's own profession of mime appears symbolic; in an early passage, she explains that when she and her partner perform, their every effort is directed toward the exclusion of speech, in an attempt to unverbalize experience: "Invested with a subtler task than those who speak classical verse or exchange witticisms in lively prose, we are eager to banish from our mute dialogues the earthbound word, the one obstacle between us and silence—perfect, limpid, rhythmic silence" (133).

The period's three novels compellingly complement *Music-Hall Sidelights,* for the protagonist of each is a music-hall dancer (or ex-dancer), skilled in a nonverbal art, who struggles in private life against loneliness, misunderstandings, and especially silence. Each heroine is characterized by a discursive self-consciousness. Chronologically first, *The Vagabond* (1910) is the most analytic and most manifestly personal of Colette's major novels, clearly reminiscent of her experiences during the years following the separation from Willy, when she was earning her lonely bread working with the mime Georges Wague. One of these events was her courtship by a wealthy young man, Auguste Hériot, whose family owned a major Paris department store, the Grands Magasins du Louvre. *The Vagabond*'s heroine, who is a performer and writer like Colette, also refuses the hand of a rich and persistent suitor. Plot joins *The Vagabond* to *The Shackle,* which appeared three years later and continues the story of its heroine. By this time Colette had married Henry de Jouvenel, and in *The Shackle* her character also settles down with a man. But thematically and formally, as well as in the use of decor, *The Vagabond* is more closely related to *Mitsou,* a novel that appeared in 1919, and I shall treat these two in tandem, before turning to *The Shackle.*

The Vagabond and *Mitsou:* Tradition

The Vagabond and *Mitsou* are anachronistic in two senses. In the first place, by virtue of preoccupations with female sexuality and work, they anticipate the most modern novels about women. In a contrary sense, by their use of letters, they recall the fiction of a much earlier period. These novels look backward, therefore, as well as forward, but the contradiction is only apparent, for the recourse to the outmoded epistolary form is in fact coherent with the attempt to express, thematically, female identity.

In the early years of its history, when the novel could perhaps aptly be described—as one critic put it half a century ago—as "women's fief,"[1] a favored pretext for literary women was the epistolary form. On both sides of the Channel, the female practitioners during its heyday, the mid- and late-eighteenth century, were many; Françoise de Graffigny, Marie Jeanne Riccoboni, Isabelle de Charrière, Sophie Cottin, Eliza Haywood, and Clara Reeve, to name only a handful, produced letter-writing heroines whose amorous adventures and intimate epistles fired the imagination of their public. Various hypotheses have been advanced as to why women writers particularly affected the letter-novel, but none is entirely satisfactory, any more than literary critics have fully explained why it is that, even in letter-novels written by men, the lone or at least the major fictional writer tends to be female—think of Guilleragues's Portuguese Nun, of Richardson's Pamela and Clarissa, of Diderot's Suzanne.

Colette's adoption of a modified letter-form, therefore, is an experiment that places her squarely in a specific feminine tradition of fiction,

that of women novelists creating analytical letter-writing women. Like
their ancestors in the corpuses of sundry eighteenth-century women
writers—Graffigny's *Lettres d'une Péruvienne* (1747), for example, or
Riccoboni's *Lettres de Mistriss Fanni Butlerd* (1757)—both novels are concerned with a young woman whose letters to a lover are the expression
of her passion and the means of coming to terms with an event of
import. The Colette works, in which the letters are addressed directly *to*
the loved one—as distinct from novels where the lover is the *subject* of
the letters, the addressee being a third party—are examples of the kind
of epistolary novel that is most dramatic (even literally, for its relation to
theater is intimate). Since the addressee is a protagonist, writing is itself
an event of moment, and letters are the means of creating emotions and
reaching decisions, not merely instruments for conveying them.

The use of an archaic device appropriated by women is significant
because the two novels in question are precisely concerned with women's
discovery and affirmation of themselves. *The Vagabond* is written as a
journal: the story of divorcée Renée Néré—as introverted and reflexive
as her name—who ekes out a living as dancer and mime. When a
wealthy and idle suitor by the name of Maxime Dufferein-Chautel proposes to her, Renée's recollections of her unhappy first marriage to a society painter named Taillandy dispose her against it, while her loneliness,
her sexual needs, and Max's sheer persistence incline her to accept. She
finally agrees that she will be his on her return from a theatrical tour
that will take her and her partner Brague through the south of France,
and she sets out on her journey full of hope. But six weeks of travel, of
keeping a diary, and of corresponding with Max persuade her that she
must reject him in favor of emotional independence and professional
autonomy. She comes back to Paris with just enough strength to flee
from him permanently.

Considerably shorter than *The Vagabond, Mitsou* is technically more
experimental. The first part of the novel is written mainly as though it
were a play (in dialogue and with stage directions), although there is also
some traditional third-person narrative. To these dramatic and narrative
forms, the novel's latter section juxtaposes a series of letters. They
recount a brief affair between another dancer, Mitsou, and a young soldier who is dressed in a blue uniform when they first meet. She happens
across him one day backstage at the "café-concert" where she works, and
although they exchange only a few sentences, Mitsou becomes infatu-
ated. So when he goes to the front she writes to him, and when he comes
home on leave they spend the night together—a single night of love,

because the simple music hall girl and the bourgeois lieutenant are from different worlds. But Mitsou's passion has increased her stature: love is an effective antidote to mediocrity. The novel's subtitle, *Comment l'esprit vient aux filles* (*How Girls Grow Wise* is one early translator's rendering of it),[2] is the title of a tale by the seventeenth-century poet La Fontaine, where "l'esprit" is a metaphor for sexual knowledge. It is an apt commentary on Colette's entire opus, where wisdom always has solid physical bases as well as emotional and intellectual ones.

Both novels are set in a theatrical milieu, and both heroines achieve self-knowledge through letter-writing and the use of mirrors. The opening scene of each work is a dressing room, a closed, close space where the performer is surrounded by her own reflection. Her very profession obliges her endlessly to contemplate her duplicate self: typically, Mitsou "looks at her own flowerlike image in the glass" (17). These initial reflections are as inauthentic as they are exact, because in this setting Renée and Mitsou are costumed, made up, literally or figuratively masked. Into this world comes an outsider who threatens its tranquillity—and one who is in some sense yet another mirror image of the heroine. Robert, Mitsou's Blue Lieutenant, is exactly her age (twenty-four), while Max is even more exactly Renée's (thirty-three and a half). For the women, the resemblances are beguiling. Robert hooks the back of Mitsou's costume, and she says thank you to the reflection in the mirror: "two young dark heads with big eyes, that might be brother and sister. Mitsou smiles, Blue Lieutenant smiles, and they look even more alike" (10). In one of her letters, she compares herself and Robert to twins. From the narcissistic setting of the theater, with its possibilities for spatial identification, the heroines return to apartments that also reflect them: Mitsou's is heteroclite, its furnishings as anomalous, as devoid of sophistication as she. Renée Néré's manifests her own ambiguity: to her suitor it appears a "charming, cozy nest," while she maintains, on the contrary, that it "gives an impression of indifference, neglect, hopelessness, almost of imminent departure" (76).

Letters

Eventually there develop the correspondences that provide the most revealing images of the heroines: verbal likenesses. In the first place, their very handwriting reflects them: as Robert comments on Mitsou's "schoolgirl's writing," so Renée speaks of her own "rapid, uneven writing which he [Max] says is like my mobile face, exhausted from expressing too much" (199). Moreover, Renée's complexity and ambivalence are reflected in her writing, as Mitsou's simplicity and eagerness are mirrored in hers. These traits are more or less apprehended by the recipients of the letters, but the more crucial function of the correspondences is to provide for the heroines themselves another reflection, an orthographic counterpart to the specular image. (The journal kept by Renée gives, of course, an additional reflection of her, but one which in a sense is less revealing, since it does not manifest the curiously telling distortions that letters contain by their very nature: written, ostensibly, for the other, letters are speech acts, not merely descriptions.) Writing is intimately associated with discovery—so much so that it even supplies the metaphors where seeing and knowing are evoked: when her internal formulation of an idea strikes her as illuminating, Renée exclaims: "This time the formula is clear. I saw it written in my mind and I see it there still, printed like a judgment in small, bold capitals" (202–3).

A dichotomy between writing and speech informs Mitsou's experience just as it does Renée's, for both are normally taciturn: Renée acknowledges that her real vocation is one of "silence and dissimulation," and Mitsou's easygoing friend Bit-of-Fluff (Petite Chose) admonishes the Blue Lieutenant at his first meeting with Mitsou: "Don't rely much on her to keep the conversation going" (9). And she herself writes him that "I am relying a lot on my silence, for when you come here and are near me" (60). Yet she composes vibrant letters, so captivating that they elicit equally long answers. Writing is posited in the two works as an unexpectedly welcome alternative to speech, even when the composition of a letter is inherently difficult, as in Mitsou's case. But while Renée, in the last analysis, writes chiefly for herself, and communicates principally with her looking-glass, Mitsou communicates with her Blue Lieutenant. Whereas Renée is "almost sincere," as she assures herself, and ready to "write—briefly, for time is short—and lie to him" (195), Mitsou proclaims her perfect sincerity, and reminds her correspondent that she writes "truthfully." Renée's engaging words are only the shadow of her thoughts, but the Blue Lieutenant can remark: "Mitsou with no grace or style, Mitsou with a schoolgirl's handwriting, you've never once failed to convey to me in your letters just exactly what you wanted to say, nothing more nor less" (51). Renée draws back from a tentative engagement and confirms her solipsism, whereas Mitsou from indifference accedes to commitment.

The form of the novels reflects these differences. *The Vagabond* contains Renée's letters to Max, but only fragments—or reflections in her own—

of his to her. *Mitsou,* on the other hand, presents a veritable exchange of letters, seven by the heroine as well as the five complete responses they elicit. Nor are the letters worked into the text as in the earlier novel; the first 11 letters of *Mitsou* appear one directly upon the other, without commentary, and the twelfth closes the volume. *The Vagabond,* then, is essentially a monologue. Max's very words are subordinated to Renée's, filtered through her consciousness. Its form is linear, there being no real exchange. *Mitsou,* however, is a duo, the two voices speaking out with equal strength, and Robert's own letters betraying a gentle bourgeois fatuousness, just as Mitsou's reveal her earnestness and love.

An epistolary exchange requires, first and foremost, a separation between the correspondents, and this necessary absence—which, according to Roland Barthes, constitutes one of the chief figures of amorous discourse—also functions differently in the two Colette novels. Barthes notes that in general it is the man who leaves, while the woman remains—waiting, sedentary, faithful. It is therefore she who experiences absence.[3] *Mitsou* presents the classic situation of which he speaks: the woman temporarily abandoned. In *The Vagabond,* on the other hand, it is Renée who leaves, Max who idly awaits her return. In the Barthesian sense, then, Renée cannot be said to suffer from absence, and for her the letter is not the means of filling a void, but rather the desired substitute for a presence.

The use of letters, objects and even characters as reflections of the protagonists is reinforced in both novels by the theme of spectatorship. The four central characters contemplate themselves and each other. Even from afar, with the mind's eye, they watch: "I see you so clearly, now that I'm far away" (191), writes Renée to Maxime. The Blue Lieutenant gets his first chance to study Mitsou when he hides in her closet and observes her as she makes up before her mirror, and Maxime falls in love with Renée while watching her—assiduously, evening after evening—perform on stage. Later he stares at Renée sleeping in her apartment. In bed, Mitsou gazes at Robert asleep; when she eventually dozes off, he awakens and they exchange roles. Renée Néré's lucidity leads her to realize that her first concession to Max is a surrender to her desire to keep "not an admirer, not a friend, but an eager spectator of my life and my person" (111). A capital moment is the one where Renée chances to find herself in the wings, observing the observers—among them her suitor: "By a curious transposition, he it is who becomes the spectacle for me" (95). The oscillation of the "spectacle" between the stage and the house attenuates Renée's experience of her alterity: for once, she is not herself the exhibition. She assimilates the moment to sleep: "I think in fact that I must have fallen asleep, or else I am just emerging from one of those moments when one's mind goes blank before some painful idea is set in motion, moments which are the prelude to a slight loss of morale" (95). It is the start of a revolution in her relation to Max because the temporary dislocation—like sleep, with its function of restoration—permits Renée to begin a reappropriation of herself.

There are, of course, other works by Colette in which letters figure importantly: the celebrated rose-cactus letter is placed at the start of *Break of Day;* and in another novel of her maturity, *Duo,* the letters from the heroine to her lover, although cited for the most part only indirectly, are crucial. But in no other work by Colette do letters occupy so much space or play so extensive a role as in the two under consideration here. Yet commentators on Colette's recourse to epistolary form normally cite only *Mitsou* and make no mention of *The Vagabond.*[4]

Mitsou does in fact put letters to a striking—and indeed traditional— use, for its heroine affirms her identity by means of her correspondence. She meets the Blue Lieutenant, as Renée does Max, the "Big-Noodle" ("Le Grand Serin"), early in the novel when he barges into her dressing-room, and the intruder is initially as unwelcome as Maxime Dufferein-Chautel. At her first writing to him, Mitsou is all the same intrigued: by the time she sends him her sixth letter, she is in love. No meeting has intervened between the first and the sixth letters, nor has the soldier, far more sophisticated than she, seduced her through his responses— Mitsou, for the most part, does not even fully grasp their meaning. It is rather her own unprecedented epistolary efforts—"I would like to impress on you that it's really something in my life for me to start writing letters, and letters to you too" (49)—that make her fall in love. Writing to the Blue Lieutenant demonstrates to Mitsou that she whose placid affair with her present lover, the "Respectable Man" ("L'Homme Bien"), has been as unproblematic as unexciting, now wants something more. Initially less self-aware than Renée, Mitsou undergoes an evolution through letters that is therefore all the more stunning, finally achieving what Colette calls a kind of "banal heroism." She learns to write as she learns to love, and this uneducated dancer acquires refinement of expression as well as of sentiment.

It is nonetheless the earlier novel that better rewards inquiry into the homologies between epistolary form and woman's search for identity. *The Vagabond* better illustrates both the form's complexity and its unique suitability for exploring questions of self-image.

Language is characteristically a central preoccupation in epistolary novels, where protagonists deal not with each other but with pen and paper, where lovers communicate not by sound and touch but through graphemes, and where articulating an emotion is therefore at least as crucial as experiencing it—if indeed emotions are not actually born of the attempt to evoke them in writing. *The Vagabond*'s heroine is a some-time novelist, diarist, and letter-writer as well as a professional mime. Written in the first person and the present tense, the novel poses the problem of language as central. Renée's dilemma with regard to the man who bursts into her life (through the door of her dressing-room), and tries to lay the world at her feet, is precisely linguistic. Her inability to come to terms with her would-be lover is symbolically revealed by her inability to find terms in which to speak to him. Accordingly, in her journal she writes:

> I don't know how to talk to you, poor Dufferein-Chautel. I hesitate between my own *personal* language, which is rather brusque, does not always condescend to finish its sentences, but sets great store on getting its technical terms exact—the language of a one-time bluestocking—and the slovenly, lively idiom, coarse and picturesque, which one learns in the music-hall, sprinkled with expressions like: "You bet!" "Shut up!" "I'm clearing out!" "Not my line!"
> Unable to decide, I choose silence. (83)

When Renée evokes the language of the music hall and contrasts it with the language of the ex-bluestocking, she is hesitating between two forms of expression, both of which would in effect trap her in a closed universe of discourse at the very moment when she is trying to find a new means of expression. The temporary choice of silence, in the absence of an idiolect, is the recognition of the inherent unsuitability of both these idioms.

How indeed is she even to address Max? Her ambivalence is translated by her refusal to accord him a Christian name; she affects instead to call him by his absurd, multi-syllabic, hyphenated family name: "I called him Dufferein-Chautel as usual, as though he had no Christian name. I always call him 'You' or 'Dufferein-Chautel'" (121–22). The definition of his relation to her is also an area of linguistic difficulty, for she must settle not only on a second-person appellation, but also on a manner of referring to him in the third person: "For I have an admirer. Only this old-fashioned name seems to suit him: he is neither my lover, nor my flame, nor my gigolo; he is my admirer" (75). The outdated "admirer" ("*amoureux*") comes closest to Renée's sense, as the old-fashioned letter-form best suits her story.

The naming of Max represents the projection onto the lover of an internal dilemma; it is an appendage of Renée's difficulty in naming herself. The novel is Renée's search for an identity. Society, her friends, her former friends, her admirer, all endeavor to label her: for her concierge, she is "a lady on her own," "an artiste," while for her bluestocking acquaintances she is "a woman of letters who has turned out badly." Renée collects these definitions, pores over them, implicitly rejects them. Max himself proposes a definition, and this turns out to be a grave error; he writes Renée that soon she "will no longer be Renée Néré, but My Lady Wife" (191). Max's avowed project of replacing a proper noun— "Renée Néré"—with another substantive can only represent a threat of alienation to her whose name would be thus canceled. This is the letter, and this ostensibly the expression, that trigger her defense mechanism and result in her ultimate decision to refuse Max. A name is a word invoking a certain code, and as much as Max himself, it is the code to which he refers and the limitations it implies that Renée rejects. The definition to which she finally acquiesces is part of a less confining code. It is the very definition proposed by the title: she is and will remain a "vagabond." This term recurs throughout the journal, considered, appraised, nuanced—"A gipsy henceforth I certainly am, and one whom tours have led from town to town, but an orderly gipsy. . . . A vagabond, maybe, but one who is resigned to revolving on the same spot like my companions and brethren" (73–74)—before being at last accepted in her own personal sense: "A vagabond, and free" (223).

The working out of her own definition for herself depends considerably on the letters addressed to Max in part three. The correspondence is motivated by Renée's departure on a 40-day tour of music halls throughout France; she has promised Max that, on her return, they will begin a new life together. Unlike speech, where Renée is prey to reservations and hesitations, constantly tempted by the alternative of silence, writing, or at least familiar letter-writing, presents little difficulty for this former novelist: "Heavens, how I write to you! I could spend my whole time writing to you, I believe I find it easier to write than to talk to you" (182). Writing appears less imperative, pleasantly nugatory and, most important, admitting of endless ambiguity: "No, I should say nothing to him. But to write is so easy. To write, to write" (199). Letters may be viewed as creating events, but since they are based on an absence, the

events created are such that the writer is excluded as a present participant in them. Hence their attraction for Renée, who prefers silence to
speech, dissimulation to frankness and absence to presence.

Her letters are the agents of the resolution of her relationship with
Max; yet far from being a veritable means of communication with him,
they are a way of keeping him at bay through concealment of the essential
truth: her growing consciousness of her own ambivalence about love, passion, marriage. These letters are as equivocal as Renée herself. In fact, she
comments that her lover's responses so little take into account her implications that she might have written the opposite of what she actually did.
On occasion, nonetheless, an unsigned one-line note from an unexpectedly
perspicacious Max—"My Renée, do you no longer love me?"—stuns her:
"I had not foreseen that gentleness and the simplicity of that question,
which confound all my literature" (216). Thus does Renée evoke the essential literarity of her enterprise: what she composes is literature in the sense
of *écriture* as opposed to expression—an exercise in writing. It is literature
too in the sense of game, literature finally because she never does find her
medium; her continuing search for an alternative to music hall discourse
and the discourse of the bluestocking bears no fruit.

The epistolary dialogue, then, is a false dialogue (even formally, since
Max's letters do not appear) and Renée's gesture is solipsistic. She even
admits on occasion to the "strange impression" that a letter she has just
posted is "on its way to a man who ought not to have read it" (187). In
the letters she writes (and rereads), Renée searches for an accurate reflection of her mind and heart. Ultimately, she is her own interlocutor, while
her words are an effort to reconstitute herself.

On the verge of deciding not to go back to Max, Renée catches from
her train window a breath of salt air and a glimpse of the sea at Sète. She
is overwhelmed by the crushing beauty of the sea that is "refusing to let
itself be possessed" (206) by the morning sun. She feels like she is skim-
ming the waves, and calls it a perfect moment—ended by the sudden
memory of Max. In her mind, she sets up an opposition between her love
for him and her sensual needs on the one hand, and, on the other, her
love of nature and language, which confers the ability to possess the
world.

Mirrors

The letter's function is duplicated and its role extended by another item
of structural importance—the mirror. The juxtaposition of the two cre-

ates a "mise en abîme"—an endless internal reflection or repetition rendering salient the work's formal structure.[5] If in her journal and letters Renée is trying out various definitions, she is interrogating her mirror at every step. Mirrors provide another kind of reflection and lead her, as do the letters, to self-awareness. As early as the fourth paragraph, she talks about the "painted mentor" who gazes at her "from the other side of the looking-glass" (5). Each of the following three sentences in the text evokes the fear and the fascination exerted by this other, this stranger, this indefatigable observer. Renée is as menaced and as mesmerized by her mirror image as she is by attempts to categorize her as an "artiste," "My Lady Wife," etc. Accidentally or intentionally, she catches and studies her reflection every few pages throughout the novel. She looks involuntarily into the mirror of her dressing-room; at home, the full-length mirror in her bedroom makes her exclaim, "Behold me then, just as I am!" (11); in the street, she quickens her pace every time she glimpses her reflection in a shop window (118); and after embracing Max, she fumbles, almost frenetically, for the small pocket mirror in her handbag. Occasionally, her physical image converges with a verbal definition: "Facing me from the other side of the looking-glass, in that mysterious reflected room, is the image of 'a woman of letters who has turned out badly'" (13). Renée gives form here to the discourse of the other, inevitably recalling Lacan's discussion of the mirror stage: discovery of the self—"identification"—through the otherness of the image.[6] The reflection is the paradoxical self/other, alienated at the moment of inception. In Renée's case, moreover, the implicit linking of mirror and letter—culminating perhaps in the last pages of the text when an "ephemeral arrangement" of her writing table results in her composing a letter as she sits beside a cheval-mirror—suggests a restitution of the primordial relation between self and language. According to Lacan, it is language that restores to the *I* its function as subject.[7]

Dressing-room mirror, bedroom mirror, hand mirror, store window, even her reflection in Max's eyes—Renée is never far from her duplicate, who not merely returns her gaze but proffers advice as well. This function of the mirror as advisor is underscored on three occasions when Renée alludes to the "mentor," painted, pitiless, staring and speaking "from the other side" (5, 6, 129). The lesson drawn from the mirror coupled with her epistolary experience compels Renée to refuse Max. In the mirror she observes change: still lovely, yet less beautiful than she once was, she sees herself declining. "How quickly everything changes!... Especially women" she exclaims, and again: "he [Max] thinks I am young too, and he does not see the *end*—my end. In his blindness he will not admit that I must change and grow old" (193). Renée herself "sees" clearly the "end" of which she speaks, for the mirror seems to have the terrifying potential for actualizing her own inevitable disappearance: "it really is me there behind that mask of purplish rouge, my eyes ringed with a halo of blue grease-paint beginning to melt. Can the rest of my face be going to melt also? What if nothing were to remain of my whole reflection but a streak of dyed colour stuck to the glass like a long, muddy tear?" (7). On the other hand, the awesome stability she senses in herself becomes clearer through her letters to Max. As she meditates on their future together, she ineluctably assimilates him to her first husband, and views their love in terms of that disastrous marriage. She grows daily older, *visibly* changes, but is at heart incapable of change. Renée eventually becomes what she has always been, the person she occasionally caught sight of in the mirror, beneath the makeup and the masks—a vagabond, herself: "have I not again become *what I was,* that is to say free, horribly alone and free?" (214). In the concluding paragraphs, she assimilates Max's love to a distorting mirror: "I refuse to see the most beautiful countries of the world microscopically reflected in the amorous mirror of your eyes" (222). In order that none of her options be diminished, she chooses solitude over engagement, and turns in on herself, just as her name, containing its own echo, turns in on itself: "Néré" is a nearly perfect reverse mirror image of "Renée." As the title of the novel foreshadows the decision that concludes it, so the repetitions in Renée Néré's very name effect a closure, suggesting from the start the choice she makes in the end.

Mitsou's name, on the other hand, intimates that her trajectory will be the opposite. The invention of her first lover, the Respectable Man, "Mitsou" is the acronym of the titles of the two corporations with which he is associated: Minoteries Italo-Tarbaises and Scieries Orléanaises Unifiées. While Renée Néré's name indicates narcissism and self-sufficiency, Mitsou's implies a bond; it is given her and freely accepted by her, apparently without an afterthought.

By historical accident, the letter as literary form is peculiarly feminine, and it is significant that Colette aligned herself early in her writing career with a host of women authors by reverting twice to the outmoded epistolary novel. The works in question are thus not merely anachronistic in the sense in which we usually understand the term (i.e., prochronistic: they anticipate the concern in fiction of recent years with female identity), they are parachronistic (for they go backwards in time)

as well. At once therefore remarkably experimental and highly traditional, these texts interweave form, theme, symbol, and autobiography.
The thematic use of the music hall, an institution with which Colette
was intimately acquainted, parallels the formal use of letters: the epistolary novel is a near relative of drama, for both theater and letter place
protagonists in a privileged position, allowing for an exchange unmedi-
ated by a narrator. The texture of these two works displays constant
plays of light and images, which illuminate the central experience: a
woman's achievement of self-knowledge.

Bondage

Renée Néré reappears in a 1913 companion novel to *The Vagabond*. A
modest inheritance from her sister-in-law has permitted her to quit
work, so instead of dancing her way around France, she now winters in
its chic watering places. Her idleness and thalassic regression signal the
unleashing of the erotic side of her nature, which had been successfully
submerged in the earlier novel. *The Shackle* (*L'Entrave*), also written in
the form of a journal, poses the same questions of sexuality, liberty, and
male-female communication as *The Vagabond,* but answers them differently. *The Shackle* has its shortcomings, too often tending to become a
disputatious analysis of the duality of love as eros and sentiment. It is
nonetheless one of Colette's more important novels, standing thematically apart from most of the others, for it equates female sexuality with
submission and implicitly defines woman as a reflection in someone else's
mirror. From a feminist standpoint, indeed from a human one, its thesis
is sad; it returns Renée from a fragile independence to conventionally
happy bondage. *The Shackle* points out the predictability of the plots
women live.

A glimpse of Max one day in Nice, three years after she has refused his
hand, leaves her tremulous, for Max has committed the sin of recovering
from her, and he takes visible satisfaction in the roles of husband and
father that a successor has bestowed on him. In contrast, Renée assesses
the stagnation of her own chastity and recognizes that travel is no substitute for self-renewal. The silent encounter with her ex-suitor triggers two
reactions: a desire for a love affair and a decision to start a diary. The diary
is the novel, the affair its story. Like Colette under Willy, Renée takes up
writing at the same time that she seems to forfeit her existence as subject.

Her perpetually vacationing companions and the "five hundred
unvarying words of their vocabulary" only barely distract her from her

interior monologue. Her friend May, vulgar in the bloom of her 25 years, both arouses and scandalizes Renée with the details of her affair with a lover named Jean. Each morning she recounts the intricacies of their love-making and displays with relish the bruises inflicted the night before. Renée marvels that Jean refuses his mistress all homage, except monetary and erotic: "Upright, May finds all the prerogatives of her sex withdrawn" (28). Masseau, a voluble opium addict, whose habit Jean subsidizes as he does May, completes the foursome.

Renée's discovery of an attraction between herself and Jean modifies the patterns of their relations and she flees, loath to betray May and still fearful of involvement. Jean pursues her as Max did not, and the next few chapters record the sultry beginning and the consummation of the liaison. *The Shackle* contains some of Colette's most erotic pages. The first amorous encounter between Renée and Jean occurs at the book's mid-point: at midnight in the deserted lobby of a Swiss hotel, he kisses the nape of her neck: "A good kiss, warm, not too devouring; warm, long and tranquil; a kiss that took time to satisfy itself and that gave me, after the first shiver right down my spine, a slightly lethargic content-ment" (112). In *The Vagabond,* Max's first kiss, sadly botched, left Renée defensive and resentful; her pliancy and compliancy in the present instance—spontaneously she leans her head forward, the better to nestle into the kiss—prefigure the ultimate terms of the relation with Jean, to whom she bends and submits. In Paris 24 hours and 20 pages later, they become lovers on the floor in front of his fireplace, where he does not bother to undress her: "Arrogant, completely assured of his triumph, he displayed a barbarous contempt of methods. . . . It was I who undid buckle and ribbon and removed pins that might hurt; it was I, lying on my back on the carpet, who made my slightly bruised body a cushion for Jean" (130).

During several weeks of late winter and early spring, Renée is deter-mined to separate the physical pleasure of love from "the rest." She remains persuaded that only passion can be shared by two people who are neither friends nor relatives. So she confides nothing to Jean except her body. But the cleavage between physical and emotional involvement proves impossible. She begins to intuit something of the absurdity of her position during a chance meeting with May, who has no idea that Renée and Jean are now lovers and exhibits her grief over the loss of Jean just as she once did her bruises. May also takes the opportunity to gloss Jean's faults. The worst thing about him, she explains in what is perhaps the novel's most comic moment, is the way he unexpectedly "f...s off": "He f...s off like no-one else and you never get him back . . . in the middle of a sentence, closing the door behind him, or else he goes out to buy cigarettes and you never see him again except in the form of a farewell letter, very well written, simply marvellous" (147–48).[8] Renée rushes back to the house: "Suppose, in my absence, Jean had 'f....d off'?"

Her alienation is translated at the level of plot and of symbol. In a strange early scene, masks set the characters eerily apart from each other. The four friends hire a car in Nice one evening for a little excursion, and as a keen wind is blowing dust in their faces, they drive silently through the twilight, half-masked with goggles, only their mouths, chins and nostrils exposed. Renée is amused and embarrassed by the spectacle of these "half-faces." And with his eyes hidden from view, she is for the first time intrigued by Jean's sultry mouth.

Renée's desire for Jean is mimetic, for she has before her, from the start, the vision of May's attachment to her brutal lover. Dispossessed of originality, Renée is even dispossessed of a home; while in *The Vagabond* she trysted with Max in her own apartment, the affair with Jean takes place in *his* houses. She puts her furniture in storage, moves into his Paris house, and continues to live there even after he has moved out! As self-conscious as ever, Renée regularly consults the mirror, where she now sees only images of alienation, not merely because they reflect the declining beauty of a troubled woman, but because they are not even *her* mirrors, but belong to hotels, restaurants, and Jean himself. Her gesture of interrogating the mirror is repeated by Masseau, the sexless, aging addict, who initially acted as go-between for her and Jean. Each time he catches sight of his reflection, he pulls himself up, pinches the corners of his lips or gesticulates clownishly, posing now as Charles Third, now as Louis XIV—as anyone but himself. In the book's last mirror allusion, Renée and Masseau are joined, appropriately and threateningly, in the full-length hall mirror of Jean's house, a tarnished image of solitude and folly.

Without a profession, Renée no longer evokes the slightest interest even in her old friend and partner Brague. On a visit to his dressing room in Geneva, she is humiliated to discover that she has been replaced on stage by a woman who also shares Brague's bed. The "act" that was once hers has thus outdistanced her. Creativity is almost completely stifled, for the former novelist no longer even writes letters—or only writes one, to Jean, which the reader never sees, a letter of recrimination from which she loosely quotes to Masseau. The only letter Jean writes, likewise withheld from us, is the letter of farewell to May, described by her to Renée. More energetic than Max, Jean refused to let Renée escape him at the start; we have a crossing of bodies rather than epistles. But communication remains just as problematical as in *The Vagabond,* for, as Renée puts it in one of many neat aphorisms, "nothing is exchanged in the sexual act." Their love is threatened with gradual extinction in silence and sex.

Her journal maps the path from eroticism to servility, a path along which she is pushed by accumulated symbols of estrangement and images of despair. The pattern is classic. She thinks she needs Jean only because he services her well, until she discovers that his services may not long be hers. Painfully she watches herself become seriously attached, and metaphors of faithful dogs at their masters' feet, prisons, chains, and shackles strew the discourse that inscribes her enslavement. When Jean leaves her, finally exasperated by her silences and her now feeble but continuing effort to resist "the rest" (everything that is not purely physical), she determines frenetically to lure him back. In a troubling and troublesome ending, Renée pretends to have left Paris to become again a dancer, then melodramatically waylays her lover late one night in his own bedroom. With the "blind, primitive instinct of the animal crying frenziedly for its master" (216), she accepts the complete submission that is her idea of femininity. She and Jean exchange functions: he will be the eager vagabond and she will gaze after him, "anchored for ever." That is what it really means, she has decided, to be a woman. Colette later called this demoralizing conclusion one in which even her heroes do not believe (*The Evening Star,* 137).

She tried to rewrite it, but never quite managed.

Chapter Four

Passages

Chéri is doubtless Colette's fictional masterpiece. Its 1920 publication was followed by *The Ripening Seed* in 1923, *The Last of Chéri* in 1926, and *Break of Day* in 1928. These are stories of passages from one life phase to another, of the rise or decline of sexuality; demonstrations that, if passion has no age, the body does.

Chéri and His Demise

In an article entitled "The Double Standard of Aging," Susan Sontag makes a critical distinction between aging and old age. The latter is an objective, "sacred" experience, while aging ("everything that comes *before* one is actually old") is subjective, "profane." Old age, moreover, is strictly egalitarian, affecting both sexes, whereas aging afflicts women more than men.[1] *Chéri* and *The Last of Chéri* (*La Fin de Chéri*) may be read as a cogent demonstration of these dichotomies: they evoke the heroine first in the throes of growing old, and then acquiescingly installed in old age.

Colette focused more than once on women at ages she seemed to consider critical. Her last heroine, Gigi, like Vinca in *The Ripening Seed,* dramatically accedes at fifteen and a half from adolescence to womanhood, while Renée Néré, between *The Vagabond* and *The Shackle,* passes from an independent 33 to an anxious and inchoately middle-aged 36. Léa, the central character of the Chéri novels, crosses in the first of them the threshold between 49 and 50.

At the novel's start, Léa is happy and beautiful, with magnificent arms and opulent bust, and a gorgeous 25-year-old lover named Chéri whom she has maintained for six years.[2] There are only a few signs of aging: she no longer goes to bed wearing her string of forty-nine pearls (one for each year), because Chéri likes to play with it when they waken, and morning light is unkind to a neck that is neither as firm nor as white as it once was. Their affair is terminated one autumn by Chéri's marriage of convenience to 18-year-old Edmée, whose mother, like his, is a former courtesan, and whose beauty, fortune, and fatherless upbringing are also compatible with his. With the honeymooners' departure from Paris, Léa attempts to escape the chilling loneliness of her big, wrought-iron bed by going off to warmer climes. Chéri gets back from Italy in mid-winter to find Léa gone and sinks into depression; he leaves his wife to haunt hotels and nightclubs with his friend Desmond and stalks his mistress's street for signs of her return. After a six-month absence, she comes back in spring, and Chéri bursts into her bedroom around midnight. The separation has taught them both to admit the depth of their love, and they spend a deliriously happy night. Léa awakens throwing caution to the wind and planning their elopement. But the morning light betrays her now. Chéri notices her rough skin and double chin, and Léa soon resigns herself to the inevitable and sends him home to Edmée. He leaves her as though he were escaping from prison, and Léa's glance falls on her mirror, where she sees a crazy old woman repeating her gestures. The mirror's role—reflection, distortion, observer, other—reinforces the novel's implicit recognition of aging as the kind of ordeal that Sontag compellingly describes as one of the imagination—"a moral disease, a social pathology."

Extraordinarily well wrought, *Chéri* is a novel of almost mythic proportions.[3] The cast is limited to a handful of characters belonging to the demimonde. Apart from Léa, Chéri, and Edmée, there are Patron, a former lover of Léa; Edmée's mother, Marie-Laure; Chéri's mother, Charlotte Peloux; and the latter's little band of toadying, degenerate old friends. The restriction of fictional time and setting enhances the novel's psychological concision. The action covers less than a year (each of the four seasons is carefully evoked) and the crucial scenes, including the first and the last, take place in Léa's overdecorated bedroom, dominated by its oversized bed. The trips—a summer in Normandy, where the liaison began, Chéri's Italian honeymoon, Léa's escape to the south—occur as flashbacks or are mentioned only indirectly, so that the foreground action never leaves Paris and its suburbs. Everything is intensely concentrated on Léa's drama.

When we meet them in the sequel, five to seven years have passed (the chronology is more impressionistic than precise). Chéri is a drifting war veteran, alienated from his socially active wife and mother. Groping for something or someone to hang on to, he decides to visit Léa, whom he has not seen in years, only to sink afterwards into still deeper despair. He seeks refuge in the home of one of Léa and Charlotte's contemporaries, La Copine, where he stares for days on end at walls covered with pictures of Léa in her younger days, listens to La Copine's recollections of

Léa's charms, and thinks about the war. In the end he shoots himself in the head.

By the time she appears in *The Last of Chéri,* Léa seems no longer a sexual being. Chéri calls on her to find a jolly, gray-haired old woman of cubic bulk, with arms like thighs. Of his beautiful mistress, only the emblematic string of pearls and the superb blue eyes remain. No longer prone to arouse desire, she is indeed no longer even female, but alternately described as masculine, virile, or asexual. The cheeks she used to powder have gone from white to red. She no longer bothers, as she did in *Chéri,* to flatter her skin with pale pink dressing-gowns, or dye her hair, or swaddle her swollen legs in tight boots. Her very clothes now proclaim her abdication from womanhood and that she has acquired a "sexless dignity" (177). This seems to correspond to what Sontag names the hallowed pain of old age, and it sets Léa in her late fifties dramatically—unreasonably—apart from the forty-nine-year-old of the earlier book. The change may seem an excessively brutal one, but apart from the fact that the brutality parallels external events (World War I and its transformation of society), it also serves to demarcate two stages of Léa's existence.[4] *Chéri* and *The Last of Chéri* are metaphorical: "parables of experience," Elaine Marks calls them.[5] The first indication of metaphoricity is the titles themselves: the chief protagonist of the first novel is Léa, yet it bears not her name but that of her lover—or rather the nickname of the lover, whose given name is Fred. The sobriquet suggests that the young man is an ideal lover, an essentially sexual being. It is also a commentary on his relation to Léa, on her love for him.

I insist on this in order to explain what commentators are wont to regard as a defect in the novel: Chéri's weakness and incomprehensibility. If Chéri appears to be two-dimensional, it is because he is the figment of Léa and the story is hers rather than his. But this is a creature surpassing his creator's comprehension. Léa is no better able than the reader to understand what makes Chéri tick. In the early months of their intimacy, they summer alone in Normandy, and Léa is profoundly perplexed by the lack of trust and candor in so young a lover. If he confides no secret to her, it is because he has none to confide. His inscrutability is ultimately his measure: Chéri is an empty shell. This impression is shared even by the hero himself, who is at one point astounded to find his splendid sole-shaped eyes filled with tears, and rhetorically asks Edmée: "Well, why shouldn't I have a heart like everyone else?" (65). Juxtaposed with Léa, surely drawn and overflowing with vigor, he may seem initially an artistic failure, vaguely disquieting.

But his nature and role develop gradually. What Léa cherishes in Chéri is the illusion he is—the illusion of her youth. This becomes clear toward the end of *Chéri* when he rushes back to her arms and for a moment it appears that they have a future together. Overwhelmed with happiness, Léa exclaims: "What a fool I was not to understand that you were my love, *the* love, the great love that comes only once!" (121). But Chéri returns next morning to Edmée. He is himself the metaphor of the aging process that Léa undergoes, and the "last of Chéri" is the end of growing old and the beginning of old age. Her hold on him in the first work is tentative, frenzied, and doomed; in the second the breach is entire, the distance between the two characters, psychological as well as physical (we see them together only once, toward the middle of the book, when her very mass keeps Chéri at bay), signifying the calm of Léa's acquiescence to age.

The sequel then is much more the story of Chéri himself, his deterioration and suicide. But although she appears only once, Léa dominates this book too. Her image haunts him and the central scene is hers. Morose and phlegmatic, Chéri cannot continue in a society that Léa has abandoned: once her sexuality has forsaken her, he too must literally die, for he was never more than her creature. Léa, who never had a biological son, gave Chéri life in the first three months of their liaison, taking an emaciated young man to her summer home in Normandy to stuff him with corn-fed chicken and fresh cream and strawberries, and to arrange for his boxing lessons with her former lover. At the end of *The Last of Chéri,* he has grown as thin and ill as he was at the start of their relation; neither eating nor sleeping, he advances sullenly toward his end. This creature of Léa does not survive her death to sex: he was the mystery, the profanity, the anguished hope of her middle age; old age externalizes, clarifies, and consecrates, and Chéri—illusion and subjectivity—disappears. He ends his life in a dismal, smoke-filled drawing room where he has been trying to live in the past—Léa's past.

The figure of the middle-aged woman is a staple of European literature, and, as Janet Whatley points out in a perceptive study of such characters in the work of Marivaux, "the aging woman who considers herself still sexually eligible . . . stands for illusion. Her complementary attribute . . . is her vulnerability to humiliation."[6] What is singular about Colette's character is her lucidity and her strength; she is neither pathetic, nor despicable, nor comical. Léa's story is optimistic, while her lover's, of course, is not. She becomes at the end a robust old woman with a double chin, happy to be alive and "freed from restraining stays"

(178). Without stays as without shackles, Léa is, in spite of her enormous size, finally free. Moreover, just as the weight Chéri gained at the start was at Léa's expense (literally speaking), so the weight she now puts on, Chéri loses. And the release and serenity that her mass confers are in counterpoint to Chéri's progressive entrapment and febrile activity as he moves toward his death.

Chéri may be said to exemplify, as Sontag affirms, the standard French account of an older woman who initiates a young man and then loses her place to a younger girl.[7] But to reduce the novel to such a schema would be to do it an injustice; the Colette work is no mere story of a demimondaine and a youthful gigolo. It is a tragedy of love and aging. What sets the series off additionally is that here the spurned older woman does not succumb to despair: her younger lover does. After the confrontation with her mirror at the end of the first novel, Léa ensconces herself comfortably in old age, and when we meet her again in *The Last of Chéri,* she is not merely resigned, she is joyful: her peculiar perfume (symbol of her ephemeral sexuality) is gone, but her rich laughter (symbol of her continuing humanity) fills the apartment. Her stance is especially remarkable since Colette has provided, for contrast, the figures of several ridiculous old women. One of them, Lilli in *Chéri,* is a courtesan of 70 who sports a sailor hat and a sulky adolescent lover. Léa accepts, as Lilli does not, her "sexual disqualification," in Sontag's phrase. But if Colette portrays her as sexless, there is equal emphasis on her dignity.

Youth's Ordeal

In a gesture that Colette's fictional universe normally represents as feminine, young Philippe Audebert in *The Ripening Seed* (*Le Blé en herbe*) contemplates his image in a window after his first night of love. He sees a tired face and eyes and "lips still smeared from contact with a rouged mouth, black dishevelled hair straggling over forehead—all signs of distress, resembling less traits of a man than those of a violated girl" (91). He reminds us of Léa in *Chéri.* She too is startled by her image one morning after a night of love—not her first, but her last. The reflection in both instances attests to the ordeal marking the beginning of a new life phase: for Léa, the end of sexual prowess; for Philippe, the passage to manhood. Features and gestures appear exaggerated or distorted, and the glass bears witness to disarray and madness: Léa sees a "crazy creature," whom she doesn't recognize, and Phil's whole appearance suggests frenzy. The transition from one age to another, involving renunciation of the perquisites of the earlier and acceptance of the circumstances of the latter, brings on a temporary alienation. Both Léa and Phil have in a sense been violated and both must evolve a new integrity.

The Ripening Seed is set among the dunes, coves, and fauna of the Brittany coast where Colette spent summers in the early 1920s, accompanied by her daughter Bel Gazou and the two adolescent sons of Henry de Jouvenel, Bertrand and Renaud.[8] The hero and heroine are Philippe Audebert and Vinca Ferret, respectively 16 and 15 years old, who have summered here since infancy, their families sharing a large rented house. The love between Phil and Vinca is the fruit of long seasons of exclusive companionship, but this year as summer draws to an end, their awkward age has brought them to the brink of crisis. The climax is precipitated by the arrival of a transient lodger in a nearby villa, Camille Dalleray, thirtyish and rapacious, who shortly initiates Phil. After Madame Dalleray's departure, a constant Vinca, fortified by a glass of champagne, willfully obliges her disconsolate friend to give her the same experience.

On the surface, this is a book about a double sexual initiation. Madame Dalleray takes Phil's virginity as he does Vinca's. (The original tale was serialized in *Le Matin* before publication in book form, but was abruptly suspended when it became clear to the editors that the author planned to give an account of a 15-year-old girl's reduction by the flesh.) It is another episode, then, in a long tradition of the novel of worldliness: a hero is initiated by an older woman, then returned to the arms of a young one, and *The Ripening Seed* actually conforms more closely to this model than does *Chéri*. But this is also a study of sex roles, their limits, overlap, and evolution. Explicit designations of femininity and masculinity, attached to traits, gestures, and actions, permeate the lexical atmosphere. At the very moment when Phil achieves what he considers manhood, he looks like a "violated girl," the smear of Madame Dalleray's lipstick across his mouth suggesting the red of sexual blood. Although his virility is never questioned, his character, a little like Julien Sorel's in *The Red and the Black,* is continually adumbrated as feminine. At his first encounter with the aggressive Madame Dalleray, he is "suddenly tired, feeble and limp, overcome by an access of femininity" (29). He soon feels ready to faint, and on the day she leaves, he does just that. Then, "like a woman," he cries.

Phil's excitability, tears, and fears, like his contemplation of his image in the window-pane, are behavior that he (like most readers of fiction) has been conditioned to associate with femininity. Vinca's, less so. Along with her lanky, adolescent beauty, she has the "unhampered agility of a boy" (48). Madame Dalleray, meanwhile, plays rapist to Phil as young virgin: her laughter is "masculine," her smile "virile," and her own beauty that of a "handsome lad." "Like a man," she jokes with Phil, and he muses that her first name, Camille, could belong to either sex.

Sexual characteristics are thus bivalent in this text, and standard roles are reversed more by qualifiers than by the action of the plot. But this implies no protofeminist revolt on Colette's part. The novel catches her young heroes at a critical moment in the process of becoming socially coded members of the bourgeoisie. Vinca's name is close to the Latin word for "chains" (*vincula*), while "ferret" is an iron rod, and "ferré" (phonetically indistinguishable) an adjective meaning bound or shod. Vinca will become a thoroughly enculturated bourgeoise. She already accepts without question her future role as homemaker, and explains to Phil that she will undertake no advanced studies. Even now she performs all the traditional female chores: she sews frocks for her little sister, and on seaside picnics she spreads the sandwiches, serves and washes up while Phil dreams of aboriginal vigor and splendor.

The difference in their reactions to physical love is the most easily apprehended aspect of the tale. His pallor, sleeplessness and loss of appetite, all testify to his self-indulgent readiness to be overwhelmed by the affair with Madame Dalleray. Vinca, in contrast, is reason, tenacity, a force of nature. If her name suggests her enculturation, it also links her to nature: "Vinca" is the botanical name of the periwinkle. Her deep blue eyes (Léa's eyes, while Phil has Chéri's enlarged eyes and pale face) ally her to the flower, the thistle, the Breton sky and the sea. Whereas Phil's distress is translated by a red smudge and a dishevelled head, Vinca's sadness is the sadness of nature; behind a window, when raindrops trickle down, they appear to stream from her eyes. The colors associated with her rival present a different configuration. Madame Dalleray is nicknamed "The Lady in White" for the color she wears. To the white are added reds, blacks, and golds. The first is for her lips and bloodstained cheek after Phil has unwittingly hit her with a bouquet of sea-holly he intends to offer in homage, and for the principal color of her living-room. It joins blacks and golds in the decor, and all three mix with the smell of incense, ripe fruits, and strong coffee. In this atmosphere, far from the peaceful blues of Vinca's clothes and eyes and the sea and sky, Phil is as though drugged and seduced. The event becomes for him "a wedge between the two periods of his existence" (129). Henceforth, everything is temporally located "before" or "after" this landmark. He believes that his own initiation is unlike that of the heroes of whose exploits he has read, and searches his literary memory in vain for a single story resembling his own. Projecting his upheaval onto his companion, he predicts that Vinca may well attempt suicide.

Nothing of the sort transpires. She reproaches him, first, for not having asked *her* instead of Madame Dalleray, and then for his priggish refusal to discuss the affair. The literary antecedent that she evokes has a different portent. While he tries to recall a fictional precedent to his own experience, she refuses his perspective because it would effectively cast their lives in a literary mold: "Phil, it's simply that I can't believe you. Otherwise the whole of our life up to now has been simply one of those soppy stories we've read in books we don't much care for" (163–64). Their mental interrogation (and rejection) of stories they have read is an attempt to differentiate their love from all others. But, of course, Phil and Vinca have invented nothing, and the text gently ironizes on their pretensions to uniqueness. The finest ironic moment occurs when Phil has initiated Vinca and anticipates a reaction that will recognize the enormity of the event: "I've heard" (in other words, "I've read") "that they always cry afterwards" (182). So the next morning, below her window, he keeps watch, only to discover, stupefied, that she comes to the window singing and calmly waters the fuchsia.

Like the lipstick smear Phil sees in his window reflection upon returning from Madame Dalleray's, the deep red flower in Vinca's window symbolizes the recent sexual act, but there is a world of difference between the symbols, the first of which suggests violence and the second, burgeoning nature. Vinca's casual acceptance of the facts of life is a worse trial for Phil than any that have preceded, and his bitter lament on this sunny morning is the novel's last line: "Neither a hero, nor an executioner . . . A little pain, a little pleasure . . . That's all I shall have given her, that and nothing else . . . Nothing" (186).

Renunciation

Break of Day (*La Naissance du jour*) is a stranger work than any of those that precede it. Colette herself appears as heroine, in a house she really owned and with the friends she really knew, and she speaks at length of her mother. But her hero is an invention and the plot a fabulation. Its resolution, moreover—the narrator's decision to give up men and sex— is at the antipodes of Colette's evolution during the period described. The question of who and what is real is omnipresent in Colette, and this work suggests that, absorbing as the problem is, it is forever indecipherable. This is an elusive, intensely poetic book, and its conclusion almost transcendental.

Like *Chéri, The Last of Chéri,* and *The Ripening Seed, Break of Day* involves the attraction between a young man and an older woman. The narrator, a well-known author in her early 50s, believes she has reached the time of life when serenity should replace passion. Valère Vial, a furniture-maker who is her Saint-Tropez neighbor and 15 years her junior, pays her assiduous court, but she manages in the space of a single night to steer him into the arms of a younger woman, Hélène Clément. Around this anecdote, the author weaves her most complicated work.

This is a self-portrait of extraordinary density and ambiguity. The most evident ambiguity is formal, in that *Break of Day* escapes generic definition. We can call it a novel, for two of the principal characters (Valère Vial and Hélène Clément) are fictitious, and its core is the story of a love that in real life never was, Vial's for Colette. But around the central fiction are arranged innumerable autobiographical elements. The narrator-protagonist bears the author's name, exercises her profession, and inhabits the house where she vacationed with Maurice Goudeket in the late 1920s, "La Treille Muscate." The flora and fauna of the Mediterranean coast are there in profusion, and the narrative conveys the texture of late summer days in what was still a sleepy fishing port. Through its pages walk Saint-Tropez acquaintances: the painters Dunoyer de Segonzac and Luc-Albert Moreau and writers Francis Carco and Paul Géraldy. In his book on Colette, Goudeket insists on the contradiction between such details and the essential fabulation:

> If ever a novel appears to be autobiographical, that one does. Everything is in it, "La Treille Muscate," the garden, the vineyard, the terrace, the sea, the animals. Our friends are called by their real names. . . . Everything is there, except that *La Naissance du jour* evokes the peace of the senses and a renunciation of love, at the moment when Colette and I were living passionate hours together, elated by the heat, the light and the perfume of Provençal summers.[9]

If we are to believe Goudeket, protagonist Colette's sworn asceticism has little to do with the real Colette's dalliance. If ever a book showed how futile it is to take novelistic truth literally, this is it. The author has simultaneously exploited and denied her own experience, projecting her persona into the future. *Break of Day* organizes the differences between possession and abstention, between introspection and anticipation, re-creating a present that absorbs the future.

The most pervasive autobiographical element is the figure of Sido, on whom turns all the narrator's meditation.[10] The first lines are a letter of Sido's dating from about a year before her death at the age of 77. She declines an invitation to visit her daughter and son-in-law on the grounds that her pink cactus is about to flower. It is a rare plant that flowers only once in four years, and Sido is too old to expect to see it happen again. Colette's own reflection follows: "Whenever I feel myself inferior to everything about me, threatened by my own mediocrity . . . I can still hold up my head and say to myself: 'I am the daughter of the woman who wrote that letter—that letter and so many more that I have kept' " (5–6). Sido's "text" thus generates Colette's, who quotes and comments on half a dozen more letters of an elderly Sido, each of which reveals new aspects of feminine charity and originality. Their significance has been suspended until an aging daughter rereads, transcribes, and elucidates them. Her attempt at self-scrutiny is verbalized as marginalia to these letters. The maternal legacy of wisdom and words inspires her to record not merely the person she is but the person she aspires to be.

Physically she resembles her mother as never before, but the essential question is one of moral resemblance. If Sido's chaste ghost were to return, would she recognize her daughter? Even if she came back one dawn and found the daughter bidding passionate farewell to a man with whom she had spent the night? Sido would doubtless take the human male for what he truly is: a less perfect avatar of the beloved plant, a variant phase of the flowering pink cactus. She would forgive the venial sins of the flesh while her daughter was still learning that sexual love, "a form of cannibalism," is not a decent sentiment.

While *My Mother's House,* another major text identifying Colette with her mother, reaches from Sido's childhood to Bel Gazou's, the temporal field of *Break of Day* extends from Sido's old age to Colette's. Yet its trajectory is from dawn to dawn, figuratively and literally. Sido is the source of the title, the giver of *jour* (day), which in some senses can be used to mean *naissance* (birth). She is at the origin of the writer's birth and the birth of day. The English word "break" suggests a cleavage, whereas the French "naissance" joins the work to the meditations on nature, natural phenomena and figurative births occurring throughout Colette's corpus.

The original dawn belongs to the maternal ghost whom Colette imagines, in the book's first pages, coming back at daybreak. But at the end of the book a new day comes after a night of unconsummated love. With the male's departure, love sloughs off its imperfect human disguise and can turn at last into one of the many forms of which Sido would approve: "a quickset hedge, spindrift, meteors, an open and unending book, a cluster of grapes, a ship, an oasis" (143). Evicted from passionate embrace, Eros takes refuge in nature and words. Colette is becoming the "great lover" Sido was: great because of her recognition of the intersections of passionate and maternal love with love of nature, great because of her transcendence of sexuality. Great finally because, like Sido, she is acquiring "the supreme elegance of knowing how to diminish" (142).

The themes, then, are resemblance, imitation, and identity; this is a text structured by mimesis and mimetic desire, which is explicit even before the pre-text (Sido's first letter). An epigraph to *Break of Day* reads, "Are you imagining, as you read me, that I'm portraying myself? Have patience, this is merely my model." The epigraph anticipates the text, its self-referentiality becoming evident when the same lines are repeated, with a slight variation, at the end of the book's fourth chapter. The dual position of these lines, both within and outside the text proper, translates the tension between a desired assimilation to the model and the inevitable dissimilation between any two things. In chapter four, the portrait-model appears as Sido, whom the narrator aspires to imitate not only as daughter and as woman, but as writer, too. Sido proposes a way of reading the world that Colette would make her own. At the book's end, the narrator asks a further question of the reader whom she apostrophized in the epigraph: "Between us two, which is the better writer, she or I? Does it not resound to high heaven that it is she?" (141). A curious question indeed and a strange demand for the reader's connivance when we recall that midway in this same book the narrator complained that Vial's love for her was imitative in origin, that his devotion mimicked that of her public. With "discouragement" and "hostility" she reproached him for doing what all her readers do: comparing her to her own heroines: "We're not concerned with my books here, Vial" (100). Yet now, at the end, she urgently wishes to establish Sido's claim as a "better writer" than she. And who after all is "Sido"? A character in Colette's books, a fictional creation who has a certain number of traits in common with the real Sidonie Landoy Colette. Moreover, the historical Sido's letters are not reducible to those appearing in *Break of Day,* having been rearranged for purposes of the book. In the real letter on which the book's first is based, Sido writes to *accept* Jouvenel's invitation, expressing only a little regret that she may miss the flowering of a plant called a sedum.

Colette's gesture imitates Vial's imitating her public: in this novelistic text, she searches for herself, sketching her identification with one of her own characters. Collected, selected, and corrected, Sido's letters with their symbolic accretions and emendations are a grid for imposing on the writer's mode of existence a sanctified pattern. They are a euphoric arrangement of the past and a blueprint for the future, a mandate to become the writer she is.

Chapter Five

Dialogues

Structurally and thematically similar, Colette's last five novels and her major novelette are all written in the third person and deal with an attempt at communication. Settings tend toward the repressive and the obsessive. Spare of description and characters, temporally and spatially condensed, these works hone the favorite themes of jealousy, dissimulation, and compromise, of woman's superiority and paradoxical cult of the male, of the sexes' incompatibility. The cumulative effect is a powerful commentary on sexual encounters.

The Other One

Neat, ingenious, at once optimistic and woeful, *The Other One* (*La Seconde,* 1929) distills several recurring Colette themes. Thirty-seven-year-old Fanny has been married for 12 years to playwright Farou, a 48-year-old womanizer. His adolescent son Jean lives with them, as does Jane, Farou's secretary—seven years Fanny's junior, but more sophisticated, with a past full of international lovers. Jane overflows with attentions for Fanny and has made herself an indispensable companion as well as factotum. The contrasts between the two women are numerous: Jane is a cool and efficient blond, Fanny a lazy, passionate, and disheveled brunette.

During a summer in Brittany, Fanny suddenly intuits that Farou and his secretary are lovers. This is by no means his first infidelity, and previously Fanny has been admired (by Jane, among others) for her philosophical acceptance of Farou's polygamy. But it is different with Jane, who lives under her roof, and Fanny's unhappiness is acute though silent. Her discovery coincides with a theater's acceptance of one of Farou's plays; the quartet abruptly returns to Paris, where the rest of the plot unravels in the anticipation and fatigue accompanying the new play's auditions and rehearsals. Only after the play's successful opening does Fanny make up her mind to have it out with Jane. "You can always see him outside," she says angrily. But Jane, momentarily confused, asks, "See who? Oh, Farou—I wasn't thinking of Farou" (134). Jane then explains that although she was unable to resist Farou's attentions, her infatuation was short-lived. Her real attachment to the family has less to do with him than with Fanny herself: "For the past four years, I've thought so much more about you than about Farou. . . . You, Fanny, are a much finer person as a woman, than Farou is as a man. Much, much finer" (139–40). It takes Fanny only one evening of reflection to resolve not to send Jane away. Farou would replace a mistress within a week; but how would she, Fanny, find another friend with whom to share the loneliness of life with Farou?

The familiar triangular structure of the novel does not have the triangle's normal tensions; victory is not at issue, nor is revenge. Here all the links are partly physical; for if Jane sleeps with Farou, she also tenderly arranges Fanny's hair, continually takes her arm and holds her hand. Fanny's very jealousy is intensely, predominantly physical in its manifestations. She faints after seeing Farou and Jane together in the bathroom, then takes a long bedrest. But the conflict is translated only by speech, and all violence is verbal: "Coming from [Jane's] lips," Fanny reflects, "extreme language is tantamount to physical violence" (12). The text traces, from one end to the other, a dialogue and a nondialogue. The first, between Fanny and Jane, opens and closes the novel, while the second is the expression of the relation between Fanny and Farou, whose "savage name" (*farouche* means "ferocious") suggests the difficulty of relating to him: "It isn't easy to talk to Farou," Fanny says (125).

Yet Farou is the professional purveyor of speech: as a dramatist, he sells not merely words, but specifically dialogue. His plays, melodramatic oversimplifications of classic conflicts, bear titles like *The Purloined Grapes, Impossible Innocence,* and *No Woman About the House.* Fanny's devotion to him does not prevent her from lucidly evaluating Farou's trivial plots and wondering if he believes that opposing positions are as clearly articulated in real life as in his plays. She also recognizes her husband's primitive notions of feminine psychology, and criticizes as unnatural the heroine who tries to take her own life after her lover's betrayal. Such a suicide, according to Fanny, is "a man's reaction and nothing else. A man's reaction!" (38). In another text published the same year, "Sido" voices a similar conviction: "once past a certain age, a woman practically never dies of her own free will" (*Sido,* 191). Much of Colette's work argues more or less that.

Fanny's comment on passion and suicide prefigures the unorthodox sanity of the position that she ultimately takes. All the text's main concerns are foreshadowed in similar manner. Fanny's intuition of Farou's infidelity with an actress precedes her discovery of his liaison with Jane; the early insomnia of Jane, who is piqued by Farou's multiple conquests, parallels Fanny's after her realization of the Jane-Farou affair. Even Fanny's jealousy has its counterpart in the muted feelings of young Jean Farou, in love with his father's secretary and resentful of her entanglement with Farou. Doubled situations, emotions, and reactions thus characterize the text, while the theatrical milieu in which the story is set provides another type of doubling. For Farou's plays echo the themes of the novel, and his profession is related to his weakness and pretensions. Writing plays—the "wrist and manly hand, shaped for plough or hoe, or to bear arms, but never wielding anything heavier than a fountain pen" (31)—suggests an abdication. This connotative emasculation impugns Farou's ostensible virility and helps explain his withdrawal from confrontation. Farou's activities are exclusively representational, his performances belletristic; "Big Farou," "Master Farou," is master of the imitative.

The theater itself is the setting for the pivotal scene of the dress rehearsal of Farou's play. Fanny dozes off during the first act. As with Renée Néré of *The Vagabond,* the catnap during a theatrical performance leads to a rejection of the meretricious and sham. Sleep restores, and it reestablishes the priority of authenticity over falsehood. Not long after the episode, Fanny decides to have her talk with Jane.

The novel belongs to a long tradition of works dealing with the opposition of love and friendship, a favored theme for centuries, especially of feminine fiction. Colette's message corroborates that of at least one 18th-century French novelist, Marie Jeanne Riccoboni, who, in a triangular situation identical to that of *The Other One*—an unheroic husband has an affair with the companion of the wife who idolizes him—makes the moral explicit: "Whatever one may think while her heart is adrift, a lover is not worth a friend."[1] Colette refines on the theme by examining the role and sense of female friendship. From the start, Fanny reflects on Jane's relation to her: "My friend?...Yes, she is my friend. All the same, to say my friend is to say a good deal" (14). When they at last admit their deepest bond, love and contempt for the male, their friendship appears perfectible. They are united, then, not—as a superficial reading might suggest—in spite of Farou, but because of him; and Fanny's stance is neither the renunciation nor the compromise it has been labeled, but a candid submission to reality. She realizes that what passed for her luxury—a feminine alliance—is in fact her necessity.

The Cat

The triangle of *The Other One*—a man between two females—recurs in a 1933 novel, *The Cat* (*La Chatte*), but here "the other one" is a cat. Alain Amparat, at 24 the last scion of a wealthy family, marries 19-year-old Camille Malmert, whose family is even more prosperous, but newer at it. While they wait for a wing to be added to Alain's mother's home, they temporarily set up house for the summer in the ninth-story apartment of a traveling friend—a flat they christen "the wedge" because its modern shape suggests a slice cut from a wheel of Brie. The tensions between the newlyweds crystallize around the figure of Alain's cat, a three-year-old female named Saha. Within weeks of the marriage, he deserts his sensual young wife's bed to sleep with Saha on a divan. One hot July night, Camille is alone on the terrace with the cat. She gives in to an obscure impulse and pursues the animal from one end of the narrow terrace to the other, forcing it, each time she turns, to seek refuge on the opposite ledge. Finally she reaches out both arms and pushes the cat off the edge. Its fall broken by a second-floor awning, the cat survives; the marriage does not. Alain packs his pet's basket and retreats to home, mother, and, metaphorically, childhood.

On the level of symbolism, the number three and the notion of triangularity recur often in *The Cat*. Robert D. Cottrell notes the extent to which these constitute a leitmotif: "The apartment is on the ninth floor, the tops of the three poplar trees that grow in the garden below are even with the apartment's three terraces, and, most important of all, the curiously shaped bedroom has three walls and is repeatedly referred to as 'the triangular bedroom.' When Alain brings his beautiful cat, Saha, to live with them, he creates a *ménage à trois*."[2] The tensions of the triangle demand the resolution, when two of the three return after three months of summer to a conventionally shaped house and the countless trees of its garden.

Novelistic technique normally valorizes the character whose perspective is privileged; that is, the reader expects to empathize with the protagonist whose thoughts are chiefly followed. Here, this is Alain, whose dreams, fantasies, and fears occupy the center of the story, and whom the text ignores only during the pivotal scene when Camille tries to kill the cat. Yet, by a stunning tour de force on the part of Colette, the reader sympathizes with the would-be murderess. Although we view Camille mainly through Alain's eyes, she, not he, appears normal and healthy. This is due in part to the occasionally palpable presence of the narrator, who emits

aphorisms like the following: "a man's sensuality is brief and seasonal and
. . . its unpredictable return is never a new beginning" (151).

Both (human) protagonists are portrayed as strongly sexual creatures.
Textual configurations in *The Cat* adumbrate the feminine side of Alain
and a masculine dimension in Camille, who shares her asexual first name
with Madame Dalleray in *The Ripening Seed,* another virile Colette heroine. Alain is as shocked by some of Camille's popular turns of speech as
he is by her sexual desires and her unselfconscious nudity, and he judges
her insufficiently afraid of his male body. Trying to articulate her over-
whelming sensuality, he tells her, "You're like the smell of roses . . . you
take away one's appetite" (133). What he cherishes in Camille is not the
vivacious, mutable beauty of a healthy young woman, but rather "some
perfected or motionless image of Camille" (77)—her shadow or her portrait. And even her portrait leaves him uneasy: shortly before their wedding, he uses a pencil to modify the look she wears in a photograph,
wishing to reduce the size of her immense eyes.

A foil to Alain's curly blond beauty, Camille is dark-haired and dark-
skinned; hers is a corporeal darkness Alain deems excessive, vaguely
obscene. It is she who loves jazz and drives their roadster. Camille is a
consuming force, and her passionate nature emasculates Alain; the first
weeks of marriage put weight on her, and he complains that she is getting fat from making love, getting fat on him. Camille seems to sap his
vitality. At the sight of a long black hair on the wash basin, he feels sick.
As she gains weight, she grows sexier. Saha, meanwhile, confined in the
apartment, becomes thinner, and Alain finds her "light and enchanting"
(152). While erecting barriers to Camille's every word and gesture, Alain
attentively interprets the language of his cat, from her "me-rrou-wa" of
displeasure to the "mouek-mouek-mouek" of good humor.

The fortune of Alain's family comes from the silk industry, a business
whose pedigree is suggested by its roots in antiquity and its associations
with refinement and luxury; but his father is dead, and the business is
now run not by Alain but by an associate. Camille, on the other hand, is
from a family involved in the manufacture of washing machines—the
symbol of progress. There are overtones of rivalry between the ancient
trade guilds, and Alain's mother condescendingly judges Camille as
slightly unmannered, a young woman from another social set, just as
Camille's family notes the Amparats' decline: they are now only barely
"in silk" and Alain is by no means the "master" of the business. His family home, a spreading building with a large garden, stands nobly in the
center of an exclusive Paris faubourg, resisting the inroads of the "new

Neuilly." The "wedge," on the other hand, where he lives with Camille, is noisy, gleaming, geometric, a ninth-floor flat of crystal and chrome. While she jokingly qualifies him as terribly "1830," Alain becomes more and more obsessed with his distaste at the prospect of seeing Camille, this "girl of today," violate the house in which he was born with her new servants and new ideas. He is relieved when her hostility toward the cat creates the pretext for a separation.

Colette treats the cat's role with discretion; in her "dignity," "modesty," "nobility," and "disinterestedness," she is at once all cats and an individualized member of the species. She is pure too in a way that Camille, highly sexed, is not. But she is also a symbol, the concrete expression, of Alain's nature. "Blue as the loveliest dreams" (189), she is his innocence, his childhood, his illusion, as his mother says. Camille gropes to understand his partiality for the cat, saying, "You're not like most people who are fond of animals. . . . You're quite different. You *love* Saha" (169). For Alain, finally, is identified with the cat. While Camille exudes the smell of roses, his is a "feline odor." Even his image mixes with Saha's: in the earliest pages, just before the wedding, while he looks at his reflection, "in the depths of the mirror, Saha gravely [watches] him from the distance" (82). At the end, Camille visits Alain in his garden, and makes a final effort to assuage him; he remains adamant, and Camille sets off again:

> She stopped short and made a movement as if to retrace her steps. But she swayed only for an instant and then walked away faster than ever. For while Saha, on guard, was following Camille's departure as intently as a human being, Alain was half-lying on his side, ignoring it. With one hand hollowed into a paw, he was playing deftly with the first green, prickly August chestnuts. (192–93)

Duo

Duo (1934) and *Le Toutounier* (1939) share their principal female protagonist. Each part of the diptych intensely concentrates subject, setting, and fictional time through lingering descriptions of such concrete physical features as a beauty mark beside a navel. Both novels are intimate accounts of the reactions to crisis of a very few characters. Yet the tales are also richly symbolic and thrust beyond the individual dramas they minutely recount. The husband-wife conflict in *Duo* is a kind of solar-lunar opposition—a global struggle between men and women—while the harmony among the sisters in *Le Toutounier* suggests an alternative to the impossible marital dialogue.

In French as in English, "duo" has the primary meaning of a musical composition for two singers or instrumentalists, but, figuratively and familiarly, it can mean a verbal exchange, as of insults. *Duo* follows a man and wife for eight days, from his discovery of her infidelity of the previous year to his suicide. Alice and Michel's milieu is that of the Farous in *The Other One:* this is another theatrical couple in financial disorder, alternately struggling to make ends meet and squandering windfalls. On the morning after their arrival at Michel's country home, Cransac, where they are to spend the Easter holiday, he surprises Alice rereading a note received months earlier and forces her to acknowledge what its content makes obvious: she has had an affair with his business associate, Ambrogio. Alice tries to cajole her husband out of his jealousy, but Michel, by turns morbidly curious, sullen, and insulting, resists her efforts to reestablish communication. Their anguish is intensified by his obsession with the gaze of others—servants, merchants, villagers. By trade a producer, he stages for the onlookers a display of conjugal entente in which he plays the lead, but in private he broods.

The novel, which Elaine Marks calls "an almost clinical study of the cerebral and physical ravages of jealousy,"[3] powerfully renders the twilight zone of suffering, the early phase of incredulity and semiforgetfulness following emotional calamity; the period when grief is intensely physical, but like an arythmic ache or a roving pain. Michel's misery harrasses him like a cat playing with a mouse. Illness punctuates the week during which he tries to come to terms with his wretchedness, and the particular form of his "mal d'amour" (a classic novelistic device) is both appropriate and humourous: Michel suffers from constipation. He pulls back from Alice and retreats into bed as a prelude to his ultimate repudiation of life and happiness.

In a final effort to placate her husband, Alice adduces the evidence of three more letters from Ambrogio, by whose explicit vocabulary and lubricious reminiscences she intends to prove that the brief liaison was entirely carnal, never affective. Whereas he found Alice's oral avowal of the affair merely harrowing, the written word—the word of the *male*—kills Michel, for whom Ambrogio's depiction of the intimacy is fatally mortifying. In the hours before his suicide, the letters haunt him: in his mind "a little phrase lifted its head in the shape of a violet-colored capital M. It looked charming for a moment, then rushed away, pulling a whole string of crude words in its wake" (125).

The sentence's purple coloration is part of a brightly variegated drama whose inception—Michel's discovery of the infidelity—is tinted violet: the original letter is written in purple ink and tucked into a purple desk blotter next to a vase of wild orchids. And the earth itself on the first morning displays the same purple hue—a purple so insistent that it catches his glance, troubles the gray-green of Alice's eyes, and incites him to demand the blotter. That afternoon they take a walk and admire the craggy purple rocks of Cransac. On the following morning, all is blue: her dress, the dew, the sky, the periwinkle. Those first two days are spring days whose promise of renewal is an illusion, for theirs is the blue of a false dawn. A furious rain begins, dropping a veritable curtain of water on Cransac, whose recluses alternately state gloomily into the fire and confusedly look out to rose-colored clusters of grapes and red hawthorne. Michel broods while Alice smokes one cigarette after another. Only the cook braves the elements to get to the butcher. The purple of Alice's sexuality thus passes through the blue of a delusory calm to the red (vegetation, fire, cigarettes, meat) of destruction and death.

Evolution occurs against the background of the dilapidated house itself, both product and symbol of the dying marriage. In his presuicidal depression, watching a cigarette burn a hole into his desk, Michel thinks, "From the attics to the cellars, Cransac is worm-eaten" (123). Cransac's smoke and worms concretize the unsalvageable state of his marriage—of marriage. His death is ultimately less a personal tragedy than a mythological vision. Alice herself is universal woman, with "occidental" green eyes and an "oriental" face. Michel assimilates her to womanhood, complaining, for example, that women are always worse than one imagines. With more eloquence than sense, he also comments on female sensuality: "For a woman, a well-balanced woman, that is, a violent sexual urge is almost always an abnormal crisis, some morbid incident. Do you understand what I'm saying, Alice?" (100). She answers politely but silently wonders why men can never address the question of a woman's sensuality without talking complete nonsense. She accuses Michel of lack of imagination and cheap histrionics.

Michel never fulminates at the erstwhile lover: with Ambrogio he acts in function of an obscure bond, directing all his rancor against Alice. For her part, she finds a fierce laconic supporter in their servant Maria. Sensing the trouble between her employers, Maria, who had previously been devoted entirely to Michel, begins to wear the new look of an ally, and Alice vaguely perceives in her "the solidarity linking wife and concubine" (86). A highly charged symbolic moment occurs in the kitchen, when Alice bandages the servant's burned arm. Maria elliptically explains that her husband took revenge on her with a hot poker. Revenge for what? "For the fact that he's my husband and I'm his wife. That's quite enough" (108). Alice will later have the opportunity to understand better when Michel behaves in a similar way, seizing and twisting the hand that gives him Ambrogio's letters, to leave her fingers injured and numb. The episode of the burned arm occurs also in an earlier text, *The Other One,* where Fanny recalls Jane's account of how one of her sadistic lovers burned her on the arm. Here as in *Duo,* the burn as an element of female memory, as an event recollected and related by one woman to another, signifies female awakening to the abyss separating woman from a fundamentally contemptible male.[4] The bandage, on the other hand, symbolizes the birth of a pure feminine alliance: Maria "bent her head and laid the white bandage close against her cheek, as she might have hugged a newborn baby in its swaddling clothes" (109). The tendencies toward sharing and patching up (literally with a bandage; figuratively in relations), so characteristic of the female, are lacking in the male, who must possess absolutely or not at all. In an oblique way, Alice's ally is a catalyst to Michel's suicide, since it is Maria who expatiates on the spring rains and the swollen river of Cransac—the waters that are shortly to take Michel's life.

Duo compellingly demarcates and characterizes male and female; all the coarse anxiety and febrile weakness are his, all the refinement of sense, healthy tenacity, and vitality are hers. In Colette's fictional universe, there is no coming to terms. The need for Alice to show the letters rather than merely tell Michel about the affair underscores the ineffectualness of dialogue; his reaction to them is the masculine refusal of female sexuality. At the end of Easter vacation—paradoxically a season of renaissance—Michel hurls himself into the river. The wife whom he was wont to describe admiringly as "long as a river" survives. There is some archetypal oscillation here, for if woman is thus identified with water, both source of regeneration and instrument of destruction, she is also, as we have seen, linked to fire where, like the phoenix, she is reborn.

Le Toutounier

The title *Duo,* with its suggestions of musicality, duplication, and reverberation, elicits the unlikely doubling of syllables in *Le Toutounier,* while foreshadowing the resemblances among its principal characters, who are physical and moral echoes of each other. The time-scarred manorhouse where the words of Alice and Michel uselessly resounded disappears with him; in the sequel a Parisian flat replaces it. And, as the setting retracts, so does the action: the second novel spans only a little over 24 hours. Some three weeks after the suicide, Alice returns to the Paris studio apartment where she was raised with her three sisters. Just as Cransac, cavernous and cold, figured the heterosexual world, so the tiny flat suggests the womb.[5] The youngest Eudes sister, Bizoute, is now making films with an impoverished husband in Polynesia, but the remaining two, Colombe and Hermine, live there still, barely supporting themselves by various paratheatrical activities. On Alice's arrival, the purples and reds of jealousy, sex, and death fade to the harmonious yellow-green of Colombe's outfit, which the new widow finds in the closet and substitutes for her black mourning attire.

If Michel spurned authentic dialogue and succumbed to the written word (Ambrogio's vivid if banal characterizations of the affair), Alice's return home corresponds to a resurgence of the power of the spoken. And while Michel's speech was predictable and trite—"When Michel starts a sentence, he could always hand it over for someone else to finish. Clause in parentheses and cliché, cliché and clause in parentheses" (99)—the refuge that her sisters provide is first of all an original, albeit regressive, infantile language, where *cigarettes* are "sisibecques," *le placard* (closet) is "le padirac," and *le plaid* (carriage robe) is "le dipla." Such arbitrary word deformations and incantations like "guézézi, guézézi" constitute a private system of discourse, codifying the exclusiveness of their community and their roots in a shared past. These locutions are in fact only part of a "tone" or "code" to which allusion is frequently made. The canon governing relations among the sisters prescribes loyalty, shared possessions, and license to joke about the personal, but a concomitant respect for psychic privacy and the avoidance of effusiveness. This mode of behavior—and especially of speech—is christened "the Toutounier code" after their invented childhood name for the battered leather divan that dominates the apartment. Thus the sisters' intimate verbal alliance, with its rigid prohibitions, is linked to their physical bond, for they sleep together on the toutounier in chaste promiscuity.

The first stage in Alice's reentry into the gynaeceum is her sodality with Maria. In *Duo,* Maria (who, like Hermine and Colombe, is significantly the same height as Alice) acts as a surrogate sister, and her kitchen strikes Alice as feminine, its disordered cleanliness conjuring up a vision of the studio apartment. At the beginning of *Le Toutounier,* Alice

tells Colombe that, after Michel's death, she and the servant slept side by
side on two sofas in the living room of Cransac, thus sealing the bond
between them. Their closeness, fulfilling and pure—Maria is clad in a
nun's nightshirt—prefigures the descent into the toutounier.

The toutounier is the deepest symbol of the gynaeceum, and the com-
forting proximity it furnishes suggests an alternative to heterosexual
love. Indeed, while Alice finds renewal in the drowsy intertwining of 12
similar limbs, with her husband she allowed only twin beds. Slumber
with her sisters functions on a more profound level than intimacy with
Michel, for, in bed with him, she sometimes forgot where she was and
sleepily called out, "move over, Colombe," or "Bizoute, what time is it?"
(202). But on their native sofa, Alice never unconsciously takes one of
the band to be Michel. Alice's sisters, then, are not substitute lovers, but
Michel can be seen as a substitute sister: sisterhood encompasses and
makes intelligible conjugal love.

Men are excluded from active participation in the "toutounier's"
eccentric eroticism. There are allusions to a father who once supported
the four girls on a music teacher's meager income, but he has long since
died. Michel of course is also dead, victim to Alice's sexuality. And even
though Colombe's drama revolves around her relations with the married
orchestra conductor for whom she works, and Hermine's around her liaison with the married boss she calls "Mr. Weekend," neither sister is in
fact her lover's mistress. Indeed, as psychologically crucial as he is, the
very name of Hermine's boyfriend suggests his marginality. Colombe
explains in the early pages of Le Toutounier that she and the man they
have nicknamed "the Balabi" are too tired to be lovers, and in the last
pages she alleges that they have no place to carry on an affair. To Alice's
suggestion that they use the toutounier, she reacts with horror, declaring that she would prefer to wear a chastity belt (201). Her indignation
and mention of the chastity belt correspond to the literal—and abnormal—inviolability of the Eudes sorority. In spite of the sisters' overriding preoccupations with men, the gynaeceum and its sofa must remain
pure, their sisterhood sterile, and their discourse an insular idiom. And
if Alice's regressive communication with her sisters is more fulfilling
than her nondialogue with Michel, the ultimate possibilities of the
female sanctuary are nonetheless illusory. The gynaeceum is provisional,
a place of renewal and repose rather than a permanent home. There is
always a male on the horizon, and the females are as inevitably
attracted by love as they are contemptuous of it. In the end, each of her
sisters prepares to leave with her man, and Alice makes her plans: she will

move into the studio, tidy it up, take care of things. Sooner or later, the others will come back. And the cycle will inevitably continue.

Of all French novelists, Colette most admired Balzac, and her own use of reappearing characters, although more limited, is not without similarities to Balzac's *Human Comedy*. Series like the Claudine novels, *The Vagabond* and *The Shackle, Chéri* and *The Last of Chéri,* and finally *Duo* and *Le Toutounier,* all allow, as do Balzac's works, a particular exploration of the relation between an individual and the world, whether it is Parisian salon society, the demimonde, or the theater. In Colette's work, however, the sequel has a special sense, for each series of novels posits the death or disappearance of the male protagonist. Chéri, like Michel, commits suicide; Renée Néré refuses the hand of her suitor Max; and Claudine's husband, Renaud, succumbs to tuberculosis. In *Le Toutounier,* the significance of the woman's survival is enhanced by its association with female language and society. Alice's salvation is her temporary reintegration into a community of women who resemble her, so that her accession to the gynaeceum, with its emphasis on twinship and childish speech, is also a regression to a mirror stage of existence.[6]

Le Toutounier was published five years after *Duo,* and there is slippage in details of chronology and plot. In *Duo,* Alice is 37 years old and Hermine is the eldest of the four sisters, but in the sequel Alice is placed chronologically between Colombe, age 34, and Hermine, now only 29. In addition, when Alice writes home in *Duo,* she addresses her letter to Bizoute, certain that it will be read by all three. But, by the second novel, set in principle only a few weeks later, Bizoute has acquired a husband, with whom she is making documentary films in the Pacific, and has been gone long enough to have sent home various photographs. The texts are otherwise, however, internally coherent, and the inconsistencies between them are only on the literal level, the sisters' essential character traits being unaltered. Thematically, the stories are of a piece, similar finally to a slightly earlier play of the era, Cocteau's *Orpheus*—another portrait of the necessary but impossible couple, the antagonism inevitable in heterosexual love, the fatal deterioration of communication between man and woman, and female solidarity.

Julie de Carneilhan

Colette's last full-length novel synthesizes all her previous fiction in its dominant themes, symbols, and structures; but to the thematic, symbolic, and structural reminiscences, it sacrifices nothing in uniqueness.

Julie de Carneilhan (1941), whose heroine shares with Claudine, Sido, and Gigi the distinction of being eponymous, is full of poetry and surprises.

Forty-five and twice divorced, Julie summarizes Colette's heroines: their beauty, robustness, wit, sterility (from Claudine on, none, except Sido, has children). But she is the most explicitly beautiful and the only aristocrat among them. Living alone in genteel poverty, Julie draws on her resources of practicality and family pride. An imperative call from her more recent ex-husband, Herbert d'Espivant, sends her to the sickbed where he is recovering from a heart attack. Herbert, whom she thought she had gotten over, turns out to be still capable of magnetizing Julie despite his illness, egotism, and history of infidelities. On her second visit a few days later, he proposes a bizarre scheme to extract money from his present wealthy wife. He wants Julie to produce an old IOU for 1 million francs, which Herbert wrote her in jest years earlier. Marianne's sense of honor will compel her to pay her husband's debt, and Herbert will use the money to get away from Marianne. Julie sends him the note, and two days later receives a visit not from a grateful Herbert, but from Marianne herself, whom he has dispatched with Julie's payment. Marianne does not know that the sealed envelope she delivers contains not the one million francs she gave her husband for the debt, but a mere hundred thousand. Herbert kept the bulk of the money and sent Julie only 10 percent—an agent's commission.

Julie's greatest scene is her encounter with the rival whose simple dignity forces her esteem. Despite their mutual jealousy and Julie's posturing, there is the suggestion of a deeper affinity between the two women than either enjoys with Herbert. After a brief hesitation, Julie chooses not to disabuse Marianne about her husband, preferring to play, in Marianne's eyes, the role of sole villain. And Herbert does not even call to say thank you. At four o'clock the morning after Marianne's visit, Julie climbs out of bed and begins rummaging about in a cupboard, where she turns up her old riding boots. She sits down under the naked bulb of the kitchen light to polish them. Not long after, she is ready to leave Paris with her brother, a horse trader, and several of his mares. In a poetic ending, they set out at dawn to ride back to their family home at Carneilhan. How long, Julie asks, will the journey last? "Three weeks ...three months...all our lives," replies her brother (135).

There are various indications that this is a *roman à clef.* Colette has evoked the atmosphere, if not the precise events, of her life in the 1920s. Reversed, Julie de Carneilhan's initials are those of Colette de Jouvenel (as she was then called), and the novel's first paragraph foregrounds them, when Julie tries to decide whether to embroider a "J" or a "C" on a cushion she is making out of an old pair of riding pants. Julie's elder brother is named Léon; Colette's of course was Léo (who had died in March 1940, the year before the novel appeared); both are bachelors, elegantly obdurate, whose principal affections are for their own distant past. The peculiar reserve characterizing Julie and Léon recalls Colette's description in *Sido* of her adult relations with Léo. Between the ages of 49 and 50, moreover, Colette divorced her second husband, Henry de Jouvenel, who, like Herbert, was an aristocrat, a diplomat, and a ladies' man; and Jouvenel replaced Colette with a wealthier wife (he married a Dreyfus). Finally, Julie's involvement with Herbert's stepson Toni recalls Colette's during the early 1920s with her stepson Bertrand de Jouvenel.

Colette's plots typically unfold in a universe temporally or spatially closed, thus accentuating the hopelessness of dialogue. *Julie de Carneilhan* covers two or three weeks in the period shortly before World War II; allusions to an impending disaster augment the feeling of closure. Most of the action takes place in two indoor settings, Julie's apartment and Herbert's house. Many of Colette's novels are similarly organized, their action oscillating between two symbolic dwellings. Léa's orderly house in *Chéri* contrasts with Charlotte Peloux's; Alain's spacious family home and garden, with the modern "wedge of cheese" apartment in *The Cat;* the rented Brittany vacation home, with the Farous' Paris residence in *The Other One;* Cransac, with the womb-like Eudes apartment in *Duo* and *Le Toutounier;* even Claudine's Montigny house and garden are evoked in counterpoint to her cramped Paris apartments. Familiar domestic spaces structure Colette's plots, spaces in which the characters resolve conflicts, assume their pasts, and strike a viable posture for the future. Functional, sterile, antiquated, or pretentious, the decors of these homes mirror the inhabitants. In *Julie de Carneilhan,* Herbert's mansion, like Herbert himself, embodies the ostentatious taste of the arriviste, betraying the fact that the recent Espivant nobility has little in common with the "ragged antiquity" of Carneilhan. Julie's studio, by contrast, is chic and practical: a corner of the kitchen lodges the bathtub and the sofa opens into a bed, requiring only one sheet folded over. This essentially bipartite schema of house and apartment is complicated, however, by the presence/absence of the Carneilhan castle, never systematically described but repeatedly evoked.

As in several other Colette novels, the claustrophobic spaces of house and apartment open out by means of mirrors and windows. Léon, Herbert, and Julie never tire of looking at their reflections, boldly when alone, furtively in company. Julie consults her mirrored self at least 15 times, or about once every nine pages. Mirrors expand the sense of external space as well as the character's consciousness of herself, but their precise role here is difficult to delineate. Their function is subtly different from that in *The Vagabond* or *Chéri*. For the earlier heroines, looking in the mirror is an exercise in self-criticism, a painful lesson in aging. To Julie, on the contrary, the mirror is unfailingly kind and the reflection of her statuesque form, blond curls and rosy complexion delights her.

In a suggestive chapter of her book on Colette, Yannick Resch discusses the function of the mirror in Colette's work. She points out, first, that in *Julie de Carneilhan* as in *Chéri,* the narrative itself is framed by mirrors, for the first and last pages of both these novels contain the description of a protagonist looking in a mirror. Resch mentions too that the proliferation of mirrors reveals the characters' taste for light, well-being, style, and comfort. But the principal thrust of her analysis is to establish that, through the mirror, knowledge of the body becomes knowledge of the self.[7] This is probably truer in *Julie de Carneilhan* than elsewhere. Each of Julie's mirror encounters produces a short pause, a moment of meditation anticipating action or decision. The mirror enables Julie to distance herself from a tedious present. It witnesses her internal struggle and helps resolve conflict, for the duality of object and image paradoxically creates a sense of wholeness. In the mirror, Julie reads her integrity and from it draws assurance. Resch notes that the mirror reflection helps Julie maintain a constantly threatened equilibrium through the coincidence of the way she wants to appear and what she actually sees.

The role of the mirror as an instrument for grasping the character's totality is crucial in a novel where the rupture between past and present is an important structuring element. The plot traces Julie's attempt to extricate herself from an emotionally and financially impoverished present and to recover a richer past. The first few pages situate her in a life whose elegance is merely symbolic: an Empire cup, a Swedish spoon, and an embroidered Turkish napkin link the shabbiness of her tiny apartment to more affluent days. Her lover of 28, a hard-working industrialist named Coco Vatard, and her friend Lucie Albert, a young nightclub performer, belong to the petite bourgeoisie, and Julie's attitude toward them is indulgent disdain. Coco's forthrightness arouses only her mockery, while she denies Lucie even a name, addressing her normally as "my pet" or "my love" ("mon petit coeur"). Like Renée Néré's friend May in

The Shackle, Lucie hardly even speaks Julie's language, staring in wonder when Julie uses words of more than two syllables.

A dual past contrasts with the makeshift friends and lodgings of Julie's present. The past is symbolized, on the one hand, by her birthplace, the rundown nine-hundred-year-old castle of Carneilhan, part manorhouse and part farmhouse; and on the other by Herbert's garish house, whose rooms have seen radical changes in decoration and use in the three years since Julie's residence there. Her brother Léon is the most evident link to Carneilhan, his visits a reminder of Julie's moral and social inheritance.

Léon extends and enriches the mirror function. In the first place, Julie resembles him in outlook and physique. They share a silent pride and an indestructible appetite, and they have the same lean form and features: "a wild look, with narrowing temples and the chin and jawbone fining down into a muzzle" (21). Anger and excitement heighten their animal affinities: their noses wrinkle and their nostrils dilate. Both self-consciously exaggerate these traits when they pass a mirror. Léon's eyes, like Julie's, are cold, deep, and blue, and their very color, he maintains, can tame animals. A mirror to Julie in more than one sense, his eyes return her image and link her visually to her ancestors while also returning her *glance:* the admiration they transmit assures her, like the mirror, of her arrogant beauty. And finally, her esteem for Léon's self-sufficiency partially motivates her decision to join him in returning to Carneilhan. For the trip, she dons a riding outfit identical to his.

At Herbert's side, Julie takes the full measure of her boredom and loneliness. Like Alice in *Le Toutounier,* she feels somehow superfluous without a man. Arriving at Espivant's, she experiences a kind of suspension in time: "for a moment she lost all sense of time. The present became meaningless, as if lost in the heart of a dream" (25). (The French is more picturesque: literally, "she lost her foothold in time" and "mistrusted the present.") Julie's equilibrium is disrupted, her very sense of time jolted. All the more so when she finds Herbert bedded down in what they once called the nursery. "Is it an attempt to make yourself seem younger?" she asks (30). She is aroused by Herbert's still potent charm, but at the same time, her bedridden host, the elaborate silver, and the meretricious decor make her feel practically a prisoner, and she confusedly seeks an escape. After two hours, she hurries back to her little apartment, and feels as though she were returning after a long absence. Herbert's reemergence elicits other ghosts belonging to the years of marriage to him. In a restaurant with Coco, she briefly glimpses

Puylamare—like Herbert, a middle-aged politician, and once her lover. She notes how dissolute and old he looks. And later, in a nightclub, she runs into the Baroness Beatrix de La Roche Tannoy, a bluestocking turned cabaret singer, and the two women exchange news of old acquaintances, mendacious confidences, and boasts: "They both gave way to the need . . . of stealing back, like burglars, into the world they had abandoned with such pointless ostentation" (54). The burglar image is suggestive. Julie becomes subtly enmeshed in a past she never effectively exorcised. She will try not only metaphorically, but also literally by becoming Herbert's accomplice, to steal it back.

Julie's weakness in the face of the man she loves links her to other Colette heroines, notably Renée of *The Shackle,* whose emancipation goes up in smoke when she falls in love. Marcelle Biolley-Godino postulates that the most interesting of Colette's female characters are those in whom coexist two contradictory tendencies: normally lucid and strong, they are unconsciously eager to find a master and submit. Biolley-Godino makes clear that nowhere is the contradiction more evident than in Julie de Carneilhan, who oscillates between domination (of partners like Coco) and abject submissiveness to Herbert's will.[8]

Another related reversal characterizes this novel: that of sexual attributes. It occurs less systematically than in *The Ripening Seed,* but Julie's virility still contrasts with Herbert's effeminacy. Her long body is leaner, harder, and more robust than his. She wears tailored suits of gray and black, keeps her hair cut short like a man, and bathes like a man too, soaping her entire body, including her head. Herbert, on the other hand, has a certain delicacy of constitution and visage, with slightly effeminate features. His need for money, moreover, specifically relates to his desire to escape his wife's sexual demands. Alleging a weak heart, he is threatened by his wife's sexuality, threatened indeed even by Julie's joking overtures in his sick-room. Julie dreams an impossible dream, that of being the ally of such a man. Her dream, like Alice's in *Duo,* Fanny's in *The Other One,* or Camille's in *The Cat,* can only fail. Emasculated by women's force or sensuality, men prefer retreat to commitment, silence to communication. In extreme cases, like Michel in *Duo,* they prefer death. Actually, Herbert's disposition is not far from Michel's. His inability to face life's disappointments and his desire to escape sexual involvement are a subtle acquiescence to death, while his illness has the lure of orgasm: he admits that his faints—"little deaths," as he dubs them—are accompanied by a feeling of well-being.

The real superiority, of course, belongs to Julie, who exhibits a kind of grandeur when she assents to his scheme: "Her secret state of mind and body was patent in her determined expression, her nostrils particularly open to the wind, and her mouth at its largest, painted a challenging red" (107). And when he fails to respond in kind, her lament is extraordinarily eloquent: "Oh Herbert, my greatest love of all, happiest part of my life, and my greatest sorrow!" (125). Herbert is seriously aroused only once: on discovering Julie's liaison with Marianne's 17-year-old son, Toni. Julie's real match is Marianne, as beautiful and avid as she, and the novel's most poignant episode is the confrontation between two women separated and betrayed by love of the same man. It recalls Fanny and Jane in *The Other One,* deliberating the fate of Farou who has been faithless to both, just as the triangular structure of man, woman, and (step)son recalls that same novel. When Julie understands that she has been duped, that there is no place for her in Herbert's future, she makes the same decision that a number of protagonists, from Claudine to Alice, made before her: she goes home. Her departure for Carneilhan is the recognition that the past must be assumed, but cannot be relived. It is the recognition of failure, but a positive attempt at a cure as well. Dawn finds Julie, like the narrator of *Break of Day,* dreaming of nature and animals as a substitute for human love.

With Julie's return to the garden Claudine left 40 years earlier, Colette's novels have come full circle.

Gigi

Gigi, which appeared in periodical form in 1941 and as the title story of a collection of short pieces in 1944, is Colette's last major work of fiction, and the locus of several contradictions. While the heroines of her later years are mostly mature (Julie de Carneilhan, for example, is 45), Gigi is an adolescent, created when Colette was nearing 70. She worked on the novelette during the war years, which were among her life's bleakest. Paris was occupied; Maurice Goudeket was arrested in 1941 and sent to a prison camp, and after his release spent months in hiding. Colette was already suffering from the lesion which would become crippling arthritis. But *Gigi* is extraordinarily optimistic for a Colette story. The title character has reached an enormous public. Americans have heard of her, seen the movie with Maurice Chevalier, and can hum the title song—but few know that Colette wrote the book. *Gigi* is such a bright, breezy story that one may incline to dismiss it as just adequate for a musical. In fact, this is a small masterpiece of stylish humor and meticulous execution. Its source is an anecdote Colette had heard in the 1920s (it occurred around 1918), but she sets her version in 1899, so that her last heroine lives in the same era as Claudine and at the time when Colette herself, under Willy's guidance, was becoming intimate with Paris and the demimonde.

The story is well known. The guileless 15-year-old product of several generations of hard-working courtesans is being groomed to follow the profession of her grandmother and great-aunt. Their efforts are about to be crowned with a lucrative arrangement. Thirty-three-year-old Gaston Lachaille, sugar tycoon and family friend (Gigi's grandmother seems to have once been the mistress of Gaston's father), wants to make Gigi his mistress. To the consternation of all, Gigi at first rejects the proposition, which strikes her as sordid. And then, just when her love for Gaston has brought her to the point of accepting, he offers her his hand in marriage instead.[9]

One of Colette's most ironic works, *Gigi* is exceptionally spare of lyricism. The constant source of humor is the contrast between her family's consecrated moral laxity, on the one hand, and on the other its rigid adherence to established codes, unvarying confidence in the reliability of signs, and enforcement of principles of order, cleanliness, and "correct" behavior. Paradoxically, their modest home without men gives proof of energetic compliance with bourgeois standards. Bed linens are changed every 10 days, meals are served at regular hours, and Madame Alvarez, the *mater familias,* rises punctually at 7:30 to wage a daily war against impropriety. She has especially inculcated in her progeny dedication to a certain ideal of bodily cleanliness: "You can, at a pinch, leave the face till the morning when traveling or pressed for time. For a woman, attention to the lower parts is the first law of self-respect" (literally, "is a woman's dignity" [142]). The reassignment of dignity from face to sexual organs is part of the code governing this society. It valorizes sex as a survival strategy: cleanliness (*propreté*) is the necessary propriety and the route to prosperity, to property (*propriété*).

When Gigi assures her great-aunt Alicia, "I understand that we don't marry" (151), she seems to endorse this sexual but nonmarital system of exchange. The operative deemphasis of marriage is so complete that, for Aunt Alicia at least, married people are by definition "ordinary" and "useless." Yet the rules for acceptable liaisons are as severe as any bourgeois rules of engagement and marriage, and Gigi understands that she must keep herself inviolate—not until her wedding day, but until her first official liaison. In preparation for her role as a wealthy man's mistress, she must watch her figure, learn to eat lobster properly, and choose cigars and evaluate jewels critically. The liaison is a transaction of paramount importance to an economy in which the family is exclusively matrilinear. Gigi is in fact related only to her mother, grandmother, and great-aunt, with Gaston (the novel's only man) in a tantalizingly ambiguous posture. His early relation to Gigi is avuncular, and the familiar French word for "uncle" that she uses to address him ("Tonton") even resonates with his name. This surrogate uncle eventually tries to withdraw from this role and become a lover. Gigi wins a victory and realigns the family when she makes of him a husband instead.

In redesigning her family tree, she transcends a social order built on scrupulous observance of an imperious sign system. For example, when Gigi wants to wear her everyday coat for the weekly call on Aunt Alicia, her grandmother declares: "That wouldn't show it's Sunday." Gigi arrives at her Aunt's to find her "wearing her little lace cap to show she had a headache" ("en signe de migraine" [138]). And when Gigi's mother opines that there is nothing extraordinary about Liane d'Exelmans, Gaston's most recent mistress: "You're wrong," retorts Madame Alvarez, "she is extraordinary. Otherwise she would not be so famous" (142). She protests again when Aunt Alicia calls Gigi a little brat: "A young girl who has held the attention of Monsieur Lachaille is not a little brat" (169). The family's faith in the appropriateness of wearing a Sunday coat on Sundays and a lace cap for migraines dovetails with their subscription to a code where appearances constitute essence and reputation is truth.

"Calling people and things by their names never did anyone any good," another of Madame Alvarez's maxims, indicates the parameters of the family's pedagogy: certain lexical items are unutterable. In the opening scene, Gigi protests wearing her skirts short on the grounds that they oblige her to be forever thinking of her "you-know-what" ("ce-que-je-pense"), which she must conceal with a minimum of fabric. Her grandmother's response:

> "Silence! Aren't you ashamed to call it your you-know-what?"
> "I don't mind calling it by any other name, only—"
> Madame Alvarez blew out the spirit lamp, looked at the reflection of her heavy Spanish face in the looking glass above the mantelpiece, and then laid down the law: "There is no other name." (127)

In a patrilinear society, the father's voice gives names, whereas Gigi's matrilinear community attempts to discredit or annihilate them. Custodian of language and sexual knowledge, her grandmother adopts a strategy that makes the female space a linguistic absence. But Gigi's sex is constantly on the verge of surfacing, and every other consideration is measured according to it. It is, in fact, the most present and powerful of signifieds, and the very refusal to name it provokes conversations foregrounding its importance. In like manner, Gaston's essential financial identity subtly surfaces in the name of the candies that he eats during his visit to her home: *agents de change.*

Madame Alvarez's mirroring of "her heavy Spanish face" is the most curious example of wordplay and the ramifications of naming, for Madame Alvarez is not Spanish. "Alvarez" is adopted, the Spanish name of a deceased lover. Her appearance has accommodated itself to the name and given the bearer pale and creamy fleshiness and lustrous, oily hair. And not only does she acquire a physiognomy to match the surname; these looks attract, in turn, a suitable Christian name: "eventually she took to calling herself Inez" (128). "Alvarez" undergoes a transformation in the next generation, for her daughter (who, to Madame Alvarez's exasperation, prefers singing to a life of gallantry), is called Andrée Alvar, "in small type on the Opéra-Comique playbills" (139). The playbill typography defines and confines Andrée, just as the Spanish suffix does her mother. The family surname will change more radically still with Gigi's acquisition of a legitimate one through marriage.

Gigi's education involves learning to acknowledge the power of the sociolect in which her mother and grandmother live their lives. Her backwardness is evidenced on the one hand by her bold invocation of the prohibited nonname—her you-know-what—and on the other by her failure to recognize and use correctly terms and names in public currency. To Gaston's astonishment, she has never heard of the playwright Feydeau. And when she has finally assimilated the fact that a demimondaine does not die when she routinely "commits suicide" at the end of an affair, Gigi still cannot sort out the social histories that give her mother and grandmother no trouble. Of Gaston's notorious ex-mistress, Liane:

> "The last time she killed herself, Grandmama, was for the sake of Prince Georgevitch, wasn't it?"
> "Where are your brains, my darling? It was for Count Berthou de Sauveterre." (143)

While those around her are deliberately ambiguous at times, they are consummately precise at others. "Let us talk briefly and to the point" (162), declares Gaston to Madame Alvarez, when he comes to say he wants Gigi for a mistress; and so they do. The terms of their negotiation are relayed only vaguely to Gigi, however, translated by her grandmother into Gaston's altruistic desire to "make Gigi's fortune." She is expected to acquiesce docilely to the euphemized scheme, but at her confrontation with Gaston, she pointedly announces, "They've drummed into my ears that I am backward for my age, but all the same I know the meaning of words" (166). Shattering the family's plans, she refuses to subscribe to a code which, by eliminating denotation, encourages sexual exploitation, and she delineates her understanding of what it means to have her "fortune" made: like all his previous mistresses, she must sleep in his bed until the day when, with great notoriety, she passes into someone else's. To Gaston's embarrassed, "Gigi, I beg of you," she counters: "But, Tonton, why should I mind speaking of it to you? You didn't mind speaking of it to Grandmama" (166).

There is, of course, no answer to Gigi's question. Why *should* she mind speaking of it? Why the ominous verbal prohibitions surrounding a transparent arrangement? Gigi's you-know-what is the elusive, problematic center of a network of financial and sexual exchange. It is simultaneously concealed (under a short skirt and a nonname) and valorized (sold intact to Gaston Lachaille); unnamed and unnamable, it is nonetheless continually evoked. Her refusal of the circumlocutions, substitutions, and silences that her family demands is the rejection of a system by which they have lived for generations, and which grants centrality to the you-know-what. Gigi is, in fact, from the start, somewhat off center, eccentric. The expression is Madame Alvarez's, who refuses in the first scene to wave Gigi's hair, maintaining that ringlets at the ends are "the maximum of eccentricity permissible for a girl your age" (my translation). Asserting finally that she will have her own "word," Gigi lays claim to a different social configuration. Her verbal and sexual triumph over Gaston rewrites the code: she imposes her own terms of exchange. Her successful attempt to communicate re-creates a family that is no longer matrilinear, and a new center emerges: love replaces commercial exchange.

The fiction of Colette's maturity, from *The Other One* to *Gigi,* is similarly eccentric, deviating from traditional fiction into a new feminocentric orbit, whose axis is a subtle investigation of sexual dialogue.

Chapter Six
Eros and Experience

Three important works underpin the novels discussed in the preceding chapter. The material of these texts comes from Colette's distant past, and the protagonists are generally long dead. All three retrospectives give permanent and final form to memories of some of the most influential figures in her life. Anecdotal and written in the first person, these memorial works may be justifiably grouped together for other reasons. Each elaborately glosses love, sensuality, and the nature of experience. The notion of purity informs *Sido* (1929), that of impurity *My Apprenticeships* (1936). *The Pure and the Impure* (1932), chronologically between them, is also their thematic middle: it adumbrates the sense of both words, stressing their relativity and ambiguities in the conclusion: "The word 'pure' has never revealed an intelligible meaning to me" (175).

The Pure and the Impure

The Pure and the Impure (*Le Pur et l'impur*, originally entitled *Ces Plaisirs*) is a discourse on forms of sexual pleasure, all the more stunning for having been written during a period when sexuality was rarely discussed openly. This is a serious piece of tourism in the land of the erotic, emphasizing the varieties of the terrain. Colette later speculated that this haunting volume would one day be recognized as her best book. It implicitly suggests a complex relation central to much literary and social theory, notably the work of Michel Foucault: the relation of discourse to sex. Colette's volume is not simply a dissertation on the practices and ravages of sex, but a sustained exercise in listening and responding. The narrator, named "Colette," records remembered or invented dialogues in order to evoke a variety of so-called "impure" love relationships. She recollects and interrogates various lovers whom she has known along with a few she has only heard of. "As if [she] were an expert," (138), she listens to and transcribes the confidences of this succession of men and women, straining to extract from the banality of whispered words their true and secret sense, their tragedy and greatness. She constantly gives us to

understand that she knows better than her speakers what they are saying, yet her own interaction with the reader is also problematic, for if she
hints at her informants' real meaning, she generally refuses to reveal it
explicitly. *The Pure and the Impure* obliquely traces a causal connection
between making love and talking about it, but also, on a more general
plane, the circuits between experience and storytelling, between author
and narrator, and perhaps above all, between pleasure and speech.

The volume is an extended meditation on a phrase from *The Ripening
Seed:* Colette examines pleasures "which are lightly called physical." The
elliptical self-quotation suggests several things. In the first place, the
body is autonomous and intractable; "it knows what it wants" (22). At
the same time, the frontier between the despotic senses and the emotions
is unstable. And, finally, words (like "pure" or "physical") do not easily
surrender all their hidden meaning, if indeed one can be sure that they
designate anything at all. Debauchery, for instance, is revealed as a thing
of the mind as well as the body, and is continually qualified and
nuanced—"what must be called debauchery," or "so-called debauchery."
It resists a simple interpretation; the word has strange affiliations—with
purity as well as pleasure—just as the practice has unforeseen consequences. Indeed, in the final analysis, the act of listening is itself "a kind
of studied debauch." And not only listening, but interpreting as well,
"the elevating to its secret meaning a litany of dull words, promoting
acrimony to grief or wild desire" (48).

The opening section is set in an opium den. Smoky, ornate, redolent,
its atmosphere assaults all the senses at once. The narrator comes not as
a seeker after pleasure, like the others, but as a novelist and journalist
"on a professional assignment." Her avowed purpose is to listen and
interpret rather than enjoy. Oriental tapestries of the kind produced for
Western consumption decorate the flat. While the text is thus under the
sign of the exotic and enigmatic East, it is a false exoticism, and the
notion of falsehood prevails along with that of mystery: signs are unwor-
thy of blind belief and truth is difficult to divine.

The narrator explores falsehood at some length in the encounter with
middle-aged Charlotte, whose "lying voice" she hears singing in this
clandestine pleasure-place. Charlotte's apparently wordless song is the
symbol of the more fundamental lies that she tells with her duplicitous
body. She explains to Colette that her lover's youth condemns her to a
diet of generous imposure: she makes the boy feel a man by feigning the
pleasure he does not give her. The voice of Charlotte, in song and then in
speech, dominates the first two chapters, early establishing the connec-

tion between words and sounds on the one hand and sex on the other. Charlotte's voice—cottony, harsh, sweet like hard and velvety peaches—resounds through the opium den, so profligate of pleasure that the listeners forbear from applauding or even from murmuring their praise. Rhythmic, harmonious, at once regular and precipitous, her song traces a kind of orgasm, expressing struggle with the invading pleasure and haste to bring it full term. The singing displeases only her young lover, who is apparently intolerant of her subliminal masturbation. A little later, in the taxi she shares with Colette, this same voice reverberates again, as Charlotte confides her sexual reservations and difficulties. They next meet at a charity book sale, where Colette autographs "for Madame Charlotte" one of her own volumes. The autographing pen seals a bond between these two middle-aged professional women with similar bisyllabic names.

At the same time, the episode reasserts the complex identity of a narrator who exists not only within the pages of *The Pure and the Impure,* but also outside and prior to them. Neither fiction nor autobiography, *The Pure and the Impure* is a prime example of a kind of writing that, more than any other, characterizes Colette. Her favored genre is a unique variant of autobiography: it is a written (-graphy) record of the self (auto-), but not necessarily of her own life (-bio-). Borrowing a term from a gesture rich in connotations (the narrator Colette signing a book with her own and the author's *real* name, for the benefit of a *fictitious* character at a *fictitious* sale), one could perhaps best call the form "autography." I mean to suggest the writing of an author who records events *in her own name and as if they were true,* but without giving anything like a self-history, without even necessarily playing the major role herself and, most important, without the commitment to veracity that characterizes the practice of traditional autobiography. I shall return in the next chapter to Colette's autography.

"For the pleasure of seeing Charlotte again" (16), Colette accepts another invitation to the opium den, where she hears more from Charlotte about her sex life. These intimate revelations are possible precisely because the two women are virtual strangers: "How nice that we know each other so little!" exclaims Charlotte; "We can talk about things one doesn't talk about with friends. Friends, women friends, if such a thing exists, never dare to confess to each other what they really and truly lack" (23). Indeed, with her best friend, Marguerite Moreno, who appears later in the volume, Colette engages in no such talk, and will note, apropos of herself and Moreno: "No one can imagine the number of subjects, the amount of words that are left out of the conversation of two women who can talk to each other with absolute freedom" (61). Intimacy of exchange is here inversely proportional to length and depth of acquaintance. In their last conversation, however, Charlotte bridles when Colette declines to endorse her policy of faking orgasm. Colette hints instead that real orgasm is not impossible and says that Charlotte would be more beautiful if she stopped lying. (The word "orgasm" is never pronounced: "the thing you lack" is their circumlocution.) It turns out that Charlotte in fact wants no part of it: "I'd be more ashamed of the truth than of the lie. Just imagine, madame...if I were to let myself go like a fool and not even know what I was doing or saying...Oh! I can't bear the idea!" (23). Piqued at Colette's refusal to approve her, Charlotte now becomes "cool and circumspect," falls back on protocol and commonplaces, and signals her definitive conversational withdrawal by pulling down her veil and leaving the studio opium den. Charlotte's "veiled face," her desire to control conversational and sexual play, her subscription to a code that confuses truth and lies—these are, as Colette suggests, a "suitable preface" to a book about pure and impure pleasures.

The recollection of Charlotte in the first pages conjures other ephemeral creatures, phantoms of the narrator's past, and so the singer's mendacious voice generates the entire book. In the succeeding chapters emerge the male and female Don Juans who have crossed Colette's path. Sadly and elliptically, they speak of themselves, pouring their doleful words into her "shadowy ear." First comes the "famous lover" who would tell her of his exploits in the private dining room of some reputable restaurant whose thick walls absorbed the sounds and magnified the silences. Again, she knows that it is only because they are *not* really intimate that he speaks to her freely, confiding the torment of the aging seducer: he is afflicted with "the neurosis that dishonors the voluptuary: the obsession with statistics." "My average is lower," he wails, then rages against the "bitches" who keep score (28). Colette interjects, "Rarely have I encountered in a woman the kind of hostility with which a man regards the mistresses who have exploited him sexually" (27). Another of the Don Juans, Damien, also bears a grudge against womankind, but his complaint is different. Fatuous, bitter, he cries out against injustice: every last one of them enjoyed it more than he did! "By what right did they always get more out of it than I did? If only I could doubt that they did! But I had only to look at them. Their satisfaction was all too real" (48). (Colette imagines with amusement Damien as the lover of

Charlotte: he would never suspect that his mate, in a spirit of kindness, characteristically faked enjoyment.)

From a consideration of the womanizer, Colette turns to the homosexual. She begins by invoking, as corollary and explanation of homosexuality, the "true mental hermaphroditism" of many strong people, male as well as female. Her thinking seems close to Virginia Woolf's, who in *A Room of One's Own,* published three years before *The Pure and the Impure,* wrote:

> I went on amateurishly to sketch a plan of the soul so that in each of us two powers preside, one male, one female; and in the man's brain, the man predominates over the woman, and in the woman's brain, the woman predominates over the man. The normal and comfortable state of being is that when the two live in harmony together, spiritually cooperating. If one is a man, still the woman part of the brain must have effect; and a woman also must have intercourse with the man in her. Coleridge perhaps meant this when he said that a great mind is androgynous. It is when this fusion takes place that the mind is fully fertilised and uses all its faculties. Perhaps a mind that is purely masculine cannot create, any more than a mind that is purely feminine.[1]

The Pure and the Impure suggests just this link between creativity and androgyny. Colette cites as evidence of hermaphroditism both her own passing predilection for men's dress and the vision of her sleeping friend, Marguerite Moreno, who dozing looks like Dante or Leonardo da Vinci's Saint John the Baptist: "Sleep brings an incalculable number of women to assume the form they would no doubt have chosen if their waking state did not keep them in ignorance of themselves. The same applies to men" (63). Colette moves from ignorance toward sapience as she implicitly questions the sense of terms like "feminine" and "masculine" and reintegrates what might be considered deviation into normalcy.

There follows a procession of male and female homosexuals. These include the "lost boys," the fabulous homosexual male secretaries of Monsieur Willy, whose virility Colette would be the last to impugn—what, after all, is virility?—and a pride of female homosexuals, including a woman from the highest stratum of society: "Her friends, as well as her enemies, never referred to her except by her title and a charming Christian name, title and name alike clashing with her stocky masculine physique and reserved, almost shy manner" (68). No doubt this is a portrait of Missy, Marquise de Belbeuf, with whom Colette lived after the separation from Willy, and whom she here chooses to call "La Chevalière." Her nobility of character and physique set her above the other members of the Paris-Lesbos circle. But the epithet, suggesting dominance and massive, overriding sexuality, belies her platonic scorn for the physical: at heart, "La Chevalière" was as timid as her masculine dress was bold. She was constantly misunderstood, and railed against her female partners in a manner befitting Damien: "I do not know anything about completeness in love," she would complain, "except the *idea* I have of it. But they, the women, have never allowed me to stop at that point" (74). If La Chevalière and Colette both dressed as men, the latter insists that she herself always remained very much a woman. Her friend, on the other hand, wished only the masculine role. Masculine garb, then, is a sign with many meanings.

Paradoxically, Colette's trio of notorious lovers—La Chevalière, Damien, and the "famous lover"—consistently want *less* than their partners do. Damien accuses all of his mistresses of going too far, and remains persuaded that he left them all with the same memory of him: "a feeling of not having had quite enough" (44); La Chevalière complains that women never let her stop at the point she would choose; and the famous lover cannot get his average as high as the "bitches" demand. All three protest that their sexual overtures elicit not responses they consider appropriate, but reactions that are incongruent, exaggerated, and unacceptable. These men and women may live on the margins of "pure" bourgeois society, but they have their own rigid notions of honor and exploitation, and they self-righteously complain when partners fail to abide by the codes governing their subcultures, thereby threatening the reciprocity of the sexual dialogue.

Colette acknowledges the naive astonishment she felt at the discovery that the somewhat banal transvestite society to which La Chevalière belonged and which haunted low-ceilinged, dimly lighted dwellings and fed on iced curaçao, serial novels, and cheap plays, "was affiliated with another group, much less clandestine, much more literary."[2] In the latter society shone the sapphic poet Renée Vivien (born Pauline Tarn, in London), whom Colette knew well in the first decade of the century. If Charlotte embodies lies, Renée Vivien incarnates mystery. The frail poet subsisted on alcohol and meager quantities of exotic foods in the sumptuous obscurity of an Oriental decor. The identity of the lover who subsidized Renée remained concealed from Colette's circle, but the biggest mystery was perhaps when and how—drunk, drugged, and half-starved amidst her Buddhas—such a poet managed to write.

Renée's poetry inhabited a "region of elevated melancholy, in which the *amies,* the female couple, daydream and weep as often as they

embrace" (92). But such a thematics was completely opposed to her conversation, for "her way of talking about physical love was rather like that
of little girls brought up for a life of debauchery: both innocent and
crude" (93). In words so explicit as to make her listener blink, she would
explain, for example, the essence of her lover's hold on her, or maintain
unselfconsciously that there are fewer ways of making love than people
say, but more than they believe. A quarrel ensues when Colette roundly
criticizes Renée's indiscreet speech, declaring "that certain frank remarks
she had made were as suitable to her as a silk hat to a monkey" (93–94).
Renée's discourse, sublimated or crude, serves on the one hand to cam-
ouflage and on the other to reveal her sexual propensities and her val-
orization of pleasure over love. And the narrator's own prudery (Colette
would call it *pudeur*) demonstrates that liberty of speech is less admissi-
ble than liberty of act. It is noteworthy, and typical of the volume, that
she records the explicitness of Renée's conversation in a manner itself
inexplicit and highly elliptical, neither repeating Renée's "frank remarks"
nor divulging the exact nature of her lesbian attachments. Here as elsewhere, Colette inclines to understatement, and the reader must surmise.

As much as Colette sympathizes with Renée, she instinctively
responds more completely to a posture more innocent and pronounce-
ments less specific, like that of the "ladies of Llangollen." These two
young Englishwomen ran away together toward the end of the eighteenth century, and shared nearly 50 years of pastoral isolation. The narrator speaks with special reverence of a creation "as perilously fragile" as
a pair of female lovers (109). This section of the book differs from the
others in that it reports not what the narrator has heard, but what she
has read, for she bases it on the diary kept by the elder of the two, Lady
Eleanor Butler. Thus the pleasure of the pair engenders the discourse of
Lady Eleanor, a sort of provincial aristocrat who writes to describe and
immortalize the delicious sameness of life with her "beloved," mention-
ing only once the words "bedroom" and "our bed." And precisely
because her pleasure remains unvoiced, Lady Eleanor's discourse engenders Colette's own pleasure, becoming in turn the cause of *her* discourse—and our reading pleasure.

The last chapter begins, as did the first, with allusions to artifice and
lure. This time the narrator voices her admiration for the false comport-
ment of certain male homosexuals: "They have so perfected their art of
dissimulation that by comparison everything else seems imperfect"
(155). Are these then "monsters"? Innocents, rather. "Error" is only our
name for the faith we do not profess.

The Pure and the Impure is the prototype of Colette's dialogues, crucial to the sense of her opus. It counterpoints interlocution and intercourse, for it is organized around two kinds of dyadic interaction, conversational and sexual. Its final effect is a reinterpretation of verbal and sexual signifiers, a redistribution of emphasis and meaning. The contrapuntal title is more than epigrammatic; its joining of opposites makes an important statement. This is not an attempt at separation—the "and" is not disjunctive—but at once an assimilation and a recognition of sexual and linguistic ambiguities, of the inadequacy of sex as well as speech. It offers, like "The Priest on the Wall," a partial explanation of the writer's vocation. Just as the child in *My Mother's House* lovingly examines, palpates, and appropriates the mysterious word "presbytery," this title suggests the writer's pleasure in considering words she does not understand. Terms like "happiness" escape a simple definition, just as there is no determining the border between the pure and the impure. Indeed, from the title's word "pure" itself, the narrator extracts no ultimate sense, and the book's concluding sentences stress only the sound: "the trembling of the plaintive 'u,' the icy limpidity of the 'r'" (174–75).

My Apprenticeships

"Apprenticeships" is what Colette calls the experiences of 13 years with Willy. Apprenticeship: learning, waiting, service, and indenture—an accurate characterization of marriage to him. In psychology "apprentissage" denotes establishing connections between certain stimuli and certain responses, the result of which is an increased adjustment of the individual to the milieu. Colette's apprenticeship was this too; there were lessons in adaptation, tolerance, and resilience. The volume chronicles less her actions than her *reactions*, her responses to a group of stimuli. Hers is the traditionally passive role of the female, and the economy in which she circulates between the ages of approximately 20 and 30 assumes that her passive masochism complements natural male aggressiveness. But her education in life is female in a positive sense too: Colette explicitly associates, in this volume and elsewhere, women and the taste for survival and self-defense.[3]

Colette was in her 60s in 1936. Her second husband, Henry de Jouvenel, had died the previous year; Willy himself in 1931. She chose the moment to reflect on her "start," in life as well as in literature. "The memories of my first and second years of marriage are clear and fantastic, like the impressions that dwell in the mind after some confused dream in which every detail, beneath its apparent incoherence, is plainly and fatally symbolic. But I was twenty-one and kept forgetting the symbols" (34). *My Apprenticeships* revives, transcribes, and interrogates the symbols "without deliberate order or plan." At a 40-year distance, the dream becomes comprehensible: the number and the confluence of the symbols led her from abjection to self-sufficiency.

Three threads run through the volume, weaving a triple apprenticeship in money, sexuality, and writing, each associated with interrelated symbols. The landscape is turn-of-the-century Paris with all its excesses, a world so shocking that its violent contrasts to village life brought the young bride to the edge of despair. Many of the symbols are human. As in *The Pure and the Impure,* friends and acquaintances play important roles. Their stories may appear digressive, but are in fact exemplary. Besides communicating the flavor of an era, they function as parables of responses to social expectations. Caroline Otéro, Marcel Schwob, Paul Masson, Polaire, all embody styles of life and attempts at self-realization.

The most important of the human symbols is Willy, who initiates, finances, and manages his wife. A caricature of patriarchal man, Willy puts the young provincial into urban circulation and determines the limits of the sphere in which she will circulate. Jealous of most female friends, Willy prefers that his wife keep company with men and homosexual boys. This "Monsieur Willy," as she calls him, is the most forceful male in all of Colette's writing. Marriage to him, as she portrays it here, consummates a rupture between past and present, country and city, happiness and suffering, between a matriarchal régime and a patriarchal one.

The center of "a haze of unhappy memories" (22), Willy introduces a radically new order, functioning under the double sign of money and sexuality. The first two chapters establish both the character's perilously close relation to money and its connections with sex and literature. For M. Willy, there exists a Book, neither the book of life nor the one he never succeeds in writing, but quite simply an account-book. He keeps it scrupulously, ominously; its margins "are sprinkled with minute calculations, figures as wee as midges, as grains of sand" (18). Colette herself hardly ever saw "the book," which seems to record not only Willy's eternal penury, but also her own humiliations. They live poorly, with Willy arbitrarily doling out household funds and refusing her a winter coat one year. "His constant cry—I know it only too well—was 'Quick, dear, quick! There's not a sou in the house!'" (16). *The Pure and the Impure* similarly characterizes the years with Willy; there she calls them "an epoch when I lived in a singular state of neglect and concealed wretchedness" (133). Sexually and financially, she is alternately neglected and exploited.

She learns of her husband's first infidelity thanks to an anonymous letter, and sets off to find him at the home of a dark-skinned little woman named Charlotte Kinceler. He and Charlotte are "not in bed but sitting in front of—yes!—an open account book. M. Willy was holding the pencil" (24). Like his conjugal life, M. Willy sprinkles his very acts of unfaithfulness with figures. Colette lingers over memories of Charlotte Kinceler, whom she grew to know and esteem: "With her came my first doubts of the man I had given myself to so trustfully, and the end of my girlhood, that uncompromising, exalted, absurd estate. From her I got my first notions of tolerance and concealment and the possibility of coming to terms with an enemy. Concentration, humility—it was an instructive time" (31). Agent of Colette's despair and of her growth, Lotte was herself to know despair, and subsequently documented her unhappiness in darkly confused letters addressed to Willy. He punched three holes in them and filed them. One day Lotte shot herself through the mouth. Colette tersely inscribes the suicide as she did the adultery, under the nummary sign: "She was twenty-six years old and had saved money" (33).

Thanks to Willy and his talent for occupying the minds and bodies of women, Colette has conceived a prodigious grudge against "the laborious, exhausting sensual pastime." The volume testifies both to an immense preoccupation with sex and to an attempt to exorcise it. Repeatedly she speaks of young girls' victimization by older men, as though her own case were paradigmatic, and the world were full of Willys and Gabrielles. But she concedes that girls like herself are hardly passive victims; they are consumed by sexual curiosity: "It is true that, at first, ridden by youth and ignorance, I had known intoxication—a guilty rapture, an atrocious, impure, adolescent impulse. There are many scarcely nubile girls who dream of becoming the show, the plaything, the licentious masterpiece of some middle-aged man. It is an ugly dream that is punished by its fulfilment" (23). An ugly dream, similar perhaps to the incoherent dream of her first years of marriage, whose details are "plainly and fatally symbolic." One of the symbols of sex's simultaneous attraction and repulsiveness is the curve—especially that of Willy's rotundity. "M. Willy was not huge, he was bulbous. The powerful skull, the slightly protuberant eyes, the nose, which was short and had no visible bridge, the drooping cheeks—every one of his features approximated to the curve" (54–55). He looked like Queen Victoria. M. Willy is a convex, tuberous monster who provides his lanky, long-haired wife with vague pleasure and clearly defined pain. Sexual images in *My Apprenticeships* consume the nubile girl, enfolding her in devouring curves: a hairy hand clasps her own, alien lips surround her mouth, a looming male shadow dwarfs her. She is transformed into "a prodigy of licentiousness" (56).

At a certain point Colette's libidinal economy must have rejected the terms of exchange on which Willy operated. She had before her a few interesting examples of young sexuality, mainly Polaire, the brilliant young actress who created the role of Claudine. One night when Polaire has a noisy spat with her lover, Willy and Colette are summoned to the rescue, but rapidly realize that they are superfluous as the other two make up: "Standing there, unwanted, almost in silence, I had had ample time to watch a strange, unknown sight—love in its youth and its violence, an outraged lover, naked to the waist, the silky woman's skin above the perfect muscles, the rippling play of light upon the proud, careless body, his easy assurance as he stepped over and then picked up the fallen body of Polaire" (95). The scene elicits in Colette an uneasy sadness that she thinks is jealousy.

Paradoxically, the instrument of her salvation would be Willy's articulated poverty. Willy wanted money, and money came from the published word. If *the* Book was a book of accounts, Willy signed his name to numerous others whose sales yielded the figures he wrote down in the profits column. His wife was to join the ranks of his ghostwriters. She was no stranger to the milieu. In Willy's company, she had frequented smoky newspaper offices and spent nights waiting for his column to appear in proof, while she breathed the gas, tobacco, printer's ink, and beer. She would doze off and awaken at the arrival of Catulle Mendès, whose capacities amazed her: "What a power it is to have no need of solitude! Mendès started writing instantly. He wrote while he talked, while he drank, while he smoked" (45). Willy was the antithesis of Mendès, and his own dubious authorship one of the great lessons of Colette's marriage. He suffered from "a sort of agoraphobia . . . a nervous horror of the blank page" (76). Colette emphasizes his underlying, paradoxical talent and devotes hilarious pages to his method. When Willy got an idea, he nurtured it no more than a moment: off it went to one of his ghostwriters, with a letter outlining how to expand it into a few pages. On its return, the idea would be laundered, purged of alien traces, and sent off to someone else, with the request to convert its substance into a short story, an article or a novel. Each time it came back, the piece would be retyped to acquire a virgin packaging and be expedited to another "therapeutist." Colette notes with irony that the letters of instruction to his ghostwriters were extraordinarily detailed, frequently several times the length of the proposed piece. Willy could write, but only if he did not think of it as writing.

As regards his wife, whom he locked in a room to make her produce, his method is considerably less funny. And if Colette tells the story now, she maintains that it is not because she enjoys the light in which it casts her, but for its "somewhat Gothic flavour and the respect due to freakish truths" (71). Her imprisonment by Willy functions as the event that welds money, sex, and literature.

"The book that should be written," she declares in the first chapter of *My Apprenticeships*, "is that man's life-story." And adds: "The trouble is that no one ever really knew him" (17). Periodically she reiterates her own and others' inability to understand him: "in my lack of knowledge of this exceptional man I am compelled to speak as a member of the crowd; to have worked for him and beside him taught me to dread, not to know him better" (61). "Work" here does multiple duty: it is literary as well as sexual, encompassing a panoply of wifely and authorial tasks. Immersion in that work precludes understanding. She cannot write the biography of Willy that ought to be written, so she writes instead, in the first instance, the Claudine and Minne books, and in the last, *My Apprenticeships* itself. They are more her story than his, but they gloss the years spent in Willy's ponderous shadow; they are her effort to identify desire, sexual pleasure, and pain, and to write about them. They selectively regroup amorous and sexual experiences, which reconstitute themselves into meaningfulness, and make sense out of fragmentation.

The identity of "the book" evolves. The schoolgirl's copy books in which she pens her first novels, Claudine's adventures, are the successors and pendants to Willy's account books. Colette finds her place in the literary and linguistic systems ordering Willy's world; the signifiers are all his. During the period, he is her jailor, her example and even her inspiration; for if the desire for money explains the novels' existence, sexual data inform them. Claudine and Minne, curious like Colette, are also punished by having their dreams fulfilled. Meanwhile, Willy's intoxication reaches "the acute, delirious phase" and he begins "to reverence, as well as to exploit, his own symbols" (70).

With Willy's adoration of his own promiscuity, Colette's apprenticeships—symbolic, social, and sexual—were nearly complete. She had broken the habit of silence, her speech growing out of, but also disrupting, a process of education. Writing had become a duty and the means to recover self-respect. With *Creature Conversations,* she allowed herself the luxury of not talking about sex and of signing her own name. She was close to 30 at that point: "the age when life musters and arrays the forces that make for duration" (101). But she was still living in Willy's space, a space of defilement, adapting her life to his syntax. He did her one last, invaluable service: he put her out. And she would be lying if she called the years of terror and delay a 'waste of time'; during those years, she had learned (like several of her heroines) an "essential art . . . not that of writing but the domestic art of knowing how to wait, to conceal, to save up crumbs, to reglue, regild, change the worst into the not-so-bad, how to lose and recover in the same moment that frivolous thing, a taste for life" (71). On her own at last, she survived.

Sido

Her mother's world is the reverse of Willy's, and *My Apprenticeships* stands with *Sido* (1929) in a relation not unlike that of *Claudine at School* to *My Mother's House.* The second work of each pair functions as a corrective to the first. Sido and Willy are the two great characters of Colette's life as of her work, and the books starring them are part of the same major effort at retrospection. The revilement of Willy finds a positive counterpart in reverence for Sido, and it seems justifiable to jolt chronology again by treating *Sido* last, although its appearance actually preceded that of *My Apprenticeships* by seven years, and even *The Pure and the Impure* by three. This order allows us to place the mother figure in its proper symbolic place: subsuming, correcting, interpreting all experience. Hers is the final word. The privileged mother-daughter relation that Colette's work traces is one of its most profoundly feminist aspects. Giving perspective to the itinerary from village to metropolis of *My Apprenticeships, Sido* illuminates the spiritual legacy that sustained Colette through the Willy years and finally helped to make her apprenticeships intelligible. From juxtaposition of the two books emerge several sets of crucial oppositions, all organized around the opposing figures of Willy and Sido: Paris and the village, marriage and chastity, impurity and purity, experience and innocence.

Like *My Mother's House,* with which commentators invariably associate it, *Sido* collects childhood memories on which the central figure confers coherence and even sanctity. These books proceed not according to chronology, but rather according to a logic of recollection, and events are secondary to the accumulated weight of sounds, sights, smells, and suggestions. In the years after her mother's death in 1912, Colette was more or less continually preoccupied with her, and *Sido,* although only half as long as *My Mother's House,* was likewise written in bits and pieces eventually gathered together for publication. After *My Mother's House* in 1922 and then *Break of Day* in 1928, the 1929 publication of *Sido* consummates the mother's hegemony. It is divided into three nearly equal parts labeled "Sido," "The Captain," and "The Savages," as Sido calls Colette's brothers.

More privileged than her male counterpart Willy, Sido gives her name both as title and subtitle to the last of the trio of books featuring her, while Willy's is submerged in the text that tries to explain him, appearing for the first time only near the end of its initial chapter. *My Apprenticeships* traces Colette's gradual separation from Willy, while *Sido* commemorates an identification, Colette's oneness with her mother: "I never thought of our resemblance, but she knew I was her own daughter" (163); "I had a habit of repeating the ends of her sentences. My voice was already lower than hers, but I used to imitate her way of talking, and I still do" (167). Blood, moral affinities, and desire attach Colette to Sido. In later life, Colette can recall her bookish father's face only vaguely, but of Sido she forgets nothing.

If Willy is loss of direction, Sido is compass, and two important themes of the book she names are geographical and climatic. Sido is the locus of happiness: "Sido and my childhood were both, and because of each other, happy at the centre of that imaginary star whose eight points bear the names of the cardinal and collateral points of the compass" (173). Her garden is at the exact center of the "eight paths of the Mariner's Chart" (174). Page after page alludes to the Zodiac, the compass points, rays of light, the beloved South, and the dreadful East wind which Sido personifies and in whose material existence her child faithfully believes. In her privileged location, Sido is at one with meteorology. She fashions rustic barometers out of grains of oats, and knows when the frost will come and when the sun will set, and if it will be a hard winter; she has seen it rain frogs. We are reminded of a brief appearance she makes in *My Apprenticeships:* Sido comes to Paris to visit in the bitter winter of 1894 or 1895 and discovers that her daughter has no outdoor coat, an index of the parsimoniousness of a man whose love is as sunless as his bachelor digs. While Sido prognosticates the weather, Willy attempts to ignore it, to deny climate and direction—geographical as well as moral. Sido points the way (and buys the coat). While symbols surround Willy, omens belong to Sido. Alive or dead, she attracts "sounds and whispers and omens," whether zodiacal, lunar, botanical, or aquatic.

My Apprenticeships associates Willy with "the book," but the Word is Sido's. An essentially oral character, she is copiously quoted throughout *Sido*. We recall Willy's frequent pose, bent over a page, meticulously making entries, or else composing endless letters and telegrams to get others to write *for* him. The irony, of course, is that Willy, quintessential author, fails at writing. His talent is indubitable, but the ideas require for execution an elaborate network of subterfuge. Sido, on the other hand, characteristically appears bent over a flower, an insect, or the face of a child; and she speaks naturally and voluminously. While Willy's own story "should" be written but cannot because, in spite of all the calculated revelations he made, "no one ever really knew him" (*My Apprenticeships,* 17), Sido's story is the record of her speech. She reminisces tirelessly about her youth and experiences, telling and retelling her own story. When Colette writes the book, she has only ostensibly to quote.

Purveyor of lubricious written words, Willy is predominantly associated with the *numbers* his titles signify for him:

> How could we have guessed . . . that figures, figures first and foremost, haunted M. Willy and his fine mathematician's brow? Most of us refused to believe it. Figures were his greatest entertainment, the source of his deepest pleasures and of his gravest guilt. To count, to amass, to hoard— even in the flood of letters that have survived him, these are his chief concerns. (*My Apprenticeships,* 17)

Willy is an inveterate counter, whereas preoccupation with numbers is foreign to Sido. "The fact is that, though she was active and always on the go, she was not a sedulous housewife. She was clean and tidy, fastidious even, but without a trace of that solitary, maniacal spirit that counts napkins, lumps of sugar, and full bottles" (152). Although she never counts in order to possess, Sido occasionally tallies for purposes of divining: no one can equal her "at separating and counting the talc-like skins of onions. 'One...two...three coats; three coats on the onions!' " (161): the winter would be difficult. Willy ciphers, reckons, and hoards; Sido tells, names, and gives.

Critics have observed that the first words of *Sido* are Sido's own, and that her voice dominates this text. The opening lines also situate *Sido* in the same time frame as *My Apprenticeships*. The first paragraph justifies considering the two texts together, both because of the coincidence of time it reveals and because of the evocation of Willy:

> It's obvious you're as proud as can be, my poor Minet-Chéri, because you've been living in Paris since your marriage. It always makes me laugh to see how proud of living in Paris all Parisians are; the real ones seem to think the mere fact ennobles them and the others imagine they've gone up in the world. . . . As for you, you give yourself airs just because you've married a Parisian. A Parisian, did I call him? Your true-born Parisians haven't so much character in their faces. You might say that Paris defaces them! (147)

One paragraph later, Colette explains, "That was the way my mother used to talk in the days when I was a very young woman" (147). Sido addresses these remarks, then, to a daughter newly married to Willy and therefore living through the events of *My Apprenticeships*. Willy himself is mentioned not by name but by definition, as it were: he is the Parisian with too much character in his face. Willy is associated here with two things: marriage, and the Paris on which Sido fixes her "spiritual gaze," a city about which she feels at one and the same time scornful and aggressively passionate. *My Apprenticeships*, of course, links him to the same institution and the same locale.

Sex, a crucial concern of *My Apprenticeships*, is by no means in the forefront of *Sido*. Elsewhere, Colette has written of Sido: "She abstained, as always, from questioning me about my most intimate troubles. The sexual side of my life inspired her, I think, with great and motherly repugnance" ("The Rainy Moon" ["La Lune de pluie"], 191). And yet a leitmotif is a related subject: marriage, which Sido seems to consider as unwholesome and indeed rather shameful.[4] Marriage is one of the formal organizers of *Sido*, whose ternary structure represents the simultaneous separation and interrelatedness among two parents and their children; and from one end of the book to the other, Sido voices her half-muted criticism. A few pages after the disdainful "since your marriage" of the second sentence, Colette records a diatribe delivered by Sido years earlier against a pair of village newlyweds, who in fact had done nothing worse than to pay a visit:

> People who've only been married four days should remain in seclusion and not stroll about out of doors, or flaunt themselves in society, or go about with the bride's or the bridegroom's mother. Are you laughing?

You've no feeling for these things. Just to have seen that four days' old
bride still makes me red all over. I'll do her the credit to say that she, at
least, was embarrassed. She looked as though she'd lost her petticoat or
sat on a newly-painted bench. (150)

Sido projects onto the bride the confused shame that Colette in *My
Apprenticeships* feels at Willy's hands, and goes on to announce what a
"horror" the bridegroom is—ugly, dissimulating, with "a memory for
figures"! *Sido* foreshadows the themes that *My Apprenticeships* elaborates.

The last pages of *Sido* return to the subject of marriage to describe the
unfortunate wedding of Sido's oldest child, ill-starred Juliette. Wedlock
is again associated with shame, but this time it is not the bride who feels
ashamed, but Colette as spectator:

I swaggered about, very proud of my eleven years, my long locks that
made me look like a little Eve, and my pink dress, highly delighted with
everything except when I looked at my sister. Very small and pale,
weighted down with white silk and tulle and trembling with nervous
weakness, she was gazing up at that unknown man with a swooning look
of such submission on her strange, Mongolian face that the sight filled me
with shame. (218)

A foreshadowing of Colette and Willy, submissive bride and unfathomable man, less than a decade later?

Nor can their brother Achille tolerate the event. He escapes Juliette's
dubious nuptial celebrations, running home to the locked house, where
he breaks a window-pane to get to his bed. Sido's gloss: "Just think of it,
it was so that he could be alone, far from those sweating people, and
sleep caressed by the night wind, that he broke the window-pane. Was
there ever a child so wise?" (218–19). The volume closes with Colette's
commentary: that wise brother must surely, in his later hard life, have
often remembered the "childish bed where he slept half-naked, chaste
and voluptuously alone" (219). Paradoxically linked to solitude, desire
seems to exclude wedlock, which is inherently unsound, indecent, and
dangerous. When Colette did her own apprenticeship in sybaritic, conjugal games, Willy and Paris did not lead her permanently astray, for she
had internalized her mother's sense of direction.

Chapter Seven
Chance Acquaintances

Colette's major volumes of short pieces include *Bella-Vista* (1937), *Chambre d'hôtel* (1940), *Le Képi* (1943), and *Gigi* (1944). The beguiling stories within their pages deserve study for their ambiguities of form and problematics of narration. Some are traditional third-person narrative, like "The Sick Child," an almost surrealistic account of a little boy's affliction with polio. But the greater number are in the first person; narrated by a woman called "Colette," they have filiations with autobiography as well as fiction, and include some of Colette's most experimental and most original pieces.[1]

The Stories of "Colette"

Elaine Marks counts 33 of the 57 titles of the complete works (*Œuvres complètes*) as narrated in the first person.[2] The later and longer stories that concern us here are related to the Claudine novels, to *"The Tendrils of the Vine," The Pure and the Impure, My Apprenticeships,* and *Break of Day*—to name only the most illustrious antecedents. But in these stories there is no obvious fictional transposition, as from Colette to Claudine; and unlike *My Apprenticeships,* most of them are not explicitly the author's own story. They have a lot in common with sections of *"The Tendrils of the Vine,"* where Colette describes visits from her "friend Valentine." In certain of the later pieces, however, it is less a question of friends than, as the title of one proclaims, of "chance acquaintances," passers-by whose dramas she witnesses. In a passage at the beginning of *My Apprenticeships,* Colette notes that, paradoxically, those features most deeply engraved in her memory "are not of people who have played decisive parts in my life. I have it in me to keep a cherished corner for the chance acquaintance as well as for the husband or relation, for the unexpected as fondly as for the everyday" (4). Throughout the short stories, she gives us to understand that fleeting encounters enriched her as woman and as writer.

Structured by the play of coincidence and only partial explanation, these pieces tend more toward anecdote than rigorously articulated narratives. Deliberate, digressive, meditative, they are internally nourished and linked to each other by their settings, and by the predominance of a single voice. In spite of a variety of incidents from the trivial to the criminal, the pieces are curiously reiterative; situations, characterizations, and obsessions reflect the historical Colette's preoccupations. They illustrate—may we say they prove?—certain of her convictions about sexuality, memory, the past, men and women. The heroines are memorable, sometimes attaining what Colette labeled in *Mitsou* a "banal heroism," and their vitality echoes the narrator's own vigor while it shapes the stories.

The tone is somewhere between journalistic and autobiographical, while the fabulations are subtle and difficult to delimit. They are all supposed to be authentic accounts of true experiences in which Colette plays the double role of observer and protagonist. The ambiguous mixture of fiction and autobiography makes for a special effect, a genre I am calling "autography," and of which *The Pure and the Impure* is another important example. The idea is bewitchingly simple: Colette tells stories about herself, only the stories are not quite true. She toys with the formal generic distinction that the twentieth century generally respects by fictionalizing *in her own name,* re-creating a self who lives a series of imagined events. Her narrator shares the writer's history as country girl, dancer, novelist, and divorcée, and the characters this "Colette" encounters allude to her past, both personal and literary—to Sido and Achille, to Claudine, Minne, and Toby-Dog. But these references are principally symbols intended to sustain credibility; they are not elaborated, their meanings rarely expanded. They are less revelations of the author than part of a codified aesthetic structure. Colette seems to enjoy the prerogative of rewriting her past by setting her stories against a detailed background of factual autobiography, while being apparently as fanciful as she pleases in the creation of character and plot. The narrator Colette, who mimics and embellishes her creator's biography, emerges as quintessentially feminine and sensitive, immensely experienced and a wise interpretor of experience. It is difficult in the final analysis to assess the overlap between *her* history and the real Colette's, to determine the precise point at which imagination begins to supplement biographical data.

"Bella-Vista"

Published in 1937 in the volume of the same name, "Bella-Vista" is dated "thirteen years ago." It presumably belongs therefore to the period after Colette's 1923 separation from Henry de Jouvenel, about the time she was discovering the attractions of Provence as a vacation spot (she bought her Saint-Tropez house, La Treille Muscate, in 1926). The psychological dating of the story is more rigorous and pertinent than the chronological:

> It is absurd to suppose that periods empty of love are blank pages in a woman's life. The truth is just the reverse. . . . When I was younger, I did not realize the importance of these "blank pages." The anecdotes with which they furnished me—those impassioned, misguided, simple or inscrutable human beings who plucked me by the sleeve, made me their witness for a moment and then let me go—provided more "romantic" subjects than my private personal drama. I shall not finish my task as a writer without attempting, as I want to do here, to draw them out of the shadows to which the shameless necessity of speaking of love in my own name has consigned them. (7)

Major first-person novels like *The Vagabond* and *The Shackle,* whose autobiographical inspiration is perceptible, may be assimilated to Colette's romances. But she insists that the short pieces she came to favor in the end reveal an equally crucial aspect of a "woman's life." Love blinds one to the fascinating discoveries that can be made in periods free of passion. Colette takes as her task both to address the subject of love and to set its limits; part of her mission is to redeem those "empty" periods of female experience that might be considered insignificant because they take no account of love. She fills in the blanks with stories about events in some ways more enthralling and more romantic than those of the novels.

In "Bella-Vista," the narrator has just purchased a modest vineyard in Provence. While the house is being modernized, she and her dog Pati spend a few weeks in a nearby hotel, the "Bella-Vista." Its middle-aged owners are Madame Suzanne, winsome but not very intelligent, and Madame Ruby, who has a thick American accent, thicker fingers, a heavy-set neck, and a T-shaped torso. There is one other guest, the sinister M. Daste, whom animals especially find antipathetic. One night Colette overhears a quarrel in the next room and discovers the owners' secret: Ruby is really Richard, a man in hiding for some reason and masquerading as a woman. And he has recently stepped so far out of his role as to get the maid pregnant. The apparently eccentric pair of lesbians who had charmed Colette are in fact just an old heterosexual couple. That same night Daste inexplicably murders all of Suzanne's parakeets and secretly moves out. As the proprietor accompanies an exasperated

Colette to the train station next morning, her predominant sentiment is annoyance: "I was on the verge of reproaching myself for ever having been taken in by this tough fellow whose walk, whose whole appearance was that of an old Irish sergeant who had dressed himself up as a woman for a joke on St. Patrick's day" (66).

Hotel life, Colette maintains, tends rapidly to become demoralizing. "The main reason for this is that people who really mean nothing to us acquire an artificial importance" (33). Daste, Suzanne, and Ruby preoccupy her unnaturally by dint of their proximity and her own isolation from normal routine. But the sociability into which they force her foregrounds an inner tension; her neighbors simultaneously attract and repel her. Her articulated misanthropy (she reiterates her preference for the company of animals to that of humans) belies an instinctive fascination with strangers. As the days draw on, she notes, "My only idea was to get away yet, against my will, I was growing used to the place. That mysterious attraction of what we do not like is always dangerous. It is fatally easy to go on staying in a place which has no soul, provided that every morning offers us the chance to escape" (35). "Fatally easy," but fatal to whom? Certainly not to Colette herself, who acts on her "keen and slightly cowardly desire to leave Bella-Vista" the very day she learns the truth about Ruby. But very likely fatal to Richard, who comes close to being discovered by Daste; and certainly fatal to the parakeets. Perhaps the ultimate fatality resides in the inevitable inscription of the story: "If the idle looker-on in me exclaimed delightedly 'What a story!,' my honourable side warned me to keep the story to myself. I have done so for a very long time" (63).

Colette intimates that seemingly ordinary people like Ruby and Suzanne appear quite extraordinary if the observer is willing to take time for careful study. But does every apparently anodine existence conceal a drama? At least three other stories, the lengthy *Chance Acquaintances,* "The Rainy Moon," and "The Photographer's Missus" ("La Dame du photographe"), suggest an affirmative answer.

Chance Acquaintances

I did not acquire my habitual mistrust of nonentities over a period of years. Instinctively, I have always held them in contempt for clinging like limpets to any chance acquaintance more robust than themselves. . . . [They] are, in fact, envoys from the nether-world, deputised to act as a liaison between ourselves and beings with no other means of approach. (141)

These curious affirmations appear at the beginning of *Chance Acquaintances* (*Chambre d'hôtel*, in a volume by that name, 1940). Colette illustrates her meaning with an anecdote from her music-hall days. Half prostitute, half actress, Lucette d'Orgeville would cross Colette's path every year or so. Now she would appear draped in sable and emeralds, now impoverished. They meet on one particular occasion when she is in the latter state. Lucette has retained a summer chalet in a mountain thermal resort in the Dauphiné, for herself and her favorite lover, the faithful Luigi. But financial wisdom forces her to change her plans and accept instead the proposition of a wealthier suitor; regretfully, she is off to America. She persuades Colette to enjoy the chalet in her stead. Colette goes but dislikes the dust and assembly-line construction, and takes a room in a nearby hotel instead, intending to return to Paris the next day.

She is hardly settled in the hotel when, through the offices of her cat, who strays across the balcony, she makes the acquaintance of Antoinette and Gérard Haume. Their voices reach her before she catches sight of the pair, and she is surprised to discover that the rasping voice is Gérard's, while the huskier, more pleasant and more virile tones are his wife's. This schematic gender reversal on the one hand recalls the more dramatic example of "Madame Ruby" in "Bella-Vista" and, on the other, reiterates numerous situations of Colette's fiction where an apparently masculine dimension in women characters formulaically connotes moral strength. It also finds an internal echo in Colette's cat, who wears "the masculine look of a she-cat who has decided to make frequent evasions of her gender" (160).

Like Lucette, the Haumes latch on to Colette. In spite of Antoinette's excessive familiarity, impersonal stylish looks and clichéd speech, Colette is drawn by the kindness of her neighbor and her courageous determination to triumph over the illness that brought the couple to the thermal waters of "X-les-Bains." From day to day, then week to week, Colette postpones her departure. Gérard remains for some time a mystery. Colette's initial assumption is that *he* must be the sick one, and her misprision is based on an accurate assessment of his weakness and propensity to self-indulgence. Eventually he confides (virtually all the characters in Colette's short fiction sooner or later confide in the narrator) that he is in despair over the silence of his Parisian mistress, Madame Leyrisse, who has not answered his letters for 18 days. He persuades Colette to return briefly to Paris at his expense to check on her, for Gérard himself cannot decently leave Antoinette. Colette reports back that his mistress has moved out, leaving no forwarding address. The distraught lover attempts suicide, broods for weeks, and perks up only when Colette introduces him to Lucette. She has returned from her transatlantic expedition raped, beaten, and with a nasty untreated wound on the nape of the neck, but still nonchalant. She and Luigi have come to occupy the villa near the hotel. A new affair begins: Luigi is still her true love, but they need money, so Lucette accommodates Gérard. But not for long. One day a terse note from Luigi brings the hotel news of Lucette's death from blood poisoning.

These "nonentities" whom the narrator condemns in fact reveal themselves as both consequential and significant, since beneath their colorless exterior lurk dangerous susceptibilities, immense reserves of energy, and inclinations to high romance and despair. Gérard's aborted suicide, of course, recalls Chéri's and Michel's successful attempts in *The Last of Chéri* and *Duo*. His charm and vanity disguise both his moral pallor and his flair for drama. Antoinette is equally contradictory, her thoughtlessness and vulgarity of dress concealing an essential superiority, just as Madame Suzanne in "Bella-Vista" turns out to be morally superior, even though intellectually inferior, to her male companion. In the short stories, like the novels, the women—strong, generous, and self-effacing—are heroic.

The narrator's own role is the most complicated aspect of *Chance Acquaintances*. Her connivance in the story takes two forms: first, she acts (grudgingly) as Gérard's intermediary with Madame Leyrisse and (unwittingly) with Lucette d'Orgeville; and, secondly, she isolates and thereby elevates to the level of story a cycle of events that would not otherwise be identified as such. All the connections between the villa and the hotel, Luigi and Gérard, and Lucette and Madame Leyrisse, are visible from no vantage point other than Colette's. Her own situation and feelings provide, moreover, a partial and problematic explanation of her role as go-between. For Colette stresses her own attitudes: her fear of strangers, on the one hand; her loneliness, impecuniousness, uneasiness, and "vague longing to be happy," on the other. She admits being piqued at Gérard Haume, who shows no interest in her as a woman. A blatant womanizer, Gérard never flirts with Colette, whom he apparently does not find attractive. Does she avenge herself by involving him in a double adventure with desertion and death? In fact, she verbalizes both her pleasure in returning from Paris with bad news about Madame Leyrisse, and her later temptation to tell Antoinette the truth about the Lucette affair. Her prolonged stay at X-les-Bains itself invites as explanation an obscure pleasure in Gérard's suffering. Her attention to him is not without consequences, as she notes: "Ghosts, even flesh and blood ghosts, do not appear unless they are summoned up. The fact of spying on your neighbor is enough to turn him into an evil-doer" (169). Obliquely, she absolves him and reproaches herself at the end: "No doubt all that was wrong with them [the Haumes] was that it had been their lot to be caught up by and steeped in their desire to become my friends" (228).

Chance Acquaintances crystallizes obscure tensions. Drama is the undersurface of ordinariness, the latter thereby containing something like its own denial. And Colette's very "fear of strangers" and "fear of displeasing strangers" paradoxically produce minatory friendships based on entrapment. There is, finally, the opposition between the narrator's articulated boredom and desire to distance herself from the events, and her involvement in the story she creates. Colette defines herself as the intermediary who lures chance acquaintances from the abyss of their nonentity, the initial allusion to the nether-world and its shadowy beings suggesting that these beings adumbrate a mysterious, and perhaps maleficent force in Colette herself.

"The Rainy Moon"

Through the most apparently ordinary acquaintance imaginable, Colette discovers the sensational event she recounts in "The Rainy Moon" ("La Lune de Pluie," also in the volume *Chambre d'hôtel*). Rosita Barberet is a typist, shortsighted, and prematurely withered. She has the solicitous appearance of "a well-trained nurse or a fashionable dentist's receptionist or one of those women of uncertain age who do vague odd jobs in beauty-parlors" (162–63). But this inoffensive young woman inhabits a murky world where devilry and witchcraft operate. Near the beginning of her narrative, Colette offhandedly recalls the astrologers, card readers, and palmists she has often consulted, only to discount their powers: "Among fortune-tellers, there are very few whom our presence momentarily endows with second sight" (160). Only much later in the story does it become clear that the point of "The Rainy Moon" is the efficacy of at least one kind of occultism.

The narrator's typist quits to get married and recommends a replacement. Colette takes her a manuscript and discovers that her Montmartre flat is one Colette herself once occupied: "it had fallen to my lot when I was alone and very far from happy" (158). Rosita Barberet lives there now with her younger and prettier sister, Délia Essendier, a semirecluse who waits day and night for the return of the husband who abandoned her. Colette does not tell them that the flat was once hers, nor does she immediately learn much about the Barberets. But her curiosity takes her obsessively back to "the scene of [her] unhappy, fascinating past" (184), where she searches for clues to the mystery of these sisters, and especially for traces of her own passage. She resolves to decipher what she terms the "enigma" of Délia—a young woman "pretending, out of sheer obstinacy and jealousy, to relive a moment of [Colette's] own life" (190). Rosita at last confides that Délia is planning her husband's death by witchcraft, and has secluded herself to cast a spell on poor Eugène, "convoking" him to die by endless repetitions of his name. Distaste supplants Colette's initial interest—"I am frightened of harmless lunatics, of people who deliver long monologues in the street without seeing us, of purple-faced drunks who shake their fists at empty space and walk zigzag" (194)—and she returns no more to the Barberet flat. But in spite of this effort to trivialize the event, she begins running into Délia in the street, "by pure chance," as it were. And the last time she spots her, Délia Essendier is wearing the black dress and white neck band of mourning.

Colette meets the Barberet sisters during one of those "empty" periods in her life. During just such a period she sojourned at the Bella-Vista, and she clearly alludes to that story when she writes in "The Rainy Moon,"

> Does one imagine those periods, during which anodynes conquer an illness one believed serious at the time, fade easily from one's memory? I have already compared them, elsewhere, to the "blanks" that introduce space and order between the chapters of a book. I should very much like—late in life, it is true—to call them "merciful blanks," those days in which work and sauntering and friendship played the major part, to the detriment of love. (165)

She notes a few pages later, "I have never had less notice taken of me by men than during those particular years whose date I dissemble here" (176). Like the narrator of *Break of Day,* she subordinates specifically sexual involvement with men to a more general interest in humanity and nature.

Among the experiences of such periods of idleness, relaxation, and virtual sexlessness, this particular anecdote is prepotent, because it is at one and the same time the story of chance acquaintances and—if not historically, then potentially and perhaps morally—her own. The play of coincidence is more personal here than in "Bella-Vista" or *Chance*

Acquaintances, because it brings her face to face with an avatar of her former self, interweaving her present state, a problematic past, and someone else's drama.

In the old building, Colette finds the familiar stairs, and in the apartment, the same window latch that spontaneously responds to her knowing grip, the same style of faded wallpaper, and the same bedroom furniture arrangement. On a daybed in one corner, Délia half reclines. Just so did an anxious Colette in lonely years past. Her entrance into the flat is a return home, a descent into her past, and her fascination with those melancholy sisters an attraction toward the young woman she was:

> To my cost, I have proved from long experience that the past is a far more violent temptation to me than the craving to know the future. Breaking with the present, retracing my steps, the sudden apparition of a new, unpublished slice of the past is accompanied by a shock utterly unlike anything else and which I cannot lucidly describe. . . . It is neither the true concern nor the natural inclination of writers to love the future. They have quite enough to do with being incessantly forced to invent their characters' future which, in any case, they draw up from the well of their own past. Mine, whenever I plunge into it, turns me dizzy. . . . Besides the person I once was, it reveals to me the one I would have liked to be. (160)

The past is the writer's obsession, then, and the woman's, too, while "The Rainy Moon" is a fable about its dangerous seductions. Colette's entire opus, from *Claudine at School* to *The Blue Lantern,* testifies to the magic of the past, to her tendency to look inward and downward. The liminary piece in *"Landscapes and Portraits"* (*Paysages et portraits*)—a posthumous collection of previously unpublished essays—reads like a gloss on "The Rainy Moon." In five pages Colette lyrically describes the irresistible attraction exerted on her by her own past and, specifically, her anguished fascination each time she drives by an apartment she once inhabited (and there were quite a few!). How she would love to resurrect the woman she was, to relive even a single hour among all those she has lived. She savors her past like a streaming cup exhaling memory, illusion, and regret (her metaphor).

What, in fact, is Délia's relation to Colette? Does the apartment autonomously breed unhappiness, or did Colette herself plant the seeds of Délia's drama? The last possibility emerges most clearly when Colette explains how a blister of glass in a windowpane catches a ray of sun and projects a tiny rainbow onto the wall opposite. During her residence there, she used to call the little planet with its seven colors her "rainy moon," and it charmed her solitude. But Délia, according to Rosita, dubs the refracted light her sad little sun: "she says it only shines to warn her something bad is going to happen" (167). Colette silently wonders, "Whatever can I have bequeathed to that reflection?" (168).

Does Délia, in her murderous design, realize a proclivity of the younger Colette? After her last visit with Rosita, Colette goes to bed early: "I kept relapsing into a nightmare in which I was now my real self, now identified with Délia. Half-reclining like her on *our* divanbed, in the dark part of our room, I 'convoked' with a powerful summons, with a thousand repetitions of his name, a man who was not called Eugène" (209–10). The dream association links the end of the story to the beginning, for her very first visit to the apartment also entails a dream image. After climbing first the hill to Montmartre and then the stairs to the mezzanine apartment, Colette looks out of the window and down into the street: "Immediately, I was conscious of the faint, rather pleasant giddiness that accompanies dreams of falling and flying" (155). Is her return to this apartment a dream of revenge for past abandonment? Her first sight of Délia jolts her, and she compares the vision, which is at once numinous and fearsome, to a dream: "I had that experience only dreams dare conjure up; I saw before me, hostile, hurt, stubbornly hoping, the young self I should never be again, whom I never ceased disowning and regretting" (173). The movements of ascent (going up to Montmartre, walking up to the mezzanine, flying) and descent (going back to her younger days, looking down into the street, falling) parallel those of "disowning and regretting." The double movement of rejection and nostalgia in a general way describes the relation to her past that characterizes Colette's work and particularly structures this story. She harbors the extravagant dream/anecdote of these passing acquaintances not in her unconscious, but in her writer's memory. Its inscription completes its exorcism.

"The Photographer's Missus"

For her suicide, Madame Armand, "the photographer's missus," goes to bed in silk stockings and black satin shoes in order to conceal her corns and crooked third toe, takes an overdose of drugs and leaves two notes. One says, "My darling Geo, don't scold me. Forgive me for leaving you. In death, as in life, I remain your faithful Georgina." A second scrap of paper, also intended for her husband, reads: "Everything is paid except the washerwoman who had no change on Wednesday" (387). But her attempt to die fails.

The narrator's acquaintance with the unhappy woman is slim. Colette gets to know her a bit only because the studio/flat of a photographer nicknamed "Big Eyes," "Geo," or "Exo," is across the hall from that of Mademoiselle Devoidy, a pearl stringer to whom Colette goes to have her necklace rethreaded. (Madame Armand's story is, like that of another of Colette's suicidal characters, Chéri, under the sign of the pearl.) Occasionally Colette notices Madame Armand encamped on the landing, with an "air of vague expectancy" (369). One day she arrives to find the building in commotion, guesses that Madame Armand is the cause, and reacts precisely as she did at the Bella-Vista and at X-les-Bains with the Haumes: "Desire to escape, slight nausea and idle curiosity struggled within me, but in the end they gave way to a strange resignation. I knew perfectly well—already out of breath before I had begun to run—I knew perfectly well that I should not stop until I reached the top landing" (385). Mademoiselle Devoidy gives her client a scaled-down version of the attempted suicide, and a few days later Colette visits the convalescent Madame Armand and hears the story from her—a story both funny and moving in its schematic evocation of a simple female existence. Madame Armand wanted to die because her life was trivial.

Structurally, "The Photographer's Missus" ("La Dame du photographe," which appeared in 1944 in the collection *Gigi*) resembles "The Rainy Moon." Its setting is a working class Parisian apartment house where Colette goes on business, and it involves three women and one man who, although crucial to the story, appears only once or twice. It too recounts disappointment and desperate resolution. In both, Colette meets the principal character through the mediation of a respectable tradeswoman. Like Rosita Barberet, Mademoiselle Devoidy is dry, unmarried, neither young nor old, and superlatively practices a humble trade.

Here as in "The Rainy Moon," Colette transcribes her ambivalence toward the actors and events. As she inevitably becomes disenchanted with Délia and Rosita, judging them, respectively, dangerous and colorless, and their home a "desert," so the moment arrives when a harsh judgment of Madame Armand and Mademoiselle Devoidy corrects a previously favorable one: the former is merely a "stale, insipid mystery," while Mademoiselle Devoidy presents only "the attraction of the void" (394). Yet Colette writes the story, as she did the Barberets', and with the same reservations about the importance to be accorded to such passers-by:

> Do those transient figures who featured in long-past periods of my life, deserve to live again in a handful of pages as I here compel them to? They were important enough for me to keep them secret, at least during the time I was involved with them. For example, my husband, at home, did not know of the existence of Mademoiselle Devoidy. . . . (384)

It is the same temporary secrecy she lavished on the Barberets: " 'I'm going to tell the Barberet story to Annie de Pène,' I mentally began. And then I told nothing at all" ("The Rainy Moon," 169); "[Sido] liked to hear the news of my men and women friends, and of any newly-formed acquaintances. I omitted however to tell her the Barberet story" ("The Rainy Moon," 191). By emphasizing that neither her mother, nor her husband, nor her friend knew anything about these "stories" at the time they occurred, Colette seems to divorce them from the material of her "real" autobiography, reminding us that neither Sido, nor Annie, nor Jouvenel could confer external authentification on events harbored in her writer's memory.

The concluding passage in "The Photographer's Missus" is interesting as part of the same problematics of "autographical" narration. When Colette relates, at the story's end, Madame Armand's own explanation of the "suicide" (the photographer's missus gives it the status of an accomplished fact), she accords the oral narrative about eight pages of almost uninterrupted direct discourse. We read pretty much what Madame Armand is supposed to have said—with an important reservation:

> It is easy to relate what is of no importance. . . . But, beginning with the words, "I have always had a very trivial life . . ." I feel absolved from the tiresome meticulousness imposed on a writer, such as carefully noting the over-many reiterations of "in one way" and "what poor creatures we are" that rose like bubbles to the surface of Madame Armand's story. Though they helped her to tell it, it is for me to remove them. It is my duty as a writer to abridge our conversation and also to suppress my own unimportant contribution to it. (396)

The writer Colette impinges here on her own persona. Her short fiction beguiles in large measure because of the interweaving of styles—autobiographical, journalistic, novelistic. Passages like these (there is a similar notation in "The Kepi," 253) underscore the tension resulting from

Colette's multiplicity of roles as participant, observer, narrator, and writer. The invocation of the writer's duty obliquely reminds us that the principal function is doubtless the last.

With simplicity, Madame Armand recites the concerns of her life as "photographer's missus": the cleaning, washing, ironing, menu-planning (she can't serve breast of veal again; they had it just last Sunday), shopping, jam-making. She insists that she never despised these tasks; but still, one day she asked herself, "Is that all? Is that the whole of my day, today, yesterday, tomorrow?" (398). She struggled against her "mania for something big," reminding herself that she had a "perfect" husband, but finally concluded that only in death would she find the desired "apotheosis" (it is her auditor, Colette, who suggests the word). So she dressed, wrote her notes, took the drug, went to bed, waited and had the "fidgets," worrying, for example, that her husband would have only a cold supper when he came in that night. Death fails her, but unlike Gérard Haume in *Chance Acquaintances,* Madame Armand does not pout. Quite the contrary, she learns an invaluable lesson: "What I am sure of is that never, never again will I commit suicide. I know now that suicide can't be the slightest use to me, I'm staying here" (404).

In her apparent frailty, in the very triviality of her life and concerns, Madame Armand, thin and solitary on her dark landing, has the solidity and grandeur of Colette's women, and is perhaps the most heroic of them all. The moral at the end is explicit: "Whenever I think of her, I always see her shored up by those scruples she modestly called fidgets and sustained by the sheer force of humble, everyday feminine greatness; that unrecognized greatness she had misnamed 'a very trivial life'" (404).

"The Kepi"

Its setting seems to attach "The Kepi" ("Le Képi," in the volume by the same name, 1944) to an earlier period than "Bella-Vista," *Chance Acquaintances,* "The Rainy Moon," or "The Photographer's Missus." Here Colette is the young wife of Willy, and the episode takes place around 1897. Thematically, it belongs, with *Chéri, The Last of Chéri,* and *Break of Day,* to the cycle of books about renunciation, suggesting that a woman's body ages tragically faster than her emotions. Marco is a middle-aged woman who is separated from her husband and earns a meager living as a ghostwriter. All day long she pores over dusty volumes at the Bibliothèque Nationale to produce manuscripts for which she gets one sou a line from a man who gets two sous a line from a chap who gets four from a fellow who gets ten. One day Marco answers, in jest, a personal ad: "Lieutenant (regular army), garrisoned near Paris, warm-hearted, cultured, wishes to maintain correspondence with intelligent, affectionate woman" (229), and it develops into a love affair, miraculously rejuvenating her. But after an idyll of under a year with Lieutenant Trallard, her 45 years catch up with her. Cavorting in bed one afternoon, she plants her young lieutenant's cap on her own head in a roguish gesture which, according to Colette's superior wisdom, only a younger woman could allow herself. Colette's message is by no means reassuring. Marco forgets for an instant, like Léa in *Chéri,* that the aging mistress of a young man must constantly monitor her looks. Relaxing her vigilance, she acts the young woman she feels like but no longer resembles. With its visor and its flat top sloping toward the eyes, the kepi throws into fearful relief all Marco's age marks, and the indiscretion costs her the lover.[3]

What has Colette to do with all this? Counselor and confidante, she follows from a lesser or greater distance the vagaries of Marco's romance. But for her, Marco is a "story" even before they meet. This is how "The Kepi" begins:

> If I remember rightly, I have now and then mentioned Paul Masson, known as Lemice-Térieux on account of his delight—and his dangerous efficiency—in creating mysteries. As ex-President of the Law Courts of Pondichéry, he was attached to the cataloguing section of the Bibliothèque Nationale. It was through him and through the Library that I came to know the woman, the story of whose one and only romantic adventure I am about to tell. (212)

My Apprenticeships is the principal intertext to speak of Masson, his friendship with the Willys, and his taste for mystification. In it, Colette describes how, one day at the shore, Masson begins to make notations on cards, explaining that he is "saving the honor of the Catalogue," by remedying lacunae and providing the titles of Latin and early Italian works "that ought to have been written." But why, she objects, if the books don't exist? "He waved an airy hand. 'Ah!' said he. 'I can't do everything' " (*My Apprenticeships,* 42–43).

In "The Kepi," she explains how Masson would visit the housebound young wife she was then, with a view to cheering her up. She appreciates his caustic wit and marvelous stories. One such story is "the lady of the Library," who writes for one sou a line, and leads a poor and chaste existence, having never had a real romance. "Her Christian name is Marco, as you might have guessed," observes Masson. "Women of a certain age, when they belong to the artistic world, have only a few names to choose from, such as Marco, Léo, Ludo, Aldo. It's a legacy from the excellent Madame Sand" (214). Intrigued to discover that the story of Marco is no mere fabulation, Colette wants to meet her. She finds her sensitive and well bred, with a "perfect voice" and "impeccable table-manners." So much so that Willy regards her as a desirable companion for his wife. Marco vacations with the Willys, and the two women become "great friends," a phrase Colette nuances to exclude serious intimacy: they talk a lot about clothes.

One day Masson proposes that he, Colette, and Marco compete at producing the best answer to an ad in the personals column. It is thus as a literary pastime that the second phase of Marco's story begins. Already a professional ghostwriter, Marco was already a part of Masson's repertory. With the sexual act, she becomes one of *Colette*'s stories, a part of *her* written text in addition to Masson's oral one. Colette narrates what she saw of the affair and what Marco told her, depending on Marco's account for the episode of the kepi. And here Colette edits and abridges Marco's words, underscoring her interference, just as she did in the suicide recital in "The Photographer's Missus": "In putting down the story that I heard, I am obliged to cut out all that made it, in Marco's version, so confused and so terribly clear" (253).

Few of Colette's narratives so starkly differentiate masculine and feminine. Exquisitely symbolic, "The Kepi" is constellated with discourse, objects, and events that are generically charged. Marco, like Délia Essendier in "The Rainy Moon," is one of Colette's doubles, for Marco and Colette share not only a profession, but the same complicated status of underling. Both write books for men to sign, both are exploited economically and professionally. Colette by no means dwells here on her victimization by Willy, but there are allusions to the unhappiness and loneliness that she glosses in *My Apprenticeships*.

Many of the conversations between Colette and Marco center on traditionally feminine concerns: fashions, makeup, interior decoration. Both as narrator and as protagonist, Colette is especially preoccupied by women's fashion, and her lines on turn-of-the-century styles are fetching and precise, echoing numerous remarks in *My Apprenticeships* on the styles of 1900. She censures Marco for betraying by her preference for ruffles and frills the fact that she "naturally belonged" to an earlier period. Although only half Marco's age, Colette plays the maternal role, counsels her on frocks and fabrics, arranges her hair, shadows her eyes, and colors her cheeks. When Marco gets a windfall from her estranged husband, Colette advises her on stylish acquisitions, and Marco becomes attractive enough to seduce a young officer.

Colette's secondhand account of the affair is striking for its precision, a woman's analysis of the changes wrought by passion in another woman. She speaks of her friend's "belated puberty," comparing her also to a "traveller who was setting off on a dangerous voyage, with no ballast but a pair of silk stockings, some pink makeup, some fruit and a bottle of champagne" (241). Marco's calm becomes fear, fever, then blissful immolation and satiety.

The last phase does her in. Marco's original beauty is discreet, firm, and slender, masculine in a word, like her name: "She looked less like a pretty woman than like one of those chiselled, clear-cut aristocratic men who adorned the eighteenth century and were not ashamed of being handsome" (217). Like those of Camile in *The Cat,* her sexual cravings arouse other desires, and satisfied love makes her grow heavier: "Her romantic love affair had already been going on for eight months. She looked so much fatter to me that the proud carriage of her head no longer preserved her chin line and her waist, visibly compressed, no longer moved flexibly inside the petersham belt, as it had done last year" (245). Her modesty and restraint disappear as well, and remarks like "A little extra flesh does make one's breasts so pretty" (245) embarrass Colette, who secretly judges moreover that her friend has "breasts like jellyfish, very broad and decidedly flabby" (247).

Her changes in weight, symbol of an active sexuality, incur the mockery of Masson and Willy. "Madame Dracula" is how Willy describes her during the early stage, when she is still thin. Colette, whose own judgments are none too favorable, nonetheless feels her "blood boil" at the critical comments of two "disillusioned" men, who make fun of her friend "as if the romance that lit up Marco's Indian summer were no more than some stale bit of gossip" (249). Masson reacts with humor and disgust to Marco's new fleshy femininity, which he dubs the phase of the dray-horse: "Marco's first, most urgent duty was to remain slender, charming, elusive, a twilight creature beaded with rain-drops, not to be bursting with health and frightening people in the streets by shouting: 'I've done it! I've done it!' " (250). When she was a dry little library mouse, Masson deemed Marco colorful, good material for his tales; when she was still a stranger to impulsiveness and indiscretion, Willy, too, found her appealing. But when Marco's sexuality is emphasized, she in some way emasculates them and their horror finds expression in cynicism. Her own severity toward the changes in Marco notwithstanding, Colette is ready to exculpate her in the face of a male onslaught.

The new and sexual Marco is *Colette*'s story—a feminine story turning on feminine words, acts, and destiny. Vestimentary concerns, traditionally female, shape Marco's fate, and an object of clothing ultimately betrays her. Not just any object of clothing but one typically masculine, military, and not subject to fashion: the kepi. Marco only confusedly perceives that the military cap is her undoing, confiding to Colette, "I can't get rid of the idea that the kepi was fatal to me. Did it bring back some unpleasant memory? I'd like to know what *you* think" (255). Colette understands instantly and replies silently:

> I saw you just as Alexis Trallard had seen you. My contemptuous eyes took in the slack breasts and the slipped shoulder-straps of the crumpled chemise. And the leathery, furrowed neck, the red patches on the skin below the ears, the chin left to its own devices and long past hope. . . . And, crowning all that, the kepi! The kepi—with its stiff lining and its jaunty peak, slanted over one roguishly-winked eye. (256)

From a man's story (Masson's) of professionalism and exploitation, Marco becomes a woman's (Colette's), the thread of which is sexuality—nascent, betrayed, moribund. "If I stick to facts," Colette notes, "the story of Marco is ended. Marco had had a lover; Marco no longer had a lover" (237). Once the kepi has put an end to the affair, Colette quickly loses touch: it is difficult, she metaphorically remarks, to hold onto someone who is losing weight fast. Marco ceases to be the subject of passion or the object of desire, and her desexing is symbolized by her weight loss and by her reentry into Masson's repertory. She is again simply "the lady of the Library," and Colette becomes again dependent on Masson for news. The concluding lines of the story, a conversation between the two principal storytellers, signify Marco's return from the sexual to the economic sphere:

> "So she's taken up her old life again," I said thoughtfully. "Exactly as it was before Lieutenant Trallard . . ."
>
> "Oh no," said Masson. "There's a tremendous change in her existence!"
>
> "What change? Really, one positively has to drag things out of you!"
>
> "Nowadays," said Masson, "Marco gets paid two sous a line." (260)

"The Tender Shoot"

"The Tender Shoot" ("Le Tendron," which also appeared in *Le Képi*) gives its name to the volume of English translations of Colette's short stories. It illustrates Colette's constant theme of female alliance against the male. But while in *The Other One, Duo,* and *Le Toutounier* the bond between women is associated with images of healing, renewal, and renaissance, here it has rather more violent overtones.

In May 1940 an elderly Colette urges her old friend Albin Chaveriat, who is also nearing 70, to leave Paris for the duration of the war, and suggests a resort in Normandy teeming with girls. Chaveriat replies that this is the very thing to put him off; by way of explanation, he tells her about an episode that took place some 17 years earlier, curing him of his taste for young flesh.

During an extended summer holiday on the country estate of a friend, Chaveriat happened across a peasant called Louisette who was herding goats nearby. She was 15 and a half years old—precisely the age of Vinca in *The Ripening Seed* and of Gigi. "I saw she was ripe for dissimulation, for forbidden collusion, in other words, for sin" (274). Sensually, their nocturnal rendezvous in the fields and bushes satisfied him completely; emotionally, much less. Louisette willingly gave her body, but rejected his gifts and refused her debonair lover the signs of affection and dependence he would normally expect from so unsophisticated a girl. At their second meeting, she tossed him neither a kiss nor a flower, but a pebble, and he reproached her for her lack of poetry. Her one overriding concern was to keep the affair secret from the mother she feared and worshiped, and Chaveriat began "getting impatient at being completely unable to understand a girl who roamed the woods at night, with [him], but sprang up as if she had been shot, turned pale and trembled at the knees if she heard the step or the voice of her mother" (287). After several weeks came a stunning climax: a downpour one night sent the lovers scurrying for refuge to Louisette's house, where they made no noise so as not to wake the mother sleeping upstairs. Chaveriat wanted only to escape as soon as possible, but Louisette fell asleep in his arms and he dared not move. Suddenly he was aware of a light shining on them and sprang to his feet at the appearance of a small woman. "Her resemblance to Louisette left me no doubt, no hope. Same frizzy hair, but already almost completely white, and faded features that would one day be Louisette's. And the same eyes, but with a wide, magnificent gaze Louisette perhaps would never have" (292). As for Louisette, she did "the only thing she could," she screamed for help: "Mamma!"

Far more certainly her mother's daughter than her lover's mistress, Louisette listened transfixed while the old woman pronounced no ordinary moral lesson, speaking neither of virtue, nor folly, nor maternal disappointment, but harping on the seducer's age: "Do you see what he's got on his temples? White hairs, Louise, white hairs just like me! And those wrinkles he's got under his eyes!" (296). The two women, the "screaming shrew" and the "adorable idiot," chased him out of their house and back toward his friend's property. When Chaveriat got to a narrow path skirting a dilapidated wall that marked the limits of his host's domain, he thought he had safely outdistanced his tormentors. But they were above the wall and heaved a large stone which grazed his shoulder. A few steps later, a second stone skinned his ear and injured his toe. Finally he retaliated, brandishing a vine-branch. (The weapon seems suited to his bacchanalian role as libertine and to his age: if Louisette is the tender shoot, Chaveriat is the hoary bough.) The aftermath of his adventure, fever and delirium, eventually passed, but Chaveriat retained, as a fitting punishment, the fear of nubile maidens.[4]

His story is a confidence he makes to Colette one night after dinner. In some sense, it perfects their friendship—a friendship, as Colette describes it, "limited by the closely-guarded secrets of Albin Chaveriat's love-life" (262). After three pages of introduction, "The Tender Shoot" is related in Chaveriat's own words, neither edited nor paraphrased by the hearer. Even the last words are Chaveriat's; Colette does not take the floor again at the end to sum up or point out a moral, as in "The Photographer's Missus." But the quotation marks that begin each paragraph are evidence of her silent role, for Chaveriat tells his story *to* her. He repeatedly invokes her presence, moreover, and responds to the objections he alone hears:

No, don't let's argue about that, I know you don't agree with me. (265)

Excuse me, what were you saying, my dear? That it was a horrid proceeding, and a classic one? Allow me to defend myself. (270)

But I observe you're looking apprehensive, not to say disapproving. (280)

Numerous asides like this translate the authorial point of view and suggest strategies for reading the text. Chaveriat tries to portray his young prey as a girl both stupid and vicious, but his allusions to the interventions of the first narrator subvert his design. Directly, Colette says nothing, but she apparently forces Chaveriat into a defensive posture that suggests another view of Louisette: as a victimized child. Indeed, as we know her, Colette cannot fail to understand the "consuming sensual audacity" (the phrase is from *My Apprenticeships,* 56) of young girls like Louisette, and to condemn old lechers who take advantage of them with geniality. The heroine of *My Apprenticeships* is just such a girl and Willy just such a man.

Apart from this filiation with Colette herself, however, Louisette is related especially to Colette's men. Her color is not the blue associated with the favored heroines, but the red and gold of young Phil in *The Ripening Seed.* Louisette has a "face like a ripe peach" (283), golden hair almost red, pink tendrils on her neck, and a body "tinged with pink" (271). Chaveriat first finds her wearing a necklace of wild pink berries, and at their second encounter offers her one of coral (which Louisette rejects with violence). They meet under a pink moon and clouds "rimmed with fire" (289). In rage she becomes red "as a nectarine, as a dahlia, as the most divinely red thing in the world" (286). And her mouth tastes of raspberries. Louisette's mother, an older version of Louisette herself, is fittingly dressed in mauve.

While red suggests here the passion and blood that Colette also associates with it elsewhere, and while the sexual initiation occurs, as elsewhere in her works, between a young partner and a much older one, still, in Louisette's case, this is no routine initiation. Chaveriat deems himself neither "ordinary" nor "careless" as a lover, for he never takes Louisette "like a straightforward normal animal, like a man who knows only one way to possess the woman he desires" (289). When he tries to exculpate himself by explaining to the mother his care not to impregnate Louisette, she asks ironically if she is supposed to say thank you. Louisette and her mother are no ordinary Colette heroines; nor is the lesson that emerges typical of Colette's works.

If the maiden shares the color associations of Phil, she is indecipherable like another male, the Willy of *My Apprenticeships.* Even her plumpness recalls Willy's rotundity. Chaveriat delights in her lack of angularity: "The expression 'well-rounded,' so long out of fashion, describes a type of beauty which, believe me, is positively intoxicating when that beauty is adolescent" (269). She is, finally, like Willy in still another way, her exploitation of her partner. There can be more than one lecher in a story of lechery, and in the last third of the narrative, Chaveriat voices the idea that has already occurred to the reader: "I used to wonder now and then whether Louisette were not exploiting me like a lecherous man who's found a willing girl" (287).

Chaveriat's insight into his own exploitation by his Lolita-like mistress is one aspect of the theme of knowledge that structures "The Tender Shoot," where the important symbols are eyes, light, and the gaze. The old woman's arrival in the room where Louisette dozes in Chaveriat's arms is heralded by the appearance of a light which he at first takes for the moon. Her look insists "on seeing everything, knowing everything" (292), and she stares at the anxious lover: "The unshaded lamp shone straight in her eyes but she did not blink" (293). Chaveriat, on the other hand, is nearly blinded by it. But it is not really to Chaveriat that she speaks—except scornfully to ask his age. Her gaze and her words are all for the daughter who is trying to hide her eyes, metaphorically trying to avoid seeing what has happened. Chaveriat is excluded from the mother's conversation (like Farou who happens to come in during the confrontation between Jane and Fanny in *The Other One*), and almost reified. Imprisoned in this female domain, he is treated like a thing Louisette must be forced at last to *see:* "Yes, now you don't want to see him any more, high time too, Louise! All the same, you've *got* to look at him! Yes, look at him, the man who was born the same year as your own father!" (296). This peasant mother can readily understand the sexual urge, and says she would condone intercourse with a *young* man. Her humiliation of Chaveriat is excruciating, for she does not judge his sexuality to be fearsome, merely ridiculous. She holds her daughter by the hair so tightly that "the little thing's eyes [are] drawn up slantwise." Louisette has no choice and does "indeed begin to look at [him]" (296). The sight seals her alliance with her mother.

"The Tender Shoot" deals with two kinds of knowledge: the first, sexual, the second and more important, intellectual and emotional. This is the knowledge forced on Louisette by her mother, and by both of them on Chaveriat. Colette's fiction frequently concerns itself with aging and with recognition of bodily limits: Léa's wrinkled neck loses her Chéri, and Renée Néré's incipient middle age causes her constant self-doubt, not to mention poor Marco in "The Kepi." But "The Tender Shoot" stands apart as the story of a *man,* a myth of male ridicule and punishment. Here for once it is the male whose vanity suffers from an accumulation of years, who finds his sexuality discredited by his wrinkles, his economic and intellectual superiority compromised by the sight and insight of a peasant woman. Chaveriat lacks what Colette calls in *Break of Day* "the supreme elegance of knowing how to diminish" (142). He goes off from his last encounter with Louisette marked by her color, red. Thanks to the rock that bloodied his ear, he wears, like Phil in *The Ripening Seed,* a red facial smudge suggesting violent initiation.

Female Autonomy

As discrete tales, these stories are haunting, while the persona who emerges from their accumulation is one of Colette's major accomplishments. The narrator is a clear, lyric voice which the reader comes to associate with wisdom, vigor, and femininity, and which suggests the sense of her opus.

The interest of the pieces is thematic as well as formal, and they are also marked by the predominance of strong female characters who write a new self-definition for women, one of the constitutive elements of which is an outright or implicit dissociation from men. Most of the heroines decline to derive identity exclusively from sexuality or from relations with men; they claim dominance over their destinies rather than allow their lives to be shaped by masculine criminality, sensuality, triviality, and fickleness. And even those whom sexuality rules are bound neither by convention nor habit, but forge responses that are consistently unexpected. When polite, reserved Marco in "The Kepi" finally has a romance, neither prudence nor decorum deters her from a total commitment to sex that can only amaze and amuse her jaded male friends. Masson, Gérard Haume, Albin Chaveriat, and Lieutenant Trallard are predictable and easily astonished, but the women are full of surprises and hard to surprise. Their analyses of situations and determined rejection of traditional perspectives serve to redistribute normal textual emphasis and to clarify and demystify male–female relations. Louisette in "The Tender Shoot" mutely spurns the role of adoring adolescent mistress, choosing and using her lover (like Lucette in *Chance Acquaintances*) and unsentimentally repudiating him at the opportune moment. Madame Armand in "The Photographer's Missus" opts for an attempt at "apotheosis" over permanent definition as a man's "missus"; it does not succeed and she returns to her housewifely chores, but her "suicide" changes her life, and her situation becomes one she consciously chooses. Délia Essendier comes out of seclusion when she has definitely eliminated her husband; the widow's band signifies successful refusal of the role of abandoned wife. Most important, the Colette of "Bella-Vista," *Chance Acquaintances,* and "The Rainy Moon" colludes with passers-by and immensely enriches her writer's memory storehouse during the periods when she has no confining entanglements with men.

Hotel-keepers, typists, pearl-stringers, goat-herds, the women are capable and productive, displaying a taste for survival and most effectively functioning as creative agents when they have established autonomy—whatever effort and anguish the process costs. They are independent signifiers in these stories, with clusters of meaning centering on them rather than on the male characters whom they surpass in almost every conceivable way. It is not simply that Antoinette's strength dwarfs Gérard's in *Chance Acquaintances,* as Suzanne's does Ruby/Richard's in "Bella-Vista," and Louisette's does Chaveriat's in "The Tender Shoot." Colette's women seem to usurp the traditionally male privilege of originating action and significance. And a woman, the narrating Colette, is of course the central figure in all the stories she discovers, glosses, and frames. The plot of "The Kepi" provides an interesting commentary on this schema, for there the young Colette's profession as writer (doubled by that of Marco as ghostwriter) contrasts with Masson's function: he inspires Colette, arousing the initial interest in "the lady of the Library," but he never makes a real (written) story of the oral anecdote. Woman-as-writer and woman-as-story thus stand in opposition to man-as-muse (or gossip), and that important paradigmatic relation traced in *My Apprenticeships* between a writing Colette and an ingenious but impotent Willy finds its echo here.

Chapter Eight
Addressing Her Age

Throughout her life, Colette kept up an enormous correspondence.[1] In spite of all her professional assignments, she managed to write several letters a day, using, from the 1920s on, fine green or blue writing paper.[2] She virtually never crossed out or revised, and almost never dated her letters.

These letters display the same meticulously calculated naturalness as her fiction, the same deliberate yet surprising responses to people and things, as well as the kind of narrative discontinuities of which she makes a high art in the texts written for publication. Indeed, Colette's correspondence fits all the more snugly into her works because of the unusually close relation between her life and the subjects of her books: the letters reflect and adumbrate the characters and events of her autobiographical vignettes, reminiscences, novels, and short stories. In the correspondence, too, the narrator "Colette" predominates, telling stories about herself to various publics and analyzing herself and the world with originality and humor. The letters, however, more spontaneous if no less thoughtful than the published works, are written for the consumption of specific individuals, and allow less margin for play with biographical reality than do other works.

The correspondence is full of riveting accounts of one woman's experiences, even if there are few authentic "revelations" about sex, family, or money. Colette typically maintained a certain epistolary discretion, even with her intimate friend Marguerite Moreno. Indeed, in their simultaneous frankness and circumspection, the letters seem to illustrate the comment made by the narrator of *The Pure and the Impure* apropos of her conversations with Moreno: "No one can imagine the number of subjects, the amount of words that are left out of the conversation of two women who can talk to each other with absolute freedom. They can allow themselves the luxury of choosing what to say" (61).[3] What Colette does choose to say in her letters reveals a rich variety of sensual, emotional, and intellectual experience. Of all the letters she wrote, those to Moreno are the most moving, and they will most often serve here as illustrations.

Marguerite Moreno was an actress whose reputation was made in sound films; she performed also in memorable stage roles, like *The Madwoman of Chaillot.* She and Colette met around 1894 and remained friends for over 50 years. One of Colette's most splendid essays is an account of their friendship, originally written for publication in *Le Figaro Littéraire* after Moreno's death in 1948, and later incorporated into *The Blue Lantern;* it is used as a sort of preface to Claude Pichois's edition of their letters. Colette writes about their first meeting when they were both young women in Paris—Colette newly married to Willy, Moreno the mistress of Catulle Mendès—and about how they remained friends throughout the years, even as they "married, unmarried, and remarried" (Moreno became the wife of the poet Marcel Schwob and then of the actor Jean Daragon); traveled; changed residences; and pursued their separate careers. With ease and pleasure they would find one another again after each separation, and take up where they left off. The letters in the published volume extend from 1902 until Marguerite Moreno's death in 1948, and in fact even beyond, since the editor adds a handful of letters written over the next several years to Marguerite's nephew, Pierre Moreno. Colette herself died in 1954, so her letters to Marguerite and Pierre Moreno cover virtually her whole adult life.

Of course, Colette also kept in touch by letter with a wide array of other friends. With Léon Hamel, who died in 1917, and later with Léopold Marchand, she had warm friendships, and in letters to them she reported regularly and almost confessionally about most of the things that mattered to her. Devoted women friends included not just the Marquise de Belbeuf,[4] but also Annie de Pène, de Pène's daughter Germaine Beaumont, couturiere Germaine Patat (one of Henry de Jouvenel's mistresses), Germaine Carco, Claude Chauvière, poet Hélène Picard, Renée Hamon (whom they called "the little pirate"), and music critic Hélène Jourdan-Morhange.

None of these correspondences has quite the impact of the letters to Moreno. Generally, Colette liked to play the roles of patron and mentor as well as friend, and did not entirely forget that she was the grande dame and that Germaine Beaumont, for example, was once her secretary at *Le Matin,* or that Hélène Picard or Renée Hamon would be touchingly grateful for a preface to one of their books. With Moreno, the relationship was of equal to equal, and there is an exceptional spontaneity in these letters. In October 1947, for instance, when she hadn't heard from Moreno for a few weeks, Colette began a letter with stunning simplicity:

"Now then, my Marguerite, what is it we're doing that we're not writing to each other?" (*LMM, 330*).

Colette's letters are anecdotal. Guided by an unfaltering interest not only in all things human but also in everything in the natural world, she loved to tell stories of encounters both momentous and slight. For her the quotidian was profound, and she wrote about it without pompousness or grandiloquence—qualities she eschewed in all things. In a passage addressed to Moreno a little over six months before the latter's death, Colette expressed the essence of friendship and of the letter-writing enterprise: "My Marguerite, I hope we aren't through exchanging 'stories' which are worthwhile because it's you and because it's me" (*LMM, 333*).

The letters testify to the personal qualities that make Colette's "stories" worth reading and reflecting on: vitality, courage, and wit; phenomenal powers of observation; an original perspective on virtually everything; and a remarkable memory. They give evidence, in short, not only of the energy, but of the sheer intellectual force of this supposedly nonintellectual woman. At the same time, they are full of the poetry of daily life, of expressions of understated wonder (and sometimes disgust) in the face of people, animals, plants, seasons, places, and even foods. Colette described with infinite pleasure what she liked to eat: raw onions, yes; grated raw carrots, no; and of course garlic and wine ("a thing so subtle and so full of memory" [*LMM, 328*]). She wrote out recipes for eating well and for keeping healthy. In the winter of 1947 she sent to an ailing Marguerite Moreno an old recipe of Sido's for treating frostbite: marinate red rose petals in good wine vinegar for a month and then apply a compress to the affected area overnight (*LFC, 210*).

Colette worked hard and vacationed hard. Occasionally she would explain that she was too busy riding horseback and picking lilacs and wild orchids to write a long letter. In the French tradition, a major annual vacation was a fact of life, and Colette loved to spend hers at the seashore—at Rozven in Brittany in the early years and at Saint-Tropez later on—declaring that nothing was comparable to the sea. Besides summers, there were also spring vacations, fall breaks, and January getaways. She wrote poetically about the Breton and Mediterranean shores, about their mists and beaches and invigorating heat. From Rozven, for example: "I am being reborn in the tide and in the sand. My former strength that was asleep is awakening" (*LHP, 36*).

On the whole, Colette didn't pay much epistolary attention to "world" events. In 1940, while Paris was occupied and in the grip of food shortages, Colette, like everyone else, was worrying about her next meal, and dashed off fervent letters about eggs, chickens, and butter she was receiving or hoped to receive. (She took unabashed advantage of two of her most devoted admirers, Yvonne Brochard and Thérèse Sourisse, the "little farmers" who kept her generously supplied with food during difficult times.[5]) But she also found the interest to discuss, in the letters she exchanged with Hélène Picard, how the latter might manage to feed her parakeets, and whether it would be better to give them to the "parakeet man," a neighbor Colette had discovered in the Palais-Royal—for he had apparently succeeded, at a very high price, in getting some birdseed. In the short and sober letter of December 1941 that announced to Hélène Picard the arrest of Maurice Goudeket, Colette also took the trouble—despite her grave preoccupations about Maurice—to inform Hélène about a visit she had made to the parakeet man (*LFC,* 185–86).

In fact, Colette's letters not only comment on the crucial events of her life, but also offer copious advice about animals and stories about animal behavior that are as compelling—if sometimes just as implausible—as the animal tales scattered throughout her publications. She writes to friends about the tortoise she finds suffering from thirst, the large green lizard who drops onto her neck, and the green tree frog who happens to cross the balcony of her sixth-floor apartment on the Champs-Elysées (reminding us of the passage in *Sido* where Colette recalls that her mother had once seen it rain frogs). She describes a cocker spaniel with "frail nerves and a persecution complex"; she reports on five hedgehogs who drink milk, and on a toad who fell into a ditch and was found hanging on to some twigs, just like a human being (*LFC,* 176, 157). She recounts how she wakes from her nap one day to find two swallows lying entwined in a fold of her blanket (*LMT,* 289). While undergoing treatment for arthritis, she writes to Moreno about one of her doctors, who has blocked the mouse holes in her bedroom to keep a mouse *in* the room, where she feeds it: that way she's not awakened by its scurrying in and out at night. Colette also knows of a nightingale who travels in the metro without a cage, and of swallows who make their nest on a shelf near an electric ceiling light and ask the caretaker to let them out each day at dawn (*LFC,* 187, 151–52). Then there is the cat who travels by train without a box, walks on a leash, does her business on command, and is ultimately cured of an aging crisis by eating raw liver: "I too am all shoddy, heavy, and aged 101," Colette adds (*LFC,* 166). The year was 1939 and Colette was in her middle 60s.

She was married to Maurice Goudeket at the time, and enjoying the calmest and probably the happiest period of her life, even if she was also coping with the mortifications of growing old. The relation with Goudeket, whom she met in 1925 and who was at her deathbed nearly three decades later, was of enormous importance to Colette, for reasons of practicality and material support as well as companionship. Her lyrical description of his sexual appeal in a May 1925 letter to Moreno— "That boy is exquisite. I prefer to add nothing more. But what masculine grace there is in a certain softness, and how touching it is to watch the inner warmth thaw the outer envelope" (*LFC,* 89)—reminds us of the strong physical attraction that had also marked the beginning of the liaison with Henry de Jouvenel, whom she nicknamed "Sidi" or "the pasha." In 1911 she had written to Christiane Mendelys, "But who told you that I have been neglecting physical culture? I just have a new method, that's all. The Sidi Method. It's excellent. But no public courses. Only private lessons... extremely private" (*LFC,* 26).

Maurice Goudeket, unlike Henry de Jouvenel, was soon transformed from her lover into her "best friend," as she called him for her last 20 years. After two husbands with egos and ambitions at least as large as her own, Colette had had the luck to meet a man 16 years younger than she who would remain in excellent health and outlive her. Whatever compensations he sought outside the marriage, he nursed Colette through her escalating illnesses. Without a career of his own, he also administered her talent,[6] but far more gently than Willy had done decades earlier. It was Goudeket who conceived and oversaw a handsome edition of her works, having secured, as she explained in a letter to Moreno, an editor's license for the purpose.

The letters written to friends during her marriage to Jouvenel are full of irony and playful exaggeration about his handsomeness, prowess, demands, and arrogance, but when later she speaks of Goudeket, it is usually with simplicity. She rarely fails to mention him in the complimentary close of letters to friends, and alludes repeatedly to her pleasure and good fortune in having him at her side. To François Mauriac she wrote, "Maurice is a man worth knowing. More than I. But he dresses in colors that fade into the woodwork, so it's not easy" (*LP,* 417).

If the efficacious and self-effacing Maurice in some ways made up for the previous two husbands, Colette's relations with other family members were not so crystalline. The Colette family was strange, by Colette's own account. While her fiction and "autobiography" appealingly portray maternal and filial love, and especially love for Sido, Colette distanced herself from her real mother and her real daughter at critical moments. An elderly Sido complained with humor and irony that Colette, preoccupied with her career and her liaison with Henry de Jouvenel, was neglecting her: "No, really, I don't see you often enough for the time that is left to me to live. See how Monsieur de Jouvenel gets a larger share of your attention than I do. And yet all he had to do was appear" (*LD,* 502). Not long afterward, Colette wrote to Georges Wague, "I am going to visit Châtillon, where my sainted mother is insupportable. Not that she is seriously ill, but she's having a crisis of 'I wish to see my daughter.' Sidi is allowing me three days—at the maximum" (*LFC,* 31).

Sido would die a month later. When Colette succinctly announced the death in a letter to Léon Hamel, she added that she didn't want to attend the burial. She didn't explain why, but she typically avoided funerals. Of course, she was also clearly overworked, with both writing and acting obligations, and preoccupied with Jouvenel, whom she would marry two and a half months later. If her stories took her constantly back to her native village, real life almost never did—any more than it took her to the town where her mother and her older brother Achille lived and died. When she had the opportunity in later life to own the house where she was born in Saint-Sauveur, she declined: once she left Burgundy, she closed that chapter in her life, while she constantly rewrote it in her books.

She did not attend the funeral of Achille, who died of cancer a year and three months after Sido. (We do not know much about Achille's feelings toward Colette, but we have to assume enough admiration to account for his naming his second daughter Colette-Claudine.) Nor did she attend that of her remaining brother Léo a quarter-century later. In the letter to Hélène Picard announcing the death of "poor old" Léo— that strange and moving creature who, according to Colette, never quite grew up—his sister wrote, "I shall no longer hear him play the piano, with chapped fingers that seemed completely numb, and from which came sounds of a smooth and scintillating quality." "My Hélène," she concluded, somewhat disconsonantly, "I bless the parakeets" (*LHP,* 201). Joanna Richardson goes so far as to describe the passage on Léo's death as "a literary comment."[7] But we must remember that Colette was a private person and preferred understatement to grandiloquence; her letters contain a large dose of what the French call *pudeur,* a kind of modesty about one's feelings. To Yvonne Brochard, exceptionally, she elaborated a little on her feelings about Léo and death: "He died in the Yonne at Bléneau. But I'm telling only my intimate friends. Death should never be a public thing. I calmly accept his end which we have seen coming for a long time" (*LFW,* 32).

She apparently skipped not just family funerals, but even the wedding of her only child, who married a certain Dr. Jauss on 11 August 1935, in the Jouvenel country house at Castel-Novel in the Corrèze. (The marriage would last only a month; Colette de Jouvenel was to be a confirmed lesbian later in her life.) Indeed, Colette de Jouvenel plays a small role in her mother's letters to friends. Colette apparently played a comparably small role in the upbringing of the child, who was raised principally by an English nurse, Miss Draper. The relation between the mother and the daughter was always cool.

Five months before her death, Colette began a letter to Hélène Jourdan-Morhange with a parenthetical remark about her daughter's failure to write her—eerily echoing Sido's own complaints about Colette in the months preceding her death:

> My Moune, I'm not writing to anyone, not even to my daughter (who moreover doesn't write to me). How can one excuse this strange family? It's Maurice who is the most civilized. I excuse myself on the grounds of my rheumatism of the feet and the forearms. A few days ago I would neither have been able nor dared to write. But my daughter is the least excusable. (*LMT,* 379)

In the correspondence are reverberations, too, of Colette's affair with her stepson Bertrand, whom she sometimes called in her letters "the little leopard." Colette spent the summer of 1920 on the coast at Rozven, in the house given to her by Missy, Marquise de Belbeuf. Here she gathered together, as usual, several women friends and, for the first time, all three children of Henry de Jouvenel: Colette de Jouvenel, then seven years old; 12-year-old Renaud, Henry de Jouvenel's son by Isabelle de Comminges; and Bertrand, a son of Jouvenel's by Claire Boas. When Boas consented, under pressure from Jouvenel, to entrust the boy to Colette's care that summer ("for his hygiene and his misfortune," as Colette joked [*LMM,* 53]), Bertrand was not quite 17 and Colette was 47. A photograph shows a gangly but dark and handsome teenager, and a fleshy woman sitting tailor-style and wearing a stern look. Colette decided that the timid boy needed to become a man. If we are to believe the account in her letters, she first intended to have either Germaine Beaumont or Hélène Picard, who were both with her at Rozven, undertake his initiation, but finally decided to do it herself. We can only guess at her deepest feelings about Bertrand, since she did not elaborate.

Was it some crisis of her incipient middle age? Was it a way of getting even with her husband for his neglect and infidelities? What can be said in defense of Colette, who seduced an adolescent stepson, half-brother to her own daughter, in a house where that daughter was also living, as was the boy's half-brother? Perhaps only that Bertrand bore her no ill will, and spoke of her with affection all his life.

These tangled experiences of motherhood notwithstanding, Colette relished giving advice on child rearing. When a daughter was born to Pierre Moreno in the summer of 1947, Colette's participation in the family's joy was expressed warmly. Her letters contain not only repeated appeals for photographs and for information about the child's appearance, health, and behavior, but also unsolicited recommendations and cautions: make sure the baby is cured of scratching, a "kind of little childish neurosis that must not be allowed to develop" (*LMM,* 341), and never let her sleep with one little ear folded back (Colette knew someone who so slept as a baby, with unfortunate results). If Pierre has a son, she added, the father "will see how much more reserved is a little male, how much deeper, more secret" (*LMM,* 332–33).

Of course, Colette was an old woman when she wrote to the Morenos about babies in 1947. Her own daughter's childhood and even that Breton summer with Bertrand were distant memories. Bertrand had become a writer and political philosopher, and Colette de Jouvenel had tried her hand at several professions, including making films and selling antiques. Cumulatively, Colette's letters convey a sense of what it meant for her to grow old as a woman and as a writer in the first half of this century. The exuberance of her earliest letters reflects the state of mind of a young woman discovering the thrills of Paris at Willy's side. She would go on to experience and write about the fears and deprivation associated with staying "at home" during two world wars and about the illnesses and deaths of friends. Despite the historical and human interest of the early letters, those written during Colette's last two decades are incomparable for the reflections born of long and thoughtful experience. They stir us by the artfulness of her analysis of human nature and her own nature, and by the way she managed the indignity of growing old and weak.

"Oh, hideous age!" she exclaimed in the winter of 1939–40 (*LFC,* 174). As her ailments accumulated, she would speak of grippe, anemia, insomnia, neuritis, enteritis, bronchitis. Pain became constant in the 1940s and the 1950s: "I'm suffering barometrically," she joked. But more often the tone was serious: to Yvonne Brochard and Thérèse Sourisse in 1947 she wrote, "I've suffered a great deal this month" (*LFW,* 160); and to Hélène Jourdan-Morhange in 1954, "I'm still suffering a great deal in the arms and the legs" (*LMT,* 302, 380). "What is this new humiliation?" she rhetorically asked as she described a bout with an ear inflammation (*LMM,* 317). Arthritis led her to seek relief from doctors in Uriage and Geneva, even while it made travel increasingly difficult. While her published work extols stoicism in the face of pain and evokes the refusal of any drugs that might dull her senses, her letters tell us that she did in fact attempt a variety of treatments to ease her misery.

Colette's aging process is accessible and visible to us not only because she wrote about it, but also because of her love of the camera. The astonishing photographic record she left—hundreds of snapshots and portraits—complements and illustrates her letters. She was copiously photographed throughout her adult life: in the early days, of course, it was thanks to Willy; later there was her own notoriety followed by her literary glory. Biographies contain dazzling photos of her: in costume (and sometimes half-naked) for her roles as mime or actress; or looking grim at Willy's side, solemn and serene with the Marquise de Belbeuf, regal with Jouvenel, peremptory with Bertrand, serious with Goudeket—but almost never smiling. The photographs provide a visual gloss both on long years of unhappiness and on the painful process of aging that her letters compellingly invoke. Indeed, there is something bewitching about the grave look she wore on that triangular face heavily made up and partly hidden by frizzy hair as she grew older.

Like most people, she widened with age; with physical inactivity, she grew fatter than most people. It was a rather spectacular change from the trim and shape-conscious woman she had been. When Colette and Willy moved to Rue de Courcelles in 1902, a gym was installed in the apartment and Colette started exercising seriously. She was already nearly 30. Soon after, perhaps sensing that the union with Willy was nearing its end and she would need a way of supporting herself, she began taking lessons in dance and mime. The disciplining of her body was in part a means to that end. It continued in earnest during the years between 1906 and 1912 when she mounted the boards professionally. After the birth of her daughter in 1913, she devoted herself more to writing and less to performing; from then on, she would return to the stage only sporadically, and her weight would gradually increase.

By March 1922, during her affair with Bertrand, she noted that Henry de Jouvenel was fat and that she herself weighed nearly 81 kilos (*LFC,* 66)! A year and a half later, when her marriage to Jouvenel was coming apart, she described a characteristic reaction to stress that helps explain both her enduring sanity and her heft: "In advance, I fight against everything by means of a methodical appetite" (*LMM,* 77). She craved seafood. Two decades later, during an attack of bronchitis she wrote: "I no longer blush to rejoice in eating" (*LFW,* 36); and at the end of a night of bombing in 1944: "At present I want to eat. . . . I want beef stew and marinated herring. To hell with tomato salad and noodles" (*LMM,* 295).[8] Arthritis gradually settled into her hip and made movement increasingly difficult; by the late 30s she was distinctly less ambulatory. Eventually she became immobilized: "you understand, my Moune," she wrote in August 1948, "I can't walk" (*LMT,* 310). The inexorable weight gain was hastened not only by immobility, but also by an indomitable appetite for good food.

She became an old woman whom one uncharitable observer would describe in the mid-1930s as a "monstrous turd on wheels."[9] Right-wing journalist Robert Brasillach recalled taking her on a visit of the Ecole Normale with her bulldog in 1929, and going everywhere but on the roofs: "she is too fat."[10] "She is no mean weight," noted a visitor to her beauty salon in 1932.[11] Actor Jean-Pierre Aumont, whose first important role was in a film for which Colette wrote the dialogue, evoked her more poetically around the same time: her body, he said, was "heavy with every food and with every love."[12] For her rare dinners at Le Grand Véfour (just below her apartment), she had to be lowered by the strong hands of friends; slim Maurice Goudeket, although he kept fit by boxing, would have been unequal to the task.

But the parallel Aumont suggests between food and love reinforces the notion that Colette's size and her vigor go hand in hand. Indeed, her transformation mimics the weight gain experienced by a number of her characters. Foreshadowing Colette's own attitude, Léa in *The Last of Cheri* gaily wears the kilos that masculinize her. Her bulk, associated with a robust laugh and fine blue eyes, becomes a sign of her humanity, even if it makes Chéri despair. To Camille in *The Cat,* and Marco in *The Képi,* satisfaction—particularly sexual—also adds weight.

The letters and pictures portraying Colette as she grew old may be read in the light of the opening lines of one of her last important works, *The Blue Lantern* (a book to which I shall return in my final chapter):

> We should not be unreasonably perturbed when our precious senses become dulled with age. I say "we," but I am the text of my own sermon. My chief concern is lest I should mistake the true nature of a condition which has come upon me gradually. It can be given a name: it keeps me in a state of vigilance, of uncertainty, ready to accept whatever may fall

to my lot. The prospect gives rise to little that is reassuring, but I have no choice. (5)

Nothing in her letters or the major works of her last few years indicates any "dulling" of her senses or her sensitivity, even if her body was declining. On the contrary, her writings are full of subtle evocations of sensual experience and the inevitable aging process.

She sensibly approached the process of growing old, by continuing not only to eat but to work. In fact, a major theme in her letters, the theme that gives shape and poignancy to the stories of sun and surf, cats and parakeets, garlic and onions, is *work*—by which she meant writing (she considered it a manual labor). All her life, she deplored the agonizing investment of time and energy required to write. It is hard to know to what extent she was posing when she spoke of her writing career as if it were a curse, insisting that she would rather soak in the sea or bake in the sun. To Marguerite Moreno, who told her in spring 1914 that she had begun to write, Colette exclaimed with humor, "She too. Now she too knows what it is to be desperate over a word instead of toasting in the sun. Now she too gnaws the tip of her pen and tears up pages" (*LFC,* 39). When Colette was in the middle of a project (and she almost always was), she would protest to friends that she was never meant to write, that it was hard to get an expression, or a plot, or an ending, just so: she had to write, rewrite, throw away, and start again. At other times she explained that if she hadn't sent a letter for a while, or if the present one was shorter than she might like, it was because of the demands of work.

Colette maintained that if she worked unremittingly, it was for the money. Given the celebrity and esteem she enjoyed, one might be inclined to dismiss such assertions as disingenuous. But in fact Colette seemed to be, or at least to think she was, always in need of money. If she kept "a vigilant watch over her career,"[13] it was not only out of some sense of personal glory, but also because of her preoccupation with finances. "My life is nothing but money worries," she complained in 1931 (*LFC,* 133). Along with the poetry of the quotidian, one finds in her letters a concern with costs, debts, salaries, and income.

In *My Apprenticeships*, explaining how Willy set her to writing, Colette quotes him as exclaiming, "Quick, dear, quick! There's not a sou in the house!" (16). That close original connection between writing and earning her bread apparently never slackened. Of course, she lived well and vacationed comfortably, but her acquisitiveness with regard to money seems to parallel her appetite for food: both drives eventually outdistanced any verifiable "need." Even elderly and increasingly infirm, and despite a doubtless substantial enough income from her books, she accepted commissions to write advertising copy or to do the translations for foreign films.

Colette was acutely aware in her later years of the paradoxical relation between life and work by which the latter gave not just pain but design and meaning—a kind of "weight"—to the former. Her letters to friends communicate that relation, both explicitly and implicitly. They make clear the central role that work played in her life, and how she came to accept that for her there was, as she put it in *The Blue Lantern*, "no other destiny" (161). At the same time, it seems that letter writing in particular somehow helped her to accept age and to manage the suffering it entailed. The correspondence itself—for the way it helps to shape her experience and her work, for what it reveals about her various appetites over half a century, as well as for the sheer and subtle beauty of the letters—represents some of her best writing.

Chapter Nine

Survival

Colette's books and letters recapitulate experience and publications, and gloss each other and the author. There are curiously symphonic effects produced by relentless repetition and transformation of themes and images (memory, childhood, love), by the circulation of characters (Maugis, Polaire, Claudine, Toby-Dog), and by the frequent return to prototypical events and figures (growing up in a village, Sido, Willy). There is an extraordinary unity about it all. John Updike speaks in a review article of "the book of life she was always composing,"[1] and indeed Colette liked to retell her own (exemplary) story—in essay, anecdote, criticism, letter and fiction.

Her last two major books especially read as a kind of summation. *The Evening Star* (*L'Etoile Vesper*, 1946) and *The Blue Lantern* (*Le Fanal bleu*, 1949) chronicle her final years and examine the sense and the successes of all the previous ones. Star and lantern throw both light and shadow on the spectacle of life to which Colette bore sensitive witness, and prove that she never lost the joy of discovery or the capacity to be surprised. She remembers her visit to a perfume factory, the acquisition of her first radio, her pregnancy, her animals. She celebrates youth and casts a hard look on her own infirm old age. A visit from a young woman named Catherine, whose mother has sent her to call on Colette, takes her back to Saint-Sauveur and Sido:

> I vividly recall my shudder of repugnance when I was very young—does Catherine feel the same with me?—at the touch of old people, and the wild delight with which at the end of the visit I made good my escape from Mme de Cadalvène or Mme Bourgneuf, old ladies of over eighty. . . . It needed every ounce of Sido's authority to force me to pick up a detested silk scarf from beside a pair of lifeless feet shod in felt slippers. . . . It was I, therefore, and not Catherine, who heard a quiet voice saying "You must be very kind to Mme Bourgneuf." (*The Blue Lantern*, 78–79)

Thus she returns at the end, as she had returned all her life, to her beginnings, seeking identities and continuities. She has become Sido, while courageous, rosy-cheeked young women have become latter-day Claudines and Minet-Chéris.

She recollects passers-by—the "transients" of her life—as well as tradesmen, admirers, and the children she has watched at play in the gardens of the Palais-Royal; friends like Hélène Picard, Renée Hamon, and Claude Chauvière; her neighbors Jean Cocteau and Jean Marais, the latter with his dog Moulouk; and her daughter's nurse, Miss Draper. Of some whom death has stolen—Léon-Paul Fargue, her brother Léo, her friend Marguerite Moreno—she speaks with some irritation: how could they have left her? She confronts her own mortality: "Am I to die without having reached the limits of my various capacities?" (*The Evening Star*, 52). She notes, "In anticipation of the time when I shall no longer be able to move, I make no effort to move. I ride at anchor beneath the blue lantern, which is quite simply a powerful commercial lamp at the end of a lengthy extensible arm, fitted with a blue bulb and a blue paper shade" (*The Blue Lantern*, 57–58).

Her writing lamp gives its name to her last major volume, and its capacity for illuminating and clarifying is symbolic. *The Blue Lantern* and *The Evening Star* are in large measure books about what it means to be a writer, about the implications of practicing a trade she labels an obsession and a compulsion. *The Evening Star* begins with a brief exchange between a solicitous Goudeket and a scribbling Colette:

> "Are you all right?"
> "Fine."
> "What's that you're writing?"
> "Oh, nothing! I scratch on the paper and then tear it up. When I can't make anything of it, I destroy it."

By the book's end, she expects to write no more: "To unlearn how to write, that shouldn't take much time" (143). But a few years later, beginning *The Blue Lantern*, she maintains, "I was honest when I called *L'Etoile Vesper* my last book. I have come to see that it is as difficult to stop writing as it is uncomfortable to go on" (6). Born (or created) half a century earlier, at Willy's insistence, Colette's imperative to write is stronger than ever. The appeal of her work resides partly in its documentation of this experience of the woman writer. Writing became for her as spontaneous and as demanding as any womanly occupation—

making love, cooking, sewing. In a provocative passage at the end of *The Evening Star*, she explicitly assimilates her exertions at writing—her "gourmet's search" for a better word—to her exertions at embroidery. Pen and needle are like a pair of horses harnessed together, falling in and out of rhythm. Both are outlets for her "creative faculties" (143). Everything seems to find its natural place in Colette's writing, and she beguiles us with her depth of understanding and her simplicity of vision.

These two books cite and arrange, in no apparent order, events of the circuit from Saint-Sauveur to the Palais-Royal. Another early passage in *The Blue Lantern* comments on her manner:

> I wanted this book to be a journal; but I do not possess the knack of writing a proper journal. . . . The art of selection, of noting things of mark, retaining the unusual while discarding the commonplace, has never been mine, since most of the time I am stimulated and quickened by the ordinary. There I was, vowing never to write anything again after *L'Etoile Vesper*, and now I have covered two hundred pages which are neither memoirs nor journal. Let my reader resign himself to it: this lantern of mine . . . throws no light on events significant enough to astonish him. (6–7)

But Colette does astonish us. Her system of narration, apparently digressive but scrupulous and rigorous, elucidates a life and a life's work. While *The Blue Lantern* is neither memoir nor journal, other books are neither autobiography nor fiction; *Break of Day* is both novel and nonnovel; some of the short pieces are both short story and reminiscence; her theater criticism is replete with autobiographical anecdotes, some of which go back several decades; her letters provide the counterpoint to autobiographical materials. Her texts are highly individuated, their specificity of form corresponding to a specificity of content and, most of all, to the female specificity that is their central message.

The paradox is that, although her published literature is relentlessly personal, it is usually less than intimate. "I am the text of my own sermon," she writes in the second line of *The Blue Lantern*, sounding like Montaigne, and she explores the dimensions of her experience, about which we know so much already. Yet she tells half-truths and remains tantalizingly veiled. This characteristic reticence creates a tension that makes it difficult to assimilate her literature to that of other female writers, where the personal is more marked and less measured. Colette steeps her works in the literarization of the personal. Endlessly, she relates information about Sido and Monsieur Willy, but in fact they are part of her literature and of her becoming literary. About Jouvenel she says less, about Goudeket less still. In *Break of Day*, she admits that she does not intend to speak much about her daughter:

> For if I see no objection to putting into the hands of the public, in print, rearranged fragments of my emotional life, it's understandable that I should tie up tight in the same sack, strictly private, all that concerns a preference for animals and—it's a question of partiality too—the child whom I brought into the world. (45)

She narrates amusing incidents from Colette de Jouvenel's childhood, but the private relations between mother and daughter are not the reader's business. At once candid and elusive, she wonders again in *Break of Day*, "Why do men—writers or so-called writers—still show surprise that a woman should so easily reveal to the public love-secrets and amorous lies and half-truths? By divulging these, she manages to hide other important and obscure secrets" (62). Likewise, in letters to friends, she gives constant advice and talks about her correspondent or seasons and places, and yet her deepest feelings may be passed over or metaphorized into literature. Her mode of self-presentation, combining discretion with exhibitionism, is her hallmark. The reader is well advised not to take it all too seriously, when even Colette's literary persona cautions that circumstances have been manipulated and fragments rearranged.

Colette's uniqueness relates on the one hand to the break with traditional genres that makes her work so enchanting and difficult to classify, and on the other to her exploration of gender differences. In Colette's writing, ordinary feminine pursuits are beautiful and heroic as well as prosaic; men are sex objects; and maternal and passionate love, heterosexual and homosexual love, the pure and the impure, drift together. The constituent element is pinpointed by her notation in *The Ripening Seed* of the female's "mission to endure," and by a line from *The Evening Star*, written in the context of the war: "The will to survive is so alive in us women and the lust for physical victory so female" (52). She was concerned with desire and common sense, eroticism and love of nature—attitudes embellished in the woman by strength of will, lust for victory, perseverance in the face of the inevitable, and the determination to survive. Colette the woman survives oppression, jealousy, scandal, arthritis, material adversity, and war. Her female characters, like Colette herself, incarnate not only Eros but also ferocity. In the line following the one quoted above from *The Evening Star*, Colette writes, "when they notice it, our men can't get over seeing us so ferocious." In a letter to Pierre

Moreno written about a year later, she echoes the idea: a baby girl is "a good and tenacious female seed that will know how to hang on to life" (*LMM,* 323). Colette knew how to hang on. Her reputation survived critics' attempts at trivialization: she is more than a surprising sensualist, a first-rate stylist, and a touching animal portraitist. Women began to catch up with Colette after her death, when the marginality of her life and the daring of her writing began to acquire respectability.

Unlike much modern feminist writing, Colette's is not anguished. Defying male bastions with naturalness and unstudied conviction, she appears to be the exception to every rule, while remaining a kind of everywoman in the range of her experience. She grants sex and sexuality a privileged position, treating them with precision, understanding, indulgence, and even some disdain. Several words sum up her writing. *Vitality,* first of all—a specifically (and enviable) feminine strength, begotten of immense curiosity, intellectual discipline, and freedom from anguish. Also, perhaps, *severity*: although zest and compassion distinguish her approach, she could judge the world with the withering look of the connoisseur and the practical eye of the bourgeoise. Finally, *subtlety*: her classical prose style, devoid of the grandiloquence she abhorred, rests on artistic understatement, ellipsis, and suggestion. The combination confers an exceptional equilibrium.

Notes and References

Chapter One

1. See Jean-Michel Adam's analysis of this section of *My Mother's House* in *Linguistique et discours littéraire*, in collaboration with Jean-Pierre Goldenstein (Paris: Larousse, 1976), pp. 28–41. He notes that "since Freud, the relation between the activity of the writer and the play of the child has been known, but what we understand here is that both consist of a nonutilitarian use of signs" (p. 40; my translation). See also Catherine Slawy-Sutton, "'Où sont les enfants?': aspects du silence dans *La Maison de Claudine*" (*The French Review* 64:2 [December 1990], 300–308), for a reading of *My Mother's House* as a meditation on the way writing mediates between two modes of communication, the child's and the adult's.

2. For much biographical information, I am in debt to Michèle Sarde, *Colette, libre et entravée* (Paris, 1978). Translated as *Colette Free and Fettered* by Richard Miller (New York, 1980).

3. A great deal of attention has been paid to the figure and role of Sido in Colette's work. The 1984 publication of the letters Colette's mother wrote her (Colette's to her mother were destroyed) provides a fascinating source of information about their historical relationship and the real Sidonie Landoy Colette. Throughout her work, of course, Colette makes unusually elaborate literary use of the material of her own life and of the figures and events of her past. In the pages that follow, my interest on the whole is not to identify strictly verifiable biographical detail, but to evoke Colette's past as she herself represented and characterized it.

4. Quoted in *Colette: catalogue de l'exposition de 1973* (Paris, 1973), p. 97 (my translation).

5. For a thorough account of Claudine's creation and an analysis of the Claudine and Minne books, see Paul d'Hollander, *Colette: ses apprentissages* (Montreal and Paris, 1978). D'Hollander maintains that Willy's part in the Claudine books was less negligible than Colette would have us believe. For a discussion of the composition and publication of *Claudine at School* and especially of Willy's role, see also the notice and notes pertaining to the novel in Colette, *Oeuvres* (Paris: Gallimard, Pléiade, 1984– , Vol. I, 1239–87). Indeed, I am indebted to the Pléiade volumes for various details about Colette's life and works.

6. William H. Gass, "Three Photos of Colette," *New York Review*, 14 April 1977, pp. 11–19. The photograph in question is reproduced on pp. 68–69 of Yvonne Mitchell's handsome biography, *Colette: A Taste for Life* (New

York: Harcourt, Brace, Jovanovich, 1975), and, in a much smaller reproduction, on p. 94 of Geneviève Dormann, *Amoureuse Colette* ([Paris]: Herscher, 1984).

7. Maurice Goudeket, *Close to Colette* (New York, 1957), p. 100.

8. For a Colette filmography and a collection of her movie criticism and her own screenplays, see *Colette au cinéma,* ed. Alain and Odette Virmaux (Paris: Flammarion, 1975). Translated as *Colette at the Movies* by Sarah W. R. Smith (New York: Frederick Ungar, 1980).

9. The narrator of *Break of Day* does remark: "So it came about that legally and familiarly, as well as in my books, I now have only one name, which is my own" (p. 19).

Chapter Two

1. Quoted in Sarde, *Colette Free and Fettered,* p. 169.

2. Ibid.

3. For the purposes of my discussion of the two works in question, I shall use their French titles throughout the rest of this chapter.

4. The significance of such an identification is stressed by Philippe Lejeune, both in *L'Autobiographie en France* (Paris: Armand Colin, 1971) and in *Le Pacte autobiographique* (Paris: Seuil, 1975).

5. Roland Barthes, *S/Z* (Paris: Seuil, 1970), p. 80.

6. Preface to *Douze Dialogues de bêtes,* in *Oeuvres complètes,* 15 vols. (Paris, 1948–50), 3:305 (my translation).

7. This piece originally appeared in *Les Vrilles de la vigne* (1908) and was incorporated into *Douze Dialogues de bêtes* in 1930.

Chapter Three

1. Jean Larnac, *Histoire de la littérature féminine en France* (Paris: Krâ, 1929), p. 251.

2. *Mitsou or How Girls Grow Wise,* tr. Jane Terry (New York: Albert and Charles Boni, 1930).

3. Roland Barthes, *Fragments d'un discours amoureux* (Paris: Seuil, 1977), pp. 17–24.

4. For example, François Jost lists *Mitsou* in his extensive inventory of letter-novels through 1966 (*Essais de littérature comparée,* vol. 2: *Europaena* [Urbana: University of Illinois Press, 1968]); and Jean Rousset, in an appendix to "Le Roman par lettres" (in *Forme et signification* [Paris: Corti, 1962]), cites only two examples for the twentieth century: *Mitsou* and Montherlant's *Les Jeunes Filles.*

5. See Lucien Dällenbach, *Le Récit spéculaire: essai sur la mise en abyme* (Paris: Seuil, 1977). Dällenbach presents the *mise en abîme* as a "modalité de la réflexion," whose "propriété essentielle consiste à faire saillir l'intelligibilité et la structure formelle de l'oeuvre" (p. 16).

6. Jacques Lacan, *Ecrits: A Selection,* tr. Alan Sheridan (New York: Norton, 1977), chapter 1: "The Mirror Stage."

7. Ibid., p. 2.

8. The specter of the lover who goes out for cigarettes and never comes back also turns up in *Mitsou.* In her last letter to the Blue Lieutenant, she writes: "In your world nobody says 'You're a thoroughly nasty woman, Miss.' You say: 'Madame, I am charmed to be with you. I must just slip out to get some cigarettes; I won't be a minute,' and you leave her there for the rest of her life" (p. 112).

Chapter Four

1. Susan Sontag, "The Double Standard of Aging," *Saturday Review* 55: 39 (October 1972), 29.

2. Chéri's genesis is discussed in detail by André J. Joubert, *Colette et Chéri* (Paris: Nizet, 1972). Chéri and Léa evolved partly from the ugly Clouk and his mistress Lulu, characters in several stories Colette published in *Le Matin* in 1911 and 1912.

3. A reading by Joan Teresa Rosasco, *"Chéri,* ou le collier de Léa," situates the novel in the framework of myth (*Teaching Language through Literature* 19: 1 [December 1979], 3–21).

4. The aging of Renaud in *Retreat from Love* is similarly abrupt. He goes to a sanatorium, exhausted but full of life, and comes back—fifty years old, like Léa in *Chéri*—a stooping "old man," the sight of whom Claudine finds intolerable.

5. Elaine Marks, *Colette* (New Brunswick, N.J., 1960), chapter xi: "Parables of Experience." Marks explains in a note that the expression is borrowed from an article by Richard Hayes.

6. Janet Whatley, "L'Age équivoque: Marivaux and the Middle-Aged Woman," *University of Toronto Quarterly* 46: 1 (Fall 1976), 68.

7. Sontag, "Double Standard," p. 29. It should be noted, however, that Léa does not literally initiate Chéri.

8. The novel has been read as a literary transposition of Colette's affair with Bertrand.

9. Goudeket, *Close to Colette,* p. 45.

10. *Break of Day*, and particularly Sido's role in it, have attracted attention from commentators, especially feminists. Marianne Hirsch gives an astute reading in *The Mother/Daughter Plot: Narrative, Psychoanalysis, Feminism* (Bloomington and Indianapolis: Indiana University Press, 1989). Valérie C. Lastinger, among others, emphasizes that the textual Sido exists independently of Colette's mother and that the book belongs to the realm of fiction (*"La Naissance du jour:* la désintégration du 'moi' dans un roman de Colette." *The French Review* 61:4 [March 1988], 542–51).

Chapter Five

1. Madame Riccoboni, *Histoire de Monsieur le marquis de Cressy,* in *Oeuvres complètes* (Paris: Volland, 1786), 2:79 (my translation).

2. Robert D. Cottrell, *Colette* (New York, 1974), p. 103. Marianna Forde's reading of *The Cat*, on the other hand, emphasizes its up/down spatial polarities and binary structure ("Spatial Structures in *La Chatte*," *The French Review* 58:3 [February 1985], 360–67).

3. Marks, *Colette*, p. 117.

4. The prototypical burned arm is that of a widowed Sido, who, in a chapter of *My Mother's House*, "My Mother and the Forbidden Fruit," reveals to her visiting daughter a newly acquired burn blister.

5. For a discussion of space in *Le Toutounier*, see Ann Leone Philbrick, "The Ambiguist Despite Herself: How Space Nurtures and Subverts Identity in Colette's *Le Toutounier*," *Modern Language Studies* 11: (Spring 1981), 32–39.

6. With her adumbration of twin speech, Colette seems to have anticipated what has become a subject of serious inquiry. Her intimate linguistic community that defines itself against the group suggests recent scientific discovery of twins developing a language with its own syntax and vocabulary.

7. Yannick Resch, *Corps féminin, corps textuel* (Paris: Klincksieck, 1973), part 3, chapter 1.

8. Marcelle Biolley-Godino, *L'Homme-objet chez Colette* (Paris: Klincksieck, 1972), p. 137.

9. Gigi's sexual appeal is the ambiguous boyish charm of Colette's earlier female adolescents, Claudine and Vinca: "At times she looked like Robin Hood, at others like a stone angel, or again like a boy in skirts; but she seldom resembled a nearly grown-up girl" (*Gigi*, p. 128).

Chapter Six

1. Virginia Woolf, *A Room of One's Own* (New York: Harcourt, Brace, 1929), pp. 170–71.

2. My translation (*Oeuvres complètes*, 9:65). The Briffault translation eliminates the entire last paragraph of the fourth chapter, where the line appears. This paragraph introduces the pages on Renée Vivien that were originally published separately in 1928.

3. For a discussion of the survival theme in *My Apprenticeships*, see Janet Whatley, "Colette and the Art of Survival," in *Colette: The Woman, The Writer*, ed. Erica Eisinger and Mari McCarty (University Park and London, 1981), pp. 32–39.

4. Mary Kathleen Benet gives a provocative reading of Colette which intersects with mine. She stresses Sido's disappointment in her marriages and her unhealthy possessiveness regarding her youngest child. Benet attributes to Colette a sense of guilt at having resisted the maternal influence that would have kept her from giving herself over into the hands of a man (*Writers in Love* [New York: Macmillan, 1977], part 3).

Chapter Seven

1.   Their sheer number makes it impossible to deal with all of Colette's short pieces. My selection of half a dozen is somewhat arbitrary, but they are among the longer stories and those I consider formally most interesting. With the exception of *Chance Acquaintances,* all those I deal with appear in *The Tender Shoot and Other Stories,* translated by Antonia White (New York: Farrar, Straus and Giroux, 1958). *Chance Acquaintances* is in the volume entitled *Julie de Carneilhan and Chance Acquaintances,* translated by Patrick Leigh Fermor (London: Secker and Warburg, 1952). My references are to those volumes. (Except for *Chance Acquaintances,* these stories are also included in *The Collected Stories of Colette,* ed. Robert Phelps, translated by Matthew Ward, Antonia White, Anne-Marie Callimachi, and others [New York: Farrar, Straus and Giroux, 1983]. Here "The Photographer's Missus" is retitled "The Photograper's Wife.")

2.   Marks, *Colette,* p. 174. Marks's chapter 14, containing a discussion of Colette's first-person narratives, was useful to my thinking.

3.   Colette must have had the idea in mind for a long time. In *The Vagabond,* which she published in 1911, Renée Néré writes: "I have seen satisfied, amorous women in whom, for a few brief and dangerous minutes, the affected ingénue reappears and allows herself girlish tricks which make her rich and heavy flesh quiver. I have shuddered at the lack of awareness of a friend in her forties who, unclothed and all breathless with love, clapped on her head the cap [*le képi*] of her lover, a lieutenant of Hussars" (pp. 199–200).

4.   For some compelling comments on the use of space in this story, see Mari McCarty, "Possessing Female Space: 'The Tender Shoot,' " *Women's Studies* 8: 3 (1981), 367–74.

Chapter Eight

1.   It has been published in part in a series of volumes including: "Letters to Hélène Picard" (*Lettres à Hélène Picard* [abbreviated hereafter as *LHP*]), "Letters to Marguerite Moreno" (*Lettres à Marguerite Moreno* [*LMM*]), "Letters from the Vagabond" (*Lettres de la vagabonde*), "Letters to the Little Pirate" (*Lettres au petit corsaire*), "Letters to Her Peers" (*Lettres à ses pairs,* [*LP*]), "Letters to the Little Farmers" (*Lettres aux petites fermières* [*LFW*]), and "Letters to Moune and the Toutounet" (*Lettres à Moune et au Toutounet* [*LMT*]). Selections from several of these volumes appear in a compact English translation edited by Robert Phelps and entitled *Letters from Colette* (*LFC*). Passages from other letters that have remained in private hands are sprinkled throughout many of the critical and biographical studies of Colette. She also wrote nearly 2,000 letters to her mother over approximately two decades between her marriage to Willy and Sido's death in 1912, but these were later destroyed by Colette's sister-in-law, Jane Robineau-Duclos (Jeannie Malige, *Colette, Qui êtes-vous?* [Lyon: La Manufacture, 1987], p. 67). Sido's letters to Colette, however (along with a few

unedited letters of Colette herself) appear in Sido, "Letters to Her Daughter" (*Lettres à sa fille* [*LD*]). Whenever possible in this chapter, I have referenced the Phelps translation (*LFC*); in the case of quotations from other volumes, the translations are my own.

2. Colette liked to write not only her letters but also her novels on colored paper. A beautiful edition of *Sido*, edited by Maurice Delcroix (Paris: Centre National de la Recherche Scientifique, 1994), reproduces the manuscript on paper of jade green and pale blue, like that which Colette used to write it.

3. Cf. the remark made to the same narrator by Charlotte: "How nice that we know each other so little! We can talk about things one doesn't talk about with friends. Friends, women friends, if such a thing exists, never dare to confess to each other what they really and truly lack" (23).

4. No correspondence between Colette and the Marquise de Belbeuf is known to survive.

5. In fact, most of her letters to the "little farmers" are hardly more than acknowledgments and thank-you notes for the provender, but Colette managed to make even her expressions of gratitude for vegetables and salt shimmer with a kind of poetry.

6. Joanna Richardson, *Colette* (London: Methuen, 1983), 167. Richardson quotes Louise Weiss's description of Willy as the administrator of Colette's talent.

7. Ibid., 179.

8. Those interested in Colette's culinary preferences might consult a handsome volume with photographs and recipes entitled *Colette gourmande* (Paris: Albin Michel, 1990) by Marie-Christine and Didier Clément, as well as a fascinating article by Mireille Rosello about the status of recipes as text. Rosello is critical of the Clément book as a hybrid volume, part biography and part cookbook ("Le Cru et l'écrit: les recettes à la Colette," in *Il Senso del nonsenso: Scritti in memoria di Lynn Salkin Sbiroli,* ed. Monique Streiff Moretti, Mireille Revol Cappelletti and Odile Martinez [Naples: Edizioni Scientifiche Italiane, 1994], pp. 469–96).

9. Richardson, op. cit., 164. The observer was Isabelle de Comminges, whom Henry de Jouvenel had left years earlier for Colette and whom they called "the panther."

10. Ibid., 133.

11. Ibid., 149.

12. Ibid., 153.

13. Ibid., 154.

Chapter Nine

1. John Updike, "An Armful of Field Flowers," review of *Letters from Colette,* selected and translated by Robert Phelps, *The New Yorker,* 29 December 1980, pp. 69–72.

Selected Bibliography

PRIMARY SOURCES

1. Complete Works

With the help of Maurice Goudeket, Colette herself prepared an edition of her works in the last few years of her life. She reviewed her texts, suppressed some, slightly modified or reworked others, added a few unpublished pieces, and wrote several new prefaces. There are short introductory notes by Goudeket for most of the texts, and a bibliography in the last volume. The edition appeared as: *Oeuvres complètes de Colette.* 15 vols. Paris: Flammarion (Le Fleuron), 1948–50. It was reedited to include, in 16 illustrated volumes, some posthumous pieces, by Editions du Club de l'Honnête Homme, 1973–76.

A welcome new edition of her *Oeuvres*—excluding, like the Fleuron edition, her countless newspaper and magazine articles—is appearing in the Bibliothèque de la Pléiade (Gallimard), under the general direction of Claude Pichois and with a formidable critical apparatus, including chronologies, bibliographies, notices, notes, and variants. Of the four planned volumes, I (1984), II (1986), and III (1991) have already appeared. (A fourth printing of volume I in 1994 and a third printing of volume II in 1993 incorporate some corrections.)

2. Selected Separate Works in Order of Publication

The following list indicates in parentheses the translations used for this study.

Claudine à l'école. Paris: Ollendorff, 1900. (*Claudine at School.* In *The Complete Claudine.* Translated by Antonia White. New York: Farrar, Straus and Giroux, 1976.)
Claudine à Paris. Paris: Ollendorff, 1901. (*Claudine in Paris.* In *The Complete Claudine.*)
Claudine en ménage. Paris: Mercure de France, 1902. (*Claudine Married.* In *The Complete Claudine.*)
Claudine s'en va. Paris: Ollendorff, 1903. (*Claudine and Annie.* In *The Complete Claudine.*)
Minne. Paris: Ollendorff, 1904.

Dialogues de bêtes. Paris: Mercure de France, 1904. (*Creature Conversations.* In *Creatures Great and Small.* Translated by Enid McLeod. New York: Farrar, Straus and Giroux, 1978.)

Les Egarements de Minne. Paris: Ollendorff, 1905.

Sept Dialogues de bêtes. Préface de Francis Jammes. Paris: Mercure de France, 1905. (*Creature Conversations.* In *Creatures Great and Small.* Translated by Enid McLeod. New York: Farrar, Straus and Giroux, 1978).

La Retraite sentimentale. Paris: Mercure de France, 1907. (*Retreat from Love.* Translated by Margaret Crosland. New York: Harcourt, Brace, Jovanovich, 1980.)

Les Vrilles de la vigne. Paris: Editions de la Vie Parisienne, 1908.

L'Ingénue libertine. Paris: Ollendorff, 1909. (*The Innocent Libertine.* Translated by Antonia White. New York: Farrar, Straus and Giroux, 1978.)

La Vagabonde. Paris: Ollendorff, 1910. (*The Vagabond.* Translated by Enid McLeod. New York: Farrar, Straus and Giroux, 1955.)

L'Envers du music-hall. Paris: Flammarion, 1913. (*Music-Hall Sidelights.* Translated by Anne-Marie Callimachi. In *Mitsou and Music-Hall Sidelights.* New York: Farrar, Straus and Giroux, 1957.)

L'Entrave. Paris: Librairie des Lettres, 1913. (*The Shackle.* Translated by Antonia White. New York: Farrar, Straus and Giroux, 1976.)

Prrou, Poucette et quelques autres. Paris: Librairie des Lettres, 1913.

La Paix chez les bêtes. Paris: Crès, 1916. New edition of preceding title. (*Creature Comfort.* In *Creatures Great and Small.* Translated by Enid McLeod. New York: Farrar, Straus and Giroux, 1978.)

Les Heures longues. Paris: A. Fayard, 1917.

Les Enfants dans les ruines. Paris: Editions de la Maison du Livre, 1917.

Dans la foule. Paris: Crès, 1918.

Mitsou ou comment l'esprit vient aux filles. Paris: A. Fayard, 1919. Also contains *En Camarades, comédie en deux actes.* (*Mitsou.* Translated by Raymond Postgate. In *Mitsou and Music-Hall Sidelights.* New York: Farrar, Straus and Giroux, 1957.)

Chéri. Paris: A. Fayard, 1920. (*Chéri.* In *Chéri and The Last of Chéri.* Translated by Roger Senhouse. Baltimore: Penguin, 1974.)

La Chambre éclairée. Paris: Edouard Joseph, 1921.

La Maison de Claudine. Paris: J. Ferenczi et fils, 1922. (*My Mother's House.* Translated by Una Vicenzo Troubridge and Enid McLeod. In *My Mother's House* and *Sido.* New York: Farrar, Straus and Giroux, 1979.)

Le Voyage égoïste. Paris: Editions d'Art Edouard Pelletan, 1922. (Selections in *Journey for Myself: Selfish Memories.* Translated by David Le Vay. New York: Bobbs-Merrill, 1972.)

Chéri, comédie en quatre actes, par Colette et Léopold Marchand. Paris: Librairie Théâtrale, 1922.

La Vagabonde, comédie en quatre actes, par Colette et Léopold Marchand. Paris: Impr. de l'Illustration, 1923.

Le Blé en herbe. Paris: Flammarion, 1923. (*The Ripening Seed.* Translated by Roger Senhouse and Herma Briffault. New York: Farrar, Straus and Giroux, 1978.)

Rêverie de nouvel an. Paris: Stock, 1923.

La Femme cachée. Paris: Flammarion, 1924. (Selections in *The Other Woman.* Translated by Margaret Crosland. New York: Signet, 1975.)

Aventures quotidiennes. Paris: Flammarion, 1924. (In *Journey for Myself: Selfish Memories.* Translated by David Le Vay. New York: Bobbs-Merrill, 1972.)

L'Enfant et les sortilèges. Musique de Maurice Ravel. Paris: Durand et Cie., 1925. (*The Boy and the Magic.* Translated by Christopher Fry. New York: Putnam, 1965.)

La Fin de Chéri. Paris: Flammarion, 1926. (*The Last of Chéri.* In *Chéri* and *The Last of Chéri.* Translated by Roger Senhouse. Baltimore: Penguin, 1974.)

La Naissance du jour. Paris: Flammarion, 1928. (*Break of Day.* Translated by Enid McLeod. New York: Farrar, Straus and Giroux, 1979.)

Renée Vivien. Abbeville: Imprimerie F. Paillart, 1928.

La Seconde. Paris: J. Ferenczi et fils, 1929. (*The Other One.* Translated by Elizabeth Tait and Roger Senhouse. New York: Farrar, Straus and Giroux, 1960).

Sido. Paris: Editions Kra, 1929. (*Sido.* Translated by Enid McLeod. In *My Mother's House and Sido.* New York: Farrar, Straus and Giroux, 1979.)

Histoires pour Bel-Gazou. Paris: Stock, 1930.

Douze Dialogues de bêtes. Paris: Mercure de France, 1930. (*Creature Conversations.* In *Creatures Great and Small.* Translated by Enid McLeod. New York: Farrar, Straus and Giroux, 1978.)

Paradis terrestres. Lausanne: Gonin et Cie., 1932.

La Treille Muscate. Paris: Jourde, 1932.

Prisons et paradis. Paris: J. Ferenczi et fils, 1932. (Selections in *Places.* Translated by David Le Vay and Margaret Crosland. New York: Bobbs-Merrill, 1971.)

Ces Plaisirs. Paris: J. Ferenczi et fils, 1932. Reedited in 1941 as *Le Pur et l'impur.* (*The Pure and the Impure.* Translated by Herma Briffault. New York: Farrar, Straus and Giroux, 1979.)

La Chatte. Paris: Grasset, 1933. (*The Cat.* Translated by Antonia White. In *Seven by Colette.* New York: Farrar, Straus and Cudahy, 1955.)

Duo. Paris: J. Ferenczi et fils, 1934. (*Duo.* In *Duo and Le Toutounier.* Translated by Margaret Crosland. New York: Dell, 1974.)

La Jumelle noire. Paris: J. Ferenczi et fils, 1934–38.

Cahiers de Colette. Paris: Les Amis de Colette, 1935–36.

Discours de réception à l'Académie Royale Belge de Langue et de Littérature Françaises. Paris: Grasset, 1936.

Mes Apprentissages. Paris: J. Ferenczi et fils, 1936. (*My Apprenticeships.* Translated by Helen Beauclerk. New York: Farrar, Straus and Giroux, 1978.)

Chats. Paris: Jacques Nam, 1936.

Splendeurs des papillons. Paris: Plon, 1936.

Bella-Vista. Paris: J. Ferenczi et fils, 1937. ("Bella-Vista," "Gribiche," "The Rendezvous," and "The Patriarch." In *The Tender Shoot and Other Stories.* Translated by Antonia White. New York: Farrar, Straus and Giroux, 1958.)

Le Toutounier. Paris: J. Ferenczi et fils, 1939. (*Le Toutounier.* In *Duo and Le Toutounier.* Translated by Margaret Crosland. New York: Dell, 1974.)

Chambre d'hôtel. Paris: A. Fayard, 1940. (*Chance Acquaintances.* In *Julie de Carneilhan and Chance Acquaintances.* Translated by Patrick Leigh Fermor. London: Secker and Warburg, 1952. "The Rainy Moon." In *The Tender Shoot and Other Stories.* Translated by Antonia White. New York: Farrar, Straus and Giroux, 1958.)

Mes Cahiers. Paris: Aux Armes de France, 1941. Includes *Cahiers de Colette,* which had appeared separately in 1935–36.

Journal à rebours. Paris: A. Fayard, 1941. (*Looking Backwards.* Translated by David Le Vay. Bloomington: Indiana University Press, 1975.)

Julie de Carneilhan. Paris: A. Fayard, 1941. (*Julie de Carneilhan.* In *Julie de Carneilhan and Chance Acquaintances.* Translated by Patrick Leigh Fermor. London: Secker and Warburg, 1952.)

De ma fenêtre. Paris: Aux Armes de France, 1942. (In *Looking Backwards.* Translated by David Le Vay. Bloomington: Indiana University Press, 1975.)

De la patte à l'aile. Paris: Editions Corrêa, 1943.

Flore et Pomone. Paris: Editions de la Galerie Charpentier, 1943.

Nudité. Paris: Editions de la Mappemonde, 1943.

Le Képi. Paris: A. Fayard, 1943. ("The Tender Shoot," "The Kepi," "Green Sealing Wax," and "Armande." In *The Tender Shoot and Other Stories.* Translated by Antonia White. New York: Farrar, Straus and Giroux, 1958.)

Broderie ancienne. Monaco: Editions du Rocher, 1944.

Gigi et autres nouvelles. Lausanne: La Guilde du Livre, 1944. (*Gigi.* Translated by Roger Senhouse. In *Gigi and Selected Writings.* New York: New American Library [Signet], 1963. "The Sick Child" and "The Photographer's Missus." In *The Tender Shoot and Other Stories.* Translated by Antonia White. New York: Farrar, Straus and Giroux, 1958.)

Trois... six... neuf.... Paris: Editions Corrêa, 1944. (Selections in *Places.* Translated by David Le Vay and Margaret Crosland. New York: Bobbs-Merrill, 1971.)

Belles Saisons. Paris: Editions de la Galerie Charpentier, 1945.

Une Amitié inattendue. Correspondance de Colette et de Francis Jammes. Introduction and notes by Robert Mallet. Paris: Editions Emile-Paul Frères, 1945.

L'Etoile Vesper. Geneva: Editions du Milieu du Monde, 1946. (*The Evening Star.* Translated by David Le Vay. London: Peter Owen, 1973.)

Pour un herbier. Lausanne: Mermod, 1948.

Trait pour trait. Paris: Editions Le Fleuron, 1949.

Journal intermittent. Paris: Editions Le Fleuron, 1949. (Selections in *Places*. Translated by David Le Vay and Margaret Crosland. New York: Bobbs-Merrill, 1971.)

Le Fanal bleu. Paris: J. Ferenczi et fils, 1949. (*The Blue Lantern*. Translated by Roger Senhouse. New York: Farrar, Straus and Giroux, 1963.)

La Fleur de l'âge. Paris: Editions Le Fleuron, 1949.

En Pays connu. Paris: Manuel Bruker, 1949. (Selections in *Places*. Translated by David Le Vay and Margaret Crosland. New York: Bobbs-Merrill, 1971.)

Chats de Colette. Paris: Albin Michel, 1949.

Gigi. Adaptation pour la scène par Colette et Anita Loos. Paris: France-Illustration, 1954.

Paysages et portraits. Paris: Flammarion, 1958. (Selections in *Places*. Translated by David Le Vay and Margaret Crosland. New York: Bobbs-Merrill, 1971. Selections also in *The Other Woman*. Translated by Margaret Crosland. New York: Signet, 1975.)

Lettres à Hélène Picard. Paris: Flammarion, 1958. (Excerpts in *Letters from Colette*. Translated by Robert Phelps. New York: Farrar, Straus and Giroux, 1980.)

Lettres à Marguerite Moreno. Paris: Flammarion, 1959. (Excerpts in *Letters from Colette*.)

Lettres de la vagabonde. Paris: Flammarion, 1961. (Excerpts in *Letters from Colette*.)

Lettres au petit corsaire. Paris: Flammarion, 1963. (Excerpts in *Letters from Colette*.)

Contes des mille et un matins. Paris: Flammarion, 1970. (*The Thousand and One Mornings*. Translated by Margaret Crosland and David Le Vay. New York: Bobbs-Merrill, 1973.)

Lettres à ses pairs. Paris: Flammarion, 1973. (Excerpts in *Letters from Colette*. Translated by Robert Phelps. New York: Farrar, Straus and Giroux, 1980.)

"Inédits en librairie." *Cahiers Colette*, no. 2. Paris: Société des Amis de Colette, 1979.

Selections from *Mes Cahiers, Contes des mille et un matins, Paysages et portraits, La Chambre éclairée, Les Vrilles de la vigne, L'Envers du music-hall, La Fleur de l'âge, La Femme cachée, Douze Dialogues de bêtes, La Maison de Claudine, La Paix chez les bêtes, Gigi, Chambre d'hôtel, Le Képi and Bella-Vista*, among other short pieces, also appear in translation in *The Collected Stories of Colette*. Ed. Robert Phelps. Translated by Matthew Ward, Antonia White, Anne-Marie Callimachi, and others. New York: Farrar, Straus and Giroux, 1983.

Lettres à Moune et au Toutounet (Hélène Jourdan-Morhange et Luc-Albert Moreau) 1929–1954. Ed. Bernard Villaret. Paris: Des Femmes, 1985.

Lettres aux petites fermières. Ed. Marie-Thérèse Colléaux-Chaurang. Paris: Le Castor Astral, 1992.

3. *Letters to Colette*

Sido. *Lettres à sa fille*. Précédé de *Lettres inédites de Colette*. Préfaces de Bertrand de
    Jouvenel, Jeannie Malige et Michèle Sarde. Paris: Des Femmes, 1984.

SECONDARY SOURCES

The number of studies dealing with Colette is immense, and this list is
necessarily selective: it is not possible to mention here all the provocative
and influential studies that have appeared. For some additional titles of
interest, consult the Notes and References section of this volume. Elaine
Marks's section on Colette in *A Critical Bibliography of French Literature*
(ed. Douglas W. Alden and Richard A. Brooks [Syracuse: Syracuse
University Press, 1980], Vol. 6: *The Twentieth Century,* part 1, 679–716)
provides a helpful annotated bibliography to 1978. For an admirably
comprehensive bibliography of publications from 1900 through 1988, a
work now indispensable to the Colette scholar, see Donna M. Norell,
Colette: An Annotated Primary and Secondary Bibliography (New York and
London: Garland, 1993). Norell organizes Colette's texts by genre and
alphabetically within genres, includes both French and English editions,
lists reviews of Colette's works and of books on Colette, and usefully
annotates both primary and secondary works.

Album Colette. Ed. Claude and Vincenette Pichois. Paris: Gallimard, Pléiade,
    1984. More than 500 illustrations of people, places and things, as well as
    excellent commentary and index.
Barbour, Sarah. "*La Naissance du jour* by Colette: Who is this Woman
    Writing?" *Australian Journal of French Studies* 27:3 (September–December
    1990), 242–53. Compellingly uses a discussion of the Oedipal structura-
    tion of narrative and of what Yannick Resch calls Colette's "pleasure-
    text" to reflect on the question that the status of *Break of Day* has posed
    for critics.
Beaumont, Germaine, and Parinaud, André. *Colette*. Paris: Seuil, "Les Ecrivains
    de Toujours," 1951. Effusive introductory essay by Beaumont, who was
    Colette's friend and secretary at *Le Matin*, followed by a selection of short
    excerpts from Colette's work. Interspersed with photographs.
Biolley-Godino, Marcelle. *L'Homme-objet chez Colette*. Paris: Klincksieck, 1972.
    Groundbreaking analysis of Colette's reversal of traditional gender roles.
Bray, Bernard, ed. *Colette: Nouvelles approches critiques* (Actes du Colloque de
    Sarrebruck, 22–23 juin 1984). Paris: Nizet, 1986. Beginning with Mieke
    Bal's shrewd psychoanalytic reading of *Chéri* and the mother-child rela-

tionship ("Inconsciences de *Chéri*. Chéri existe-t-il?"), this is a varied and often cited collection.

Cahiers Colette, nos. 3/4 (Colloque de Dijon, 1979). Saint-Sauveur en Puisaye: Société des Amis de Colette, 1981. A collection of papers delivered at the first academic colloquium devoted entirely to Colette.

Cohen, Susan D. "An Onomastic Double Bind: Colette's *Gigi* and the Politics of Naming," *PMLA* 100:5 (October 1985), 793–809. An excellent study of the importance and function of names, both proper and common, as an aspect of the relation of women to discourse and power. Views the conclusion of *Gigi* as not nearly so sanguine as is normally thought.

Colette: catalogue de l'exposition de 1973. Paris: Bibliothèque Nationale, 1973. Prepared for the Colette centennial exhibit at the Bibliothèque Nationale, this catalog reproduces letters, photographs, and other documents.

Cothran, Ann. "The Dryad's Escape: Female Space in *La Vagabonde*," *Modern Language Studies* 21:2 (Spring 1991), 27–35. A perceptive survey of the "landscape" of space, both figurative and literal, including the space of possession and the space of restitution, in one of Colette's most popular novels.

Cottrell, Robert D. *Colette*. New York: Frederick Ungar, 1974. A concise, intelligent, and well-written study, concentrating on the major novels.

Crosland, Margaret. *Colette: The Difficulty of Loving*. New York: Dell, 1973. A readable biography, suggesting that Colette's obsessive love for Sido made it difficult for her to love anyone else effectively.

Davies, Margaret. *Colette*. New York: Grove Press, 1961. A lively general introduction with some pertinent observations—for example, on *Break of Day*.

D'Hollander, Paul. *Colette: ses apprentissages*. Montreal: Presses de l'Université de Montréal [also Paris: Klincksieck], 1978. An account of the genesis of the Claudine and Minne books and especially of Willy's role, based on exhaustive biographical research and manuscript study.

Dobbs, Annie-Claude. "Enquête sur une déviance syntaxique dans *Les Vrilles de la Vigne* de Colette," *Romanic Review* 80:3 (May 1989), 434–44. A fascinating account of the way editors have imposed their own moralizing vision on Colette through a typographical detail in editions of two short pieces from *Tendrils of the Vine*: the agreement (masculine or feminine) of a past participle.

Dormann, Geneviève. *Amoureuse Colette*. [Paris]: Herscher, 1984. (Published in English as *Colette, A Passion for Life*. Translated by David Macey and Jane Brenton. New York: Abbeville Press, 1985.) This coffee-table volume emphasizes the anecdotal and the scandalous in Colette's life, but it is sumptuously illustrated.

Dranch, Sherry A. "Reading through the Veiled Text: Colette's *The Pure and the Impure*," *Contemporary Literature* 24:2 (Summer 1983), 176–89. Studies the ways in which experiences and obsessions that are denied overt expression are conveyed in a book about sexual satisfaction and lesbian desire.

Eisinger, Erica, and McCarty, Mari, Eds. *Charting Colette*, special issue of *Women's Studies* 8:3 (1981). A collection of articles using Marxist, Lacanian, Jungian, linguistic, and textual approaches.

————. *Colette: The Woman, The Writer*. University Park and London: Pennsylvania State University Press, 1981. A collection of articles dealing with different aspects of Colette's work.

Evans, Martha. "Colette: *The Vagabond*," in *Masks of Tradition: Women and the Politics of Writing in Twentieth-Century France*. Ithaca and London: Cornell University Press, 1987, 36–74. A detailed interpretation of the masks and the game of hide-and-seek in a novel, published a few years after Colette's separation from Willy, in which the heroine (like Colette herself) seeks her own voice.

Flieger, Jerry Aline. *Colette and the Fantom Subject of Autobiography*. Ithaca and London: Cornell University Press, 1992. Uses psychoanalytic and feminist approaches to examine Colette's relation to "fictional autobiography."

Goudeket, Maurice. *Près de Colette*. Paris: Flammarion, 1956. (Translated as *Close to Colette*. Introduction by Harold Nicolson. New York: Farrar, Straus and Cudahy, 1957.) An anecdotal account by Colette's third husband of her personality and habits during their years together.

Holmes, Diana. *Colette*. New York: St. Martin's Press, 1991. A feminist reading, and a clear and compact introduction to the work.

Huffer, Lynn. *Another Colette: The Question of Gendered Writing*. Ann Arbor: University of Michigan Press, 1992. A provocative study of Colette "as an (en)gendered text"; addresses complex questions of subjectivity, gender, and representation.

Jouve, Nicole Ward. *Colette*. Bloomington: Indiana University Press, 1987. A remarkable and wide-ranging account of Colette's life and works. Written in a highly personal style, it engagingly asks the question, "What difference does it make that she was a *woman* writer?"

Ketchum, Anne A. *Colette ou la naissance du jour: étude d'un malentendu*. Paris: Minard, 1968. The "malentendu" of the subtitle refers to critical misunderstanding of Colette, which this study proposes to correct by a phenomenological reading.

————. "Defining an Ethics from a Later Short Story by Colette," in *Continental, Latin American and Francophone Women Writers*, ed. Eunice Myers and Ginette Adamson. Lanham, MD: University Press of America, 1987, 71–77. A reading of *The Tender Shoot*, with its May 1940 setting, as an account of female dignity and maternal protection from lecherous male aggression.

Lachgar, Lina. *Colette*. Paris: Henri Veyrier, 1983. A photography album with an elegant introductory essay, a chronology, and fine photographs of Colette and some of her friends, acquaintances, and contemporaries.

Ladimer, Bethany. "Colette: Rewriting the Script for the Aging Woman," in *Aging and Gender in Literature: Studies in Creativity*, ed. Anne M. Wyatt-Brown and Janice Rossen. Charlottesville: University Press of Virginia, 1993, 242–57. Focuses on the sensory pleasure of the gaze in Colette's later works and the erotic pleasure of writing about it.

Lottman, Herbert. *Colette*. Boston: Little, Brown, 1991. The most thorough biography of Colette to date.

Marks, Elaine. *Colette*. New Brunswick: Rutgers University Press, 1960. The first important study for readers of English and a thorough, original, and influential introduction to Colette.

Massie, Allan. *Colette*. Harmondsworth, England: Penguin, 1986. Although not a scholarly work (quotations are not referenced), this short biographical portrait is elegantly written.

Mercier, Michel, Ed. *Europe* 59 (November–December 1981), 631–32. A special issue on Colette containing articles about her life and work, as well as a chronology and several of her previously unpublished pieces.

Miller, Nancy K. "The Anamnesis of a Female 'I': In the Margins of Self-Portrayal," in *Colette: The Woman, the Writer*, ed. Erica Eisinger and Mari McCarty. University Park and London: Pennsylvania State University Press, 1981, 164–75. A frequently referenced essay that explores, with special attention to the *gender* of genre, the ways in which *Break of Day* replicates and inflects features of the "autoportrait."

———. "Woman of Letters: The Return to Writing in Colette's *The Vagabond*," in *Subject to Change: Reading Feminist Writing*. New York: Columbia University Press, 1988, 229–64. A finely detailed reading of *The Vagabond* as a story about the refusal of a fixed identity and of nostalgia for integrity, and as an account of a return to writing published under the signature of a woman writer.

———. "Women's Autobiography in France: For a Dialectics of Identification," in *Women and Language in Literature and Society*, ed. Sally McConnell-Ginet, Ruth Borker, and Nelly Furman. New York: Praeger, 1980, 258–73. Uses *Break of Day* with its much-cited epithet as point of departure for an astute discussion proposing a mode of reading that privileges neither the autobiography nor the fiction, but takes the two together in their status as text.

Phelps, Robert. *Belles Saisons: A Colette Scrapbook*. New York: Farrar, Straus and Giroux, 1978. A handsome pictorial biography, making extensive use of excerpts from Colette's own writings.

———. *Earthly Paradise: An Autobiography Drawn from Her {Colette's} Lifetime Writings*. New York: Farrar, Straus and Giroux, 1966. Rather than being a real autobiography, this is Phelps's selection and ingenious arrangement of autobiographical passages in Colette's writings.

Plottel, Jeanine Parisier. "Colette's Love Triangles," *L'Esprit créateur* 34:3 (Fall 1994), 92–98. A short essay on ambiguity, eroticism and violence in Colette's writing, especially in *Claudine Married*.

Raaphorst-Rousseau, Madeleine. *Colette: sa vie et son art*. Paris: Nizet, 1964. A good general study, with bibliography. Treats love, nature, and animal themes as well as style.

Resch, Yannick. *Corps féminin, corps textuel: essai sur le personnage féminin dans l'oeuvre de Colette*. Paris: Klincksieck, 1973. An influential statistical and interpretive analysis of Colette's use of the vocabulary for the human body in five novels about communication within a couple: *Duo, Julie de Carneilhan, The Other One, The Cat*, and *Chéri*.

Reymond, Evelyne. *Le Rire de Colette*. Paris: Nizet, 1988. Categorizes sources of humor—for example, scatology; farce; caricature; slang; and dress, situations, or behavior that Colette finds droll (humans who resemble animals or animals with human traits)—in passages from Colette's work. Does not reference the passages cited.

Richardson, Joanna. *Colette*. London: Methuen, 1983. (Reissued, New York: Franklin Watts, 1984.) While it may overuse information and interpretations supplied by Bertrand and Renaud de Jouvenel, this readable and frequently mentioned biography provides much useful information.

Sarde, Michèle. *Colette, libre et entravée*. Paris: Stock, 1978. (Translated by Richard Miller as *Colette Free and Fettered*. New York: William Morrow, 1980.) An original and provocative feminist biography that has had a great deal of success.

Slawy-Sutton, Catherine. "Lies, Half-truths, Considerable Secrets: Colette and Re-Writing the Self," in *Redefining Autobiography in Twentieth-Century Women's Fiction*, eds. Janice Morgan and Colette T. Hall. New York and London: Garland, 1991, 23–44. Deftly examines the blurring of autobiography and fiction, the interplay between revelation and disguise in Colette's writing, to argue that her works fall mostly under the rubric of "autobiographical fiction."

Stivale, Lezlie Hart. "Colette and Autobiography: The Film Version," *Women in French Studies* (Fall 1994), 67–77. An interesting article on a rarely treated topic: Yannick Bellon's 1950 documentary film, *Colette*, on which Colette herself collaborated.

Strand, Dana. *Colette: A Study of the Short Fiction*. New York: Twayne, 1995. A welcome and intelligent introduction to the short fiction, with its rich ambiguities and heterogeneity. Includes a short essay on Colette's view of the difficult process of writing, with substantial excerpts from Colette herself, and a selection of critical essays on Colette's stories.

———. "The 'Third Woman' in Colette's 'Chance Acquaintances,' " *Studies in Short Fiction* 29:4 (Fall 1992), 499–508. Takes a little-discussed story as the basis for a cogent and discerning analysis of how Colette, using a vision that is gendered male, manages to divert the course of conventional plots.

Tinter, Sylvie. *Colette et le temps surmonté*. Geneva: Slatkine, 1980. An essay on old age in Colette's works, emphasizing oedipal desire, asymmetrical couples, and the importance of the mother figure.

Whatley, Janet. "Colette's *Le Pur et l'impur*: On Real and Phony Mysteries," *Modern Language Studies* 13:3 (Summer 1983), 16–26. An exquisite and compelling analysis of the mystifications of one of Colette's most enigmatic works.

Index

The Author

Joan Hinde Stewart, who holds the Ph.D. degree from Yale University, is professor of French at North Carolina State University. She has published articles and books on eighteenth- and twentieth-century literature, including *The Novels of Mme Riccoboni* (Chapel Hill: North Carolina Studies in the Romance Languages and Literatures, 1976), and *Gynographs: French Novels by Women of the Late Eighteenth Century* (Lincoln: University of Nebraska Press, 1993), as well as editions of Marie Riccoboni's *Lettres de Fanni Butlerd* (Geneva: Droz, 1979) and, with Philip Stewart, of Isabelle de Charrière's *Lettres de Mistriss Henley publiées par son amie* (New York: Modern Language Association, 1993).